Stopping Terror Finance: Securing The U.S. Financial Sector

REPORT PREPARED BY THE STAFF OF THE
TASK FORCE TO INVESTIGATE TERRORISM FINANCING,
COMMITTEE ON FINANCIAL SERVICES, U.S. HOUSE OF REPRESENTATIVES

Michael Fitzpatrick
Chairman, Task Force to Investigate Terrorism Financing

Stephen F. Lynch,
Ranking Member, Task Force to Investigate Terrorism Financing

114th Congress, Second Session
December 20, 2016

This report, prepared by the Republican and Democrat Staff of the Task Force to Investigate Terrorism Financing, has not been officially adopted by the Task Force or the Committee on Financial Services and may not necessarily reflect the views of the Members of the Task Force or Committee.

Task Force to Investigate Terrorism Financing
114th Congress
Michael G. Fitzpatrick, Pennsylvania, *Chairman*

Robert Pittenger, North Carolina, *Vice Chairman*
Peter T. King, New York
Steve Stivers, Ohio
Dennis A. Ross, Florida
Ann Wagner, Missouri
Andy Barr, Kentucky
Keith J. Rothfus, Pennsylvania
David Schweikert, Arizona
Roger Williams, Texas
Bruce Poliquin, Maine
French Hill, Arkansas
Jeb Hensarling, Texas, *ex officio*

Stephen F. Lynch, Massachusetts, *Ranking Member*
Brad Sherman, California
Gregory W. Meeks, New York
Al Green, Texas,
Keith Ellison, Minnesota
James A. Himes, Connecticut
Bill Foster, Illinois
Daniel T. Kildee, Michigan
Kyrsten Sinema, Arizona
Maxine Waters, California, *ex officio*

The Task Force to Investigate Terrorism Financing would like to express appreciation to the United States Secret Service, the United States Army, and the Congressional Research Service (CRS) for their invaluable assistance in the preparation of materials for, and the conduct of, the Task Force. The Secret Service detailed two top Special Agents, William S. You and Matthew J. Fishler, whose insights helped guide Task Force Members' work. Army Lt. Col. Christopher D. L'Heureux and Majors Peter A. Thomas, Bryan S. Whittier and Brent Weece worked tirelessly on complex logistics for Task Force fact-finding delegations, and CRS Specialist in International Crime and Narcotics Liana Rosen, along with Martin Weiss, Specialist in International Trade and Finance, provided countless hours of research and prepared a detailed series of reports on various aspects of the terror financing threat that appear in Appendix A of this report.

Table of Contents

Appendix A: Further Reading

Appendix B: Hearing Summaries

Appendix C: "A Survey of Global Terrorism and Terrorist Financing" (Apr. 22, 2015)

Appendix D: "A Dangerous Nexus: Terrorism, Crime, and Corruption" (May 21, 2015)

Appendix E: "Evaluating the Security of the U.S. Financial Sector" (Jun. 24, 2015)

Appendix F: "The Iran Nuclear Deal and Its Impact on Terrorism Financing" (July 22, 2015)

Appendix G: "Could America Do More? An Examination of U.S. Efforts to Stop the Financing of Terror" (Sept. 9, 2015)

Appendix H: "Trading with the Enemy: Trade-Based Money Laundering is the Growth Industry in Terror Finance" (Feb. 3, 2016)
[Appendix H is on file with the Committee. A link will be added when available].

Appendix I: "Helping the Developing World Fight Terror Finance" (Mar. 1, 2016)
[Appendix I is on file with the Committee. A link will be added when available].

Appendix J: "Preventing Cultural Genocide: Countering the Plunder and Sale of Priceless Cultural Antiquities by ISIS" (Apr. 19, 2016)
[Appendix J is on file with the Committee. A link will be added when available].

Appendix K: "Stopping Terror Finance: A Coordinated Effort" (May 24, 2016)
[Appendix K is on file with the Committee. A link will be added when available].

Appendix L: "The Enemy in Our Backyard: Examining Terror Funding Streams from South America" (June 8, 2016)
[Appendix L is on file with the Committee. A link will be added when available].

Appendix M: "The Next Terrorist Financiers: Stopping Them Before They Start" (June 23, 2016)
[Appendix M is on file with the Committee. A link will be added when available].

Introduction

      Terrorist financing describes a form of financial crime in which an individual or entity solicits, collects, or provides funds "with the intention that [these funds] may be used to support terrorist acts or organizations."[1] While terrorists can benefit from big donations of deep-pocketed financiers sympathetic to their cause, terrorist financing often involves relatively small-dollar amounts and itself is just a subset melting into the larger stream of all financial crime occurring in the international financial system. The threat to national security from terrorist financiers is real, so while U.S. policymakers have long recognized the idea that "following the money" through the retail banking system can help combat terrorism and related forms of illicit finance, new financing technologies have arisen since the September 11, 2001, terror attacks that require constant renewal of detection and disruption methods.[2]

      In December 2015, the intergovernmental Financial Action Task Force (FATF) warned that "further concerted action urgently needs to be taken ... to combat the financing of ... serious terrorist threats...."[3] Two months later, in February 2016, FATF noted that the scope and nature of terrorist threats had "globally intensified considerably."[4] According to the U.S. Department of the Treasury (Treasury Department), these threats collectively represent a source of risk generally to the United States, and to the financial system in particular.[5] Specifically, Treasury concludes:

> [t]he central role of the U.S. financial system within the international financial system and the sheer volume and diversity of international financial transactions that in some way pass through U.S. financial institutions expose the U.S. financial system to TF [terrorist financing] risks that other financial systems may not face.[6]

---

[1] International Monetary Fund, *Anti-Money Laundering / Combating the Financing of Terrorism – Topics, available at* https://www.imf.org/external/np/leg/amlcft/eng/aml1.htm.

[2] U.S. Dep't of the Treasury, *National Terrorist Financing Risk Assessment* 2 (2015), [hereinafter Treasury TF Risk Assessment] *available at* https://www.treasury.gov/resource-center/terrorist-illicit-finance/Documents/National%20Terrorist%20Financing%20Risk%20Assessment%20–%2006-12-2015.pdf.

[3] Financial Action Task Force, "FATF's strategy on combating terrorist financing," *available at* http://www.fatf-gafi.org/publications/fatfgeneral/documents/terroristfinancing.html.

[4] Financial Action Task Force, *Consolidated FATF Strategy on Combatting Terrorist Financing* 1 (Feb. 19, 2016), [hereinafter Consolidated FATF Strategy Report] *available at* http://www.fatf-gafi.org/publications/fatfgeneral/documents/terroristfinancing.html.

[5] Treasury TF Risk Assessment, *supra* note 2.

[6] *Id.* at 2-3.

The bipartisan Task Force to Investigate Terrorism Financing of the Financial Services Committee (Task Force) was authorized for two six-month terms during the 114th Congress to probe the growing terrorist financing problem.[7] The Task Force held eleven hearings, and its 21 Members systematically examined how select terror groups and actors acquire and move funds illicitly.[8] The hearings featured expert testimony from current and former U.S. government employees, with witnesses from both the U.S. and overseas, on a wide range of topics. The Task Force recently concluded its work with two wrap-up hearings, one of which featured testimony from two senior Treasury Department officials on how the agency is coordinating its efforts to fight terrorist financing.

During its first six-month term, the Task Force held five targeted hearings to survey terrorist funding sources and networks. At a hearing on April 22, 2015, witnesses testified to the diversity and scope of today's terrorist financing threats, which have become more varied since the September 11, 2001, terrorist attacks.[9] On May 21, 2015, the Task Force explored the nexus of terrorism, corruption, and transnational crime, especially drug trafficking.[10] A June 24, 2015, Task Force hearing paid specific attention to U.S. financial sector security by focusing on expanded and diversified criminal schemes exploited by terrorist groups to finance their activities, including the use of anonymized shell corporations and cyber-attacks.[11] A July 22, 2015, hearing specifically explored the implications of the July 2015 Joint Comprehensive Plan of Action (JCPOA) on Iran's terrorist financing capabilities and intent.[12] On September 9, 2015, the Task Force explored whether

---

[7] The Task Force has examined terrorism financing issues within the jurisdiction of the Financial Services Committee as established by Rule X of the House of Representatives. The Task Force was first established to run from March 25, 2015, through September 25, 2015, and was renewed for a second iteration from January 5, 2016, through July 5, 2016.

[8] On March 25, 2015, a resolution establishing the Task Force for its initial six-month period starting March 25, 2015, and expiring on September 25, 2015, passed unanimously for a voice vote; http://financialservices.house.gov/calendar/eventsingle.aspx?EventID=398821. On December 8, 2015, a second resolution re-establishing the Task Force for another six-month period starting on January 5, 2016, and running through July 5, 2016, was agreed to by a voice vote; http://financialservices.house.gov/calendar/eventsingle.aspx?EventID=400034.

[9] *See* prepared statement of Juan. Zarate, Senior Adviser, Center for Strategic and International Studies, for *A Survey of Global Terrorism and Terrorist Financing: Hearing before the Task Force to Investigate Terrorism Financing, H. Comm. on Fin. Serv.* 114th Cong. 8-10 (Apr. 22, 2015), [hereinafter *Hearings*] (A Survey of Global Terrorism and Terrorist Financing) *available at* http://financialservices.house.gov/calendar/eventsingle.aspx?EventID=398891.

[10] *A Dangerous Nexus: Terrorism, Crime and Corruption: Hearing before the Task Force to Investigate Terrorism Financing, H. Comm. on Fin. Serv.* 114th Cong. (May 21, 2015), [hereinafter *Hearings*] (A Dangerous Nexus: Terrorism, Crime and Corruption) *available at* http://financialservices.house.gov/calendar/eventsingle.aspx?EventID=399069.

[11] *Evaluating the Security of the U.S. Financial Sector: Hearing before the Task Force to Investigate Terrorism Financing, H. Comm. on Fin. Serv.* 114th Cong. (June 24, 2015), [hereinafter *Hearings*] (Evaluating the Security of the U.S. Financial Sector) *available at* http://financialservices.house.gov/calendar/eventsingle.aspx?EventID=399267.

[12] *The Iran Nuclear Deal and Its Impact on Terrorism Financing: Hearing before the Task Force to Investigate Terrorism Financing, H. Comm. on Fin. Serv.* 114th Cong. (July 22, 2015), [hereinafter

the U.S. was using the tools at its disposal to inhibit terrorist financing, as well as how to improve interagency and private sector coordination to diminish terrorist financing.[13]

During its second six-month term, the Task Force took a more granular look at some less well-publicized terrorist financing methodologies. On February 3, 2016, the Task Force heard testimony on the widespread use of trade-based money laundering (TBML) and the importance of trade transparency.[14] Treasury's efforts to help developing countries strengthen anti-money laundering (AML) and counter terrorist financing (CFT) defenses were explored in a hearing held on March 1, 2016.[15] An April 19, 2016, hearing discussed the increased plundering of arts and antiquities by terrorists, especially the Islamic State of Iraq and Syria (ISIS),[16] and how stolen cultural objects can fund terror either through direct sale, or as a store of value that can be traded.[17] At a May 24, 2016, hearing, the Task Force heard testimony from two Treasury officials including the head of the country's "financial intelligence unit," the Financial Crimes Enforcement Network (FinCEN), and explored Treasury's *National Terrorist Financing Risk Assessment*, which details the exposure of the U.S. financial system to terrorist financing risks.[18] On June 8, 2016, the Task Force examined terrorist funding streams from South America in

---

Hearings] (The Iran Nuclear Deal and Its Impact on Terrorism Financing) *available at* http://financialservices.house.gov/calendar/eventsingle.aspx?EventID=399373.

[13] *Could America Do More? An Examination of U.S. Efforts to Stop the Financing of Terror: Hearing before the Task Force to Investigate Terrorism Financing, H. Comm. on Fin. Serv.* 114th Cong. (Sept. 9, 2015), [hereinafter *Hearings*] (Could America Do More? An Examination of U.S. Efforts to Stop the Financing of Terror) *available at* http://financialservices.house.gov/calendar/eventsingle.aspx?EventID=399633.

[14] *Trading with the Enemy: Trade-Based Money Laundering is the Growth Industry in Terror Finance: Hearing before the Task Force to Investigate Terrorism Financing, H. Comm. on Fin. Serv.* 114th Cong. (Feb. 3, 2016), [hereinafter *Hearings*] (Trading with the Enemy: Trade-Based Money Laundering is the Growth Industry in Terror Finance) *available at* http://financialservices.house.gov/calendar/eventsingle.aspx?EventID=400192.

[15] *Helping the Developing World Fight Terror Finance: Hearing before the Task Force to Investigate Terrorism Financing, H. Comm. on Fin. Serv.* 114th Cong. (Mar. 1, 2016), [hereinafter *Hearings*] (Helping the Developing World Fight Terror Finance) *available at* http://financialservices.house.gov/calendar/eventsingle.aspx?EventID=400338.

[16] ISIS is also known as the Islamic State, or IS, the Islamic State of Iraq and the Levant, or ISIL, or Daesh.

[17] *Preventing Cultural Genocide: Countering the Plunder and Sale of Priceless Cultural Antiquities by ISIS: Hearing before the Task Force to Investigate Terrorism Financing, H. Comm. on Fin. Serv.* 114th Cong. (Apr. 19, 2016), [hereinafter *Hearings*] (Preventing Cultural Genocide: Countering the Plunder and Sale of Priceless Cultural Antiquities by ISIS) *available at* http://financialservices.house.gov/calendar/eventsingle.aspx?EventID=400550.

[18] *Stopping Terror Finance: A Coordinated Government Effort: Hearing before the Task Force to Investigate Terrorism Financing, H. Comm. on Fin. Serv.* 114th Cong. (May 24, 2016), [hereinafter *Hearings*] (Stopping Terror Finance: A Coordinated Government Effort) *available at* http://financialservices.house.gov/calendar/eventsingle.aspx?EventID=400670.

particular[19] before calling on previous witnesses to testify again at a final hearing on June 23, 2016.[20]

The recent massacres in San Bernardino, California, and Orlando, Florida, were the deadliest on U.S. soil since the terrorist attacks of September 11, 2011. While none of these attacks was expensive to execute, each required specific and targeted funding. Against this backdrop, the Task Force remains committed to ensuring that the United States is doing everything in its power, and is as efficient as possible in seeking to prevent extremist terror groups, and so-called "lone wolves," from accessing the global financial system. It is the Task Force's hope that this report will serve as a useful summary of the key points illuminated by Task Force hearings regarding the terrorist financing threat, and current efforts to combat it. Fighting the last terrorist threat without anticipating the next attack is not unlike fighting the last war instead of preparing for the next one, so it is also the Task Force's hope that this report will underscore that continued vigilance is necessary to stop the constantly evolving terrorist financing threat.

---

[19] *The Enemy in our Backyard: Examining Terror Funding Streams from South America: Hearing before the Task Force to Investigate Terrorism Financing, H. Comm. on Fin. Serv.* 114th Cong. (June 8, 2016), [hereinafter *Hearings*] (The Enemy in our Backyard: Examining Terror Funding Streams from South America) *available at* http://financialservices.house.gov/calendar/eventsingle.aspx?EventID=400715.

[20] *The Next Terrorist Financiers: Stopping Them Before They Start: Hearing before the Task Force to Investigate Terrorism Financing, H. Comm. on Fin. Serv.* 114th Cong. (June 23, 2016), [hereinafter Hearings] (The Next Terrorist Financiers: Stopping Them Before They Start) *available at* http://financialservices.house.gov/calendar/eventsingle.aspx?EventID=400810.

Nature of the Terror Finance Threat

Terror Financing Methods

The first step to disrupting the financing of terrorism is to properly identify the key actors and the various methods at their disposal. According to a frequently cited typologies report released by FATF, the most common sources of terrorist financing include state sponsors, private donors, charitable entities, self-funding mechanisms, and various criminal activities.[21] The Islamic State's unprecedented ability to generate financing—which is uniquely different from financing typical of Al-Qaeda and thus from the terror finance typologies FATF-style screening sought to identify—was a significant factor that drove FATF to re-evaluate its analysis of terrorist finance methods. Recognizing that terrorists frequently evolve as better methods of funding and finance arise, FATF re-evaluated terrorist financing methods in late-2015, finding that groups are increasingly fundraising through social media, the exploitation of new payment products (like virtual currencies), and the appropriation of natural resources and cultural items such as arts and antiquities, for profit.[22] Additionally, earlier this year, Director of National Intelligence (DNI) James Clapper identified the Internet in particular as a critical platform used by modern terrorist groups like ISIS "to organize, recruit, spread propaganda, collect intelligence, raise funds and coordinate operations."[23]

State Sponsors

Although there are fewer countries today identified as official State Sponsors of Terrorism by the U.S. Department of State (State Department), three governments currently remain active—Iran, Syria, and Sudan.[24] The most recent *Country Reports on Terrorism* stated that Iran remained the world's leading sponsor of terrorism last year.[25] The issue of Iran's role in terrorist financing as it

---

[21] *See* Financial Action Task Force, *Terrorist Financing* (Feb. 29, 2008), [hereinafter Terrorist Financing FATF report] *available at* http://www.fatf-gafi.org/publications/methodsandtrends/documents/fatfterroristfinancingtypologiesreport.html.

[22] *See* Financial Action Task Force, *Emerging Terrorist Financing Risks* (Oct. 21, 2015), *available at* http://www.fatf-gafi.org/publications/methodsandtrends/documents/emerging-terrorist-financing-risks.html.

[23] Prepared statement of James Clapper, Director of National Intelligence, for *Worldwide Threat Assessment of the U.S. Intelligence Community: Hearing before S. Comm. on Armed Services* 3 (Feb. 9, 2016), *available at* https://www.dni.gov/index.php/newsroom/testimonies/217-congressional-testimonies-2016/1313-statement-for-the-record-worldwide-threat-assessment-of-the-u-s-ic-before-the-senate-armed-services-committee-2016.

[24] U.S. Dep't of State, *Country Reports on Terrorism 2015*, 299-302 (June 2016), *available at* http://www.state.gov/j/ct/rls/crt/2015/.

[25] *Id.* at 10.

specifically relates to sanctions relief from the JCPOA featured prominently in a July 2015 Task Force hearing.[26] During this hearing, Mark Dubowitz—Executive Director of the Foundation for Defense of Democracies (FDD)—said that it is "very likely" that Iran increasingly would "spend money on terrorism..." because the JCPOA specifically authorizes the release of billions of dollars of Iranian funds held overseas and previously unavailable to Iran's Revolutionary Guard because of international sanctions released by the agreement.[27] Another witness at the hearing, Ilan Berman—Vice President of the American Foreign Policy Council—warned of Iran's increased support of terrorists following the JCPOA, because "we don't have the ability ... to exact tactical punishments from the Iranians for instances of malfeasance, including additional funding for terrorism."[28]

Charities and Donors

Terrorists also receive funding from both individual donors and charitable foundations.[29] While some donors are sympathetic to radical causes, others are unaware that their funds are being diverted or commingled for illicit purposes.[30] Notably, the Administration has pointed out that Al-Qaeda's main sources of financial support to orchestrate the September 11, 2001, attacks were wealthy private donors and charity organizations in the Arabian Peninsula.[31] More recently, the Treasury Department reported an emerging trend in which terror financiers prey on well-intentioned donors to solicit funds "under the auspices of charity" often online and make use of personal accounts and other "informal channels," but they are in fact "unaffiliated with any charitable organization recognized by the U.S. government."[32]

The Treasury Department has also identified Kuwait and Qatar as particularly permissive environments for donor-driven terrorist financing.[33] In an

---

[26] *Hearings, supra* note 12 (The Iran Nuclear Deal and Its Impact on Terrorism Financing).

[27] Additionally, Mr. Dubowitz remarked, "I don't think Iran is going to spend all of its money on terrorism. Iran will spend some of its money on terrorism. And as a small percentage of hundreds and hundreds of billions of dollars means that Iran can keep Bashar Assad in power for some time. It costs Iran about $6 billion a year ... to keep Bashar Assad in power, not to mention the hundreds of millions of dollars available for Hezbollah and other terrorist organizations...." Testimony of Mark Dubowitz, Executive Director, Foundation of the Defense of Democracies, and Director, Center on Sanctions and Illicit Finance, *Hearings, supra* note 12 (The Iran Nuclear Deal and Its Impact on Terrorist Financing).

[28] Testimony of Ilan Berman, Vice President, American Foreign Policy Council, *Hearings, supra* note 12 (The Iran Nuclear Deal and Its Impact on Terrorist Financing).

[29] Terrorist Financing FATF Report at 11-3, *supra* note 21.

[30] *Id.*

[31] *See* The White House, *National Strategy for Counterterrorism* (June 2011), *available at* https://www.whitehouse.gov/blog/2011/06/29/national-strategy-counterterrorism.

[32] Treasury TF Risk Assessment, *supra* note 2, at 41-4.

[33] *Id.*

April 2015 Task Force hearing examining global terrorist financing, Dr. Jonathan Schanzer—Vice President for Research at FDD—testified:

> One thing that has not changed at all is the challenge of deep-pocket donors in the Gulf states. We knew that this was a problem in the immediate aftermath of 9/11, and ... we continue to see challenges out of Saudi Arabia, Kuwait, Qatar, et cetera. This is an issue that we have not fully tackled yet. There has been better cooperation in some cases, but in some cases we continue to see these intransigent countries where they are not cracking down enough....[34]

At the same April 2015 hearing, Juan Zarate—former Deputy Assistant to the President and Deputy National Security Adviser for Combating Terrorism during the George W. Bush administration[35]—elaborated on the issue of donors: stating, "[w]e know some of them. And we also aren't always sure we know what their motivations are. In the context of Syria, this is what makes it so complicated."[36]

Criminal Activities

Terrorist funding from self-generated profits is also common—while some include proceeds from legitimate business ventures, other funds come from illicit activities, such as drug trafficking, kidnapping for ransom, and extortion or even garden-variety petty crimes.[37] For instance, the terror cell suspected of planning the March 22, 2016, bombings in Brussels was comprised mostly of petty criminals who largely immigrated to Europe to pledge allegiance to ISIS.[38] Various observers have asserted that transnational terrorism, crime, and corruption interact in varied and significant ways, and regardless of whether the funds are intended to commit an act of terror or are the proceeds of drug or sex trafficking, white-collar crime, or official corruption, they all move in the same illicit channels.[39] In Congressional

---

[34] Testimony of Dr. Jonathan Schanzer, Vice President for Research, FDD, *Hearings, supra* note 9 (A Survey of Global Terrorism and Terrorist Financing).

[35] Mr. Juan Zarate is currently a Senior Advisor with the Center for Strategic and International Studies, chairman and cofounder of the Financial Integrity Network and a visiting lecturer in law at the Harvard Law School. He also serves as chairman and senior counselor for FDD's Center on Sanctions and Illicit Finance (CFIS). Mr. Zarate was the first ever assistant Secretary to the Treasury for Terrorist Financing and Financial Crimes.

[36] *Hearings, supra* note 9 (A Survey of Global Terrorism and Terrorist Financing), statement of Mr. Juan Zarate.

[37] *Id.*

[38] For instance, according to news reports, French officials investigating the November 2015 Paris terror attacks identified the majority of the masterminds as being French or Belgian nationalists with criminal records and ties to ISIS; *See, e.g.,* "Paris Attacks: Who Were the Attackers?'" BBC NEWS, (Apr. 27, 2016), *available at* http://www.bbc.com/news/world-europe-34832512.

[39] *Hearings, supra* note 10 (A Dangerous Nexus: Terrorism, Crime and Corruption).

testimony from February 2016, for instance, DNI Clapper identified terrorism and transnational organized crime as among the top eight global threats to U.S. national security.[40] The Administration's most recent *National Security Strategy* also echoed that terrorism, crime, and corruption represent mutually reinforcing and interconnected threats[41]—as did a May 21, 2015, Task Force hearing on the financial implications of this nexus.[42]

Over the past decade, the Treasury Department's Office of Terrorism and Financial Intelligence (TFI), the Department of Justice's Drug Enforcement Administration (DEA), and the Department of Defense (DOD) have participated in various efforts to establish foreign-deployed "threat finance cells" as an interagency mechanism "to identify and disrupt financial networks related to terrorism … narcotics trafficking and corruption."[43] The first such threat finance cell was established in 2005 in Iraq and the second in 2008 in Afghanistan.[44] The Afghanistan Threat Finance Cell (ATFC) was reportedly instrumental in discovering the illicit hawala-related financial activities of the New Ansari Exchange,[45] "a major money laundering vehicle for Afghan narcotics trafficking organizations" with ties to known terrorists, including Osama bin Laden.[46] According to Celina Realuyo—Professor of Practice at the William J. Perry Center for Hemispheric Defense Studies at the National Defense University—intelligence and law enforcement operations such as the ATFC should be maintained and used as a model against "emerging crime-terrorism hybrid threats" like ISIS.[47] Juan Zarate reinforced this suggestion in an April 2015 hearing before the Task Force, stating:

---

[40] *Hearing before U.S. Senate Select Committee on Intelligence,* 114th Cong. (Feb. 9, 2016), *available at* http://www.intelligence.senate.gov/hearings/open-hearing-worldwide-threats-hearing.

[41] *See* The White House, *National Security Strategy,* (Feb. 1, 2015), *available at* https://www.whitehouse.gov/sites/default/files/docs/2015_national_security_strategy.pdf; The Obama Administration released its second National Security Strategy on February 6, 2015; the first was published in May, 2010, as part of a Congressional mandate in the Goldwater-Nichols Department of Defense Reorganization Act of 196 (P.L. 99-433, § 603/50 U.S. C. §3043).

[42] *Hearings, supra* note 10 (A Dangerous Nexus: Terrorism, Crime and Corruption).

[43] *See* U.S. Dep't of the Treasury, *Fact Sheet: Combating the Financing of Terrorism, Disrupting Terrorism at its Core,* (Sept. 8, 2011), *available at* https://www.treasury.gov/press-center/press-releases/Pages/tg1291.aspx.

[44] Written Testimony of Daniel L. Glaser, Treasury Assistant Secretary, for *Combating Terrorism Post-9/11: Oversight of the Office of Terrorism and Financial Intelligence: House Fin. Serv. Subcomm. on Oversight and Investigations* (Sept. 6, 2011), *available at* https://www.treasury.gov/press-center/press-releases/Pages/tg1287.aspx.

[45] U.S. Dep't of the Treasury, *Treasury Designates New Ansari Money Exchange* (Feb. 18, 2011), *available at* https://www.treasury.gov/press-center/press-releases/Pages/tg1071.aspx.

[46] Yaroslav Trofimov, "Al Ansari Exchange Finds Itself Embroiled in Terror Investigation," WALL ST. J. (Nov. 1, 2001), *available at* http://www.wsj.com/articles/SB1004652055539614360.

[47] Testimony of Celina Realuyo, Professor of Practice, William J. Perry Center for Hemispheric Defense Studies, National Defense University, *Hearings, supra* note 10 (A Dangerous Nexus: Terrorism, Crime and Corruption).

The first thing I would do ... is reinstate the Iraq Threat Finance Cell, which we had created in 2006, to look at how Al-Qaeda in Iraq and the insurgents were funding themselves. They are engaged in bank robbery, oil smuggling, kidnap-for-ransom. All the things we are talking about now, they were doing on a micro-scale then. And you need the intelligence and analysis to map it....[48]

Experts generally acknowledge that terrorist organizations are becoming more willing to interact with criminal organizations, even when the entities may have divergent goals or ideologies. According to Richard Barrett—Senior Vice President of the Soufan Group—this willingness has developed because terrorist organizations simply will "do whatever is easiest and most effective" to fund operations.[49] Mr. Barrett offered additional insight into this relationship at the Task Force's May 2015 hearing, stating:

Increasingly, terrorists are attracted to less-governed areas of the world where they can establish bases and control territory. And inevitably too, these areas are ones that criminals use for their own trans-shipments of drugs or other contraband and things like that. And to this extent, terrorists have established a close relationship both with crime and with criminal gangs, though in my view they are more likely to take a cut from the criminal gangs than to join their rackets or compete with them....[50]

In testimony during the same hearing, Douglas Farah—President of IBI Consultants LLC—also identified the "convergence of terrorism, transnational crime, and corruption [as] ... a significant strategic threat to the United States."[51] Mr. Farah described how a bloc of countries in South America, led by Venezuela, are operating transnational organized criminal networks, creating alliances across the globe with terrorist organizations, including Hezbollah and the Revolutionary Armed Forces of Columbia (FARC), often using profits from drug trafficking as their revenue source.[52] Professor Realuyo also offered additional background and specific examples on the nexus between terrorism, crime, and corruption, stating that the "Haqqani Network in Afghanistan, the FARC in Colombia, Hezbollah, and ISIL" all exhibit the hybrid terror-crime behavior.[53]

---

[48] Testimony of Mr. Juan Zarate, *Hearings, supra* note 9 (A Survey of Global Terrorism and Terrorist Financing).
[49] Testimony of Richard Barrett, Senior Vice President, Soufan Group, *Hearings, supra* note 9 (A Survey of Global Terrorism and Terrorist Financing).
[50] *Id.*
[51] Testimony of Douglas Farah, President, IBI Consultants LLC, *Hearings, supra* note 9 (A Survey of Global Terrorism and Terrorist Financing).
[52] Mr. Farah refers to this movement as "the Bolivarian alliance," noting it has "been successful." *Id.*
[53] Testimony of Celina B. Realuyo, Professor of Practice, William J. Perry Center for Hemispheric Defense Studies, *Hearings, supra* note 10 (A Dangerous Nexus: Terrorism, Crime and Corruption).

Key Terrorist Financiers

The terrorist groups that pose the highest threat as a consequence of their financial capabilities include well-funded groups like ISIS; Nigerian-based Boko Haram; Al-Shabaab, a Somalian fundamentalist group; the Lebanese-Shiite Muslim political party Hezbollah; Palestinian Sunni-Islamic fundamentalist organization Hamas; and FARC.[54] The Task Force's efforts revealed how these and other terrorist groups use diverse methods—some involving the formal banking sector—to generate and move funds to support their agendas and activities.

ISIS

While recent assessments indicate that both ISIS's income and financial assets have declined from the reportedly two billion dollars available at the group's peak in late 2014 to early 2015, ISIS fundraising methods have continued to evolve.[55] According to Daniel Glaser—Treasury's Assistant Secretary for Terrorist Financing—oil revenue, which is ISIS's largest source of income, has dropped from approximately $500 million per year to "probably… about half of what they previously have been making,"[56] and much of this oil has crossed clandestinely into Turkey.[57]

Notwithstanding the constriction of its main funding source, ISIS has innovated in its fundraising efforts with alarming success.[58] Notably, ISIS has profited from looting antiquities from cultural sites in Iraq and Syria.[59] During testimony at the Task Force's April 19, 2016, hearing, Robert M. Edsel—Chairman of the Board of the Monuments Men Foundation—explained that the "profitability

---

[54] The degree to which all of these terrorist organizations finance their activities was explored in several Task Force hearings.

[55] Testimony of Seth G. Jones, Director of the International Security and Defense Policy Center, RAND Corporation, *Hearings, supra* note 9 (A Survey of Global Terrorism and Terrorist Financing).

[56] Foundation for Defense of Democracies, "State of Play: Combating Today's Illicit Financial Networks" (May 11, 2016), transcript *available at* http://www.defenddemocracy.org/events/conversation-with-daniel-glaser-and-juan-zarate/.

[57] Mr. Schanzer stated that, at its peak, between $1-2 million worth of oil was reportedly smuggled daily to Turkey's border area to be sold through middlemen…." *See* Testimony by Dr. Jonathan Schanzer, Vice President for Research at FDD, *Hearing, supra* note 9 (A Survey of Global Terrorism and Terrorist Financing); *see also* Testimony by Professor Celina B. Realuyo, *Hearing, supra* 10 (A Dangerous Nexus: Terrorism Crime and Corruption). .

[58] Testimony of Seth G. Jones, Director of the International Security and Defense Policy Center, RAND Corporation, *Hearing, supra* note 9 (A Survey of Global Terrorism and Terrorist Financing).

[59] *Id. See also* Mark Vlasic, "Islamic State sells 'blood antiquities' from Iraq and Syria to raise money," WA Po, (Sept. 14, 2014), *available at* http://www.washingtonpost.com/opinions/islamic-state-sells-blood-antiquities-from-iraq-and-syria-to-raise-money/2014/09/14/49663c98-3a7e-11e4-9c9f-ebb47272e40e_story.html.

of art and antiques and sometimes their relatively small size facilitates movement" by criminals and terrorist groups, often by moving proceeds out of the purview of taxing authorities.[60] Although there is not an exact estimate of how much ISIS profits overall from looting antiquities,[61] Iraqi officials claimed in 2015 that ISIS could be generating as much as $100 million annually.[62] In March 2016, Russian officials also sent a letter to the president of the United Nations Security Council (UNSC) stating "[t]he profit derived by the Islamists from the illicit trade in antiquities and archaeological treasures is estimated at as much as $150-200 million per year."[63] Furthermore, according to Dr. Patty Gerstenblith of DePaul University College of Law, the United States is "the single largest market for art in the world, with 43 percent market share," adding that the United States is also "the largest ultimate market for antiquities," meaning that a good portion of stolen arts and antiquities could end up in the country with an overall share of the market. [64]

During an April 2015 hearing, Seth G. Jones—Director of the International Security and Defense Policy Center at the RAND Corporation—testified that ISIS might also have one to two percent of its assistance coming from outside donors.[65] In a fashion similar to its predecessor, Al-Qaeda in Iraq, ISIS also raises several million dollars per month through a sophisticated extortion and taxation racket.[66] According to the U.S. Government Accountability Office (GAO), sales receipts from ISIS' Antiquities Division uncovered in the U.S. raid of Abu Sayyaf—dubbed as ISIS' "chief financial officer"—indicate that the terrorist group had earned more than $265,000 "in taxes on the sale of antiquities over a 4-month period in late 2013

[60] Testimony by Robert M. Edsel, Chairman of the Board, Monuments Men Foundation, *Hearings, supra* note 17 (Preventing Cultural Genocide: Countering the Plunder and Sale of Priceless Cultural Antiquities by ISIS).

[61] *Id.*

[62] *Id.* In June 2014, *The Guardian (UK)* reported that the Iraqi forces raided the home of an ISIS military leader near Mosul and collected "more than 160 computer flash sticks" with details on the organization's finances. The article quoted an Iraqi intelligence office as stating that ISIS had generated "$36 million from al-Nabuk alone" and that "the antiquities there are up to 8,000 years old." This assertion has generated debate among observers, who question whether the $36 million figure represented only antiquities looting or included other sources of revenue. *See* Martin Chulov, "How an Arrest in Iraq Revealed ISIS's $2bn Jihadist Network," THE GUARDIAN (June 15, 2014), *available at* https://www.theguardian.com/world/2014/jun/15/iraq-isis-arrest-jihadists-wealth-power.

[63] *Hearings, supra* note 17 (Preventing Cultural Genocide: Countering the Plunder and Sale of Priceless Cultural Antiquities by ISIS); UNSC, *Smuggling of Antiquities by the International Terrorist Organization Islamic State in Iraq and the Levant,* letter and annex from the Permanent Representative of the Russian Federation to the United Nations addressed to the President of the Security Council, S/2016/298, (Mar. 31, 2016).

[64] Testimony of Dr. Patty Gerstenblith, Ph.D., Distinguished Professor, DePaul University College of Law, *Hearings, supra* note 17 (Preventing Cultural Genocide: Countering the Plunder and Sale of Priceless Cultural Antiquities by ISIS).

[65] Testimony of Seth G. Jones, Director of International Security and Defense Policy Center at the RAND Corporation, *Hearings, supra* note 9 (A Survey of Global Terrorism and Terrorist Financing).

[66] Remarks by David Cohen, Under Secretary for Terrorism and Financial Intelligence, U.S. Dep't of the Treasury, *Attacking ISIL's Financial Foundation* (Oct. 23, 2014), *available at* https://www.treasury.gov/press-center/press-releases/Pages/jl2672.aspx.

and early 2015."[67] Assistant Secretary Glaser estimates that the Islamic State generates approximately $360 million per year broadly in "taxation."[68] Kidnapping and ransom payments tend to be fairly irregular, but each one can be a significant source of revenue as well.[69]

Boko Haram

To fund its operations, the Nigerian-based Boko Haram deploys a system of couriers to move cash inside Nigeria and across the border from neighboring African states.[70] Boko Haram's annual net income has been estimated at $10 million.[71] These funds have been raised primarily through kidnapping and extortion.[72] Some U.S. officials have estimated that the group was paid as much as $1 million for the release of a wealthy Nigerian.[73] Foreigners have fetched higher ransoms—in February 2013, Boko Haram was paid $3 million for the release of a French family of seven kidnapped in northern Cameroon.[74] The group has also smuggled drugs to raise funds. In 2012, the DEA indicated that Boko Haram was becoming increasingly involved in cocaine trafficking to raise money for its activities, or was being bankrolled by the traffickers in exchange for support. [75] The Treasury Department also has evidence that Al-Qaeda has financially supported Boko Haram.[76] The amount of this support, however, is dwarfed by the millions of dollars the group makes through its kidnapping and ransom activities. For instance, one U.S. estimate of financial transfers from Al-Qaeda in the Islamic Magreb (AQIM), which is "an offshoot of the jihadist group founded by Osama bin Laden," was in the low hundreds of thousands of dollars.[77]

---

[67] *See*, U.S. Gov't Accountability Office, *Cultural Property: Protection of Iraqi and Syrian Antiquities*, GAO-16-673, 9 (Aug. 2016), *available at* http://www.gao.gov/assets/680/679061.pdf.

[68] Foundation for Defense of Democracies, "State of Play: Combating Today's Illicit Financial Networks" (May 11, 2016), transcript *available at* http://www.defenddemocracy.org/events/conversation-with-daniel-glaser-and-juan-zarate/.

[69] *Id.*

[70] Phil Stewart and Lesley Wroughton, "How Boko Haram is Beating U.S. Efforts to Choke Its Financing," REUTERS (July 1, 2014), *available at* http://www.reuters.com/article/2014/07/01/us-usa-nigeria-bokoharam-insight-idUSKBN0F636920140701.

[71] Farouk, Chothia, "Boko Haram Crisis: How Have Nigeria's Militants Become So Strong?" BBC News (Jan. 26, 2015), *available at* http://www.bbc.com/news/world-africa-30933860.

[72] *Id.*

[73] *Id.*

[74] *Id.*

[75] Ntaryike Divine, Jr., "Drug Trafficking Rising in Central Africa, Warns Interpol," VOICE OF AMERICA (Sept. 8, 2012), *available at* http://www.voanews.com/content/drug-trafficking-rising-in-central-africa-warns-interpol/1504026.html.

[76] Phil Stewart and Lesley Wroughton, "How Boko Haram is Beating U.S. Efforts to Choke Its Financing," REUTERS (July 1, 2014), *available at* http://www.reuters.com/article/2014/07/01/us-usa-nigeria-bokoharam-insight-idUSKBN0F636920140701.

[77] *Id.*

Counterterrorism experts say Somalia-based Al-Shabab has benefited from several different sources of income over the years, including revenue from other terrorist groups, state sponsors of terrorism, some members of the Somali diaspora, charities, piracy, kidnapping, and the extortion of local businesses.[78] The governments of Eritrea, Iran, Saudi Arabia, Syria, Qatar, and Yemen have been cited as financiers—although most officially deny these claims. [79] Domestically, the group built an extensive racketeering operation in Kismayo, Somalia, after seizing control of the southern port city and its economy in 2008.[80] A major fundraising source is the trade of charcoal, which is essential to the city's commerce.[81] A Kenya-led assault liberated Kismayo from Al-Shabaab control in October 2012—a victory that many experts say strategically crippled the jihadi group.[82] However, an October 2014 UN Security Council report says Al-Shabaab's illicit charcoal trading has not been interrupted by "the military offensive against the group" and continues in Kismayo and nearby Barawe.[83]

---

[78] *See* Jonathan Masters and Mohammed Aly Sergie, *Al-Shabaab, Council on Foreign Relations Backgrounders* (Mar. 5, 2015), *available at* http://www.cfr.org/somalia/al-shabab/p18650.
[79] *Id.*
[80] *Id.*
[81] *Id.*
[82] *Id.*
[83] *Id.*

Hezbollah

Since 2010, Lebanese-based Hezbollah has been linked with South American drug trafficking organizations.[84] Hezbollah has primarily used the proceeds from trafficking cocaine into Europe and the Middle East to finance its operations.[85] Like many criminal organizations, Hezbollah has established itself firmly within the vastly unregulated, virtually lawless region defined by the confluence of the Paraná and Iguazú rivers in Paraguay, and Argentina and Brazil, known as the Tri-Border region.[86] Hezbollah also continues to become more efficient at smuggling drugs from the Andean region of South America in Chile, Bolivia, and Peru, where it is shipped to European markets through West and North Africa.[87] Michael Braun—Managing Partner at SGI Global—provided his analysis on the topic to the Task Force in testimony for a hearing held on June 8, 2016:

> Hezbollah is not the same organization that they were 15 … years ago. In the early 2000s, they began moving small quantities of cocaine from the tri-border area of Latin America into fledgling markets … in Europe and the Middle East…. [F]ifteen years later, they are now moving multi-tons of cocaine into Europe in an attempt to satisfy the ever-increasing demand…. [T]hey possess a demonstrated ability to move … hundreds of tons of cocaine over that 15-year period and move massive amounts of currency, hundreds of millions, perhaps billions of dollars in currency around the world in the most sophisticated money laundering scheme[s] that we have ever witnessed. They have metastasized into a hydra with international connections that … ISIS and groups like al Qaeda could only hope to have.[88]

FARC

Terrorist groups like the Foreign Terrorist Organization (FTO)-designated FARC, which controls the majority of the world's illicit cocaine cultivation and production, cooperate with corrupt government officials in Latin American countries

---

[84] Clare Ribando Seelke et. al, "Latin America and the Caribbean: Illicit Drug Trafficking and U.S. Counterdrug Programs," *CRS Report R41215* (Apr. 30, 2010), *available at* http://assets.opencrs.com/rpts/R41215_20100430.pdf.

[85] Edwin Mora, "State Dep't: Hezbollah Raising Funds Through Drug Cartels in South America But 'No Credible Information' of Terrorist Operations There," CNS NEWS (June 9, 2010), *available at* http://cnsnews.com/news/article/state-dept-hezbollah-raising-funds-through-drug-cartels-south-america-no-credible.

[86] Testimony of Dr. Emanuele Ottolenghi, Senior Fellow, Center on Sanctions and Illicit Finance, FDD, *Hearings, supra* note 19 (The Enemy in Our Backyard: Examining Terror Funding Streams from South America).

[87] Testimony of Michael A. Braun, Co-Founder and Managing Partner, SGI Global, LLC, *Hearings, supra* note 19 (The Enemy in Our Backyard: Examining Terror Funding Streams from South America).

[88] *Id.*

such as Venezuela to carry out their illicit deeds.[89] FARC obtains funds from extortion, kidnapping for ransom, and drug trafficking. According to recent testimony, drug proceeds benefitting FARC may range from $200 million to $3 billion per year.[90] In recent years, FARC diversified into illegal mining, especially gold mining as gold prices rose.[91] In April 2016, *The Economist* reported that an unpublished Colombian study estimated that FARC had stockpiled some $11 billion in assets by 2012.[92] After nearly four years of negotiations, the Columbian government and FARC reached a peace deal to end their 52-year war in August 2016; however, it is too soon to tell if the agreement will be effective.[93]

An additional concern is ISIS's infiltration of Latin American terrorist organizations. Specifically, Admiral Kurt Tidd, U.S. Commander of Southern Command (SOUTHCOM), pointed out the connection between Latin America and ISIS, emphasizing that international terrorist organizations also profit from criminal activity in Latin America, but that the terrorist threat often is underestimated in relation to terrorism in other parts of the world.[94]

---

[89] Vanda Felbab-Brown, *Shooting Up: Counterinsurgency and the War on Drugs* (Jan. 13, 2010), *available at* https://www.brookings.edu/book/shooting-up/.

[90] Prepared statement of Michael Shifter, President of the Inter-American Dialogue, for *Terrorist Groups in Latin America: The Changing Landscape: Hearing before the H. Foreign Affairs Subcomm. on Terrorism, Nonproliferation and Trade* (Feb. 4, 2014), *available at* https://foreignaffairs.house.gov/hearing/subcommittee-hearing-terrorist-groups-in-latin-america-the-changing-landscape/.

[91] *See* Juan Carlos Garzón and Julian Wilches, "The Reasons for the Surge in Coca Cultivation in Colombia," Wilson Center for International Studies (Aug.25, 2015), *available at* https://www.wilsoncenter.org/article/the-reasons-for-the-surge-coca-cultivation-colombia.   (examining the idea that coca cultivation and gold price are correlated and finding that these activities may be complementary).

[92] *See* "Unfunny Money," ECONOMIST (Apr. 16, 2016), *available at* http://www.economist.com/news/americas/21697008-government-may-never-get-its-hands-guerrillas-ill-gotten-gains-unfunny-money.   Notably, Colombian officials have not corroborated this estimate since *The Economist* article was published. FARC has also reportedly denied the accuracy of the figure as well.

[93] *See, e.g.,* Steven Pinker and Juan Manuel Santos, "Columbia's Milestone in World Peace," N.Y. TIMES, (Aug. 26, 2016), *available at* http://www.nytimes.com/2016/08/26/opinion/colombias-milestone-in-world-peace.html?_r=0.

[94] *Hearings, supra* note 19 (The Enemy in our Backyard: Examining Terror Funding Streams from South America).

U.S. Policy Responses to Terrorist Financing

Policy Responses in Historical Perspective

The foundations of contemporary U.S. efforts to stop the financing of terror are grounded in anti-money laundering regimes that date back to enactment of the Bank Secrecy Act of 1970 (BSA).[95] Designations and prohibitions against State Sponsors of Terrorism and Foreign Terrorist Organizations first emerged in the late 1970s and evolved through the 1990s to include statutes that criminalized "material support" of terrorists, designated terrorist organizations,[96] and established targeted financial sanctions against FTOs and terrorist groups. Immediately following the September 11, 2001, terror attacks, departments, bureaus, and agencies throughout the U.S. government additionally sought to enhance coordination in the fight to curtail terrorist financing, and Congress enacted several landmark measures that provided additional tools to counter the convergence of terror financing methodologies. The United States also ratified the Terrorist Financing Convention UN resolution in June 2002.[97]

Agency Efforts to Combat Terrorist Financing

The Federal Bureau of Investigation (FBI) established the Terrorism Financing Operations Section (TFOS) within its Counterterrorism Division immediately after the September 11, 2011, terrorist attacks to coordinate and centralize its efforts to track the financial underpinning of terrorist activity.[98] The National Security Council (NSC) established the interagency Terrorist Financing Working Group (TFWG) in 2001, which is chaired by the State Department and tasked with coordinating the interagency delivery of training and technical assistance to combat terrorist financing. The group, which has been on hiatus since at least late 2012 or early 2013 due to organization restructuring within Counterterrorism,[99] has been criticized for gaps in coordination on counter terrorist financing training and technical assistance.[100] However, experts like Professor

---

[95] 12 U.S.C. §1829b, 12 U.S. C. §§1951-9, and 31 U.S.C. §§5311-14, 5316-32.

[96] *See* 18 U.S.C. §§ 2339(A)-(B).

[97] *International Convention for the Suppression of the Financing of Terrorism*, 9 G.A. Res. 109, U.N. GAOR 54th Sess., 76th mtg., U.N. Doc. A/RES/54/109 (2000) (Dec. 9, 1999).

[98] *See* Federal Bureau of Investigation, *Terrorism, available at* https://www.fbi.gov/investigate/terrorism.

[99] *See* U.S. Gov't Accountability Office, "Combating Terrorism: State Should Evaluate its Countering Violent Extremism Program and Set Time Frames for Addressing Evaluation Recommendations," GAO-15-684, July 2015), *available at* http://www.gao.gov/products/GAO-15-684.

[100] The State Dep't alerted the Committee that the Bureaus of International Narcotics and Law Enforcement Affairs and Counterterrorism still speak regularly and coordinate on terrorism financing issues like preparation for FATF meetings. *See, e.g.*, U.S. Gov't Accountability Office, *Agencies Can Improve Efforts to Deliver Counter-Terrorism-Financing Training and Technical*

Realuyo recommended reviving the TFWG. In testimony before the Task Force on May 21, 2015, she stated TFWG is necessary "to coordinate U.S. government efforts to combat terrorist financing via designations, the enforcement of sanctions and technical assistance and capacity building programs."[101]

After the creation of the Department of Homeland Security (DHS) in November 2002, the Treasury Department also underwent several institutional changes that emphasized counterterrorism finance.[102]

Treasury's Counter Terrorist Financing Authorities and Organization

On May 8, 2004, Treasury's Office of Terrorism and Financial Intelligence was established to marshal Treasury's policy, enforcement, regulatory, and intelligence functions.[103] Sections within TFI include the Office of Terrorist Financing and Financial Crimes (TFFC), and the Office of Intelligence and Analysis (OIA),[104] which is a formal member of the U.S. Intelligence Community that contributes all-source financial threat assessments and products. OIA's analysts have been central in interagency efforts such as the Afghanistan and Iraq Threat Finance Cells.[105] TFFC is the policy development and outreach office for TFI, which, among other priorities, leads the U.S. delegation to FATF.[106] TFI, headed by an Under Secretary, also includes a separate bureau, FinCEN, which collects and analyzes data on financial crimes, and the Office of Foreign Assets Control (OFAC), which administers multiple sanctions programs to block transactions and freeze assets within U.S. jurisdiction of specified foreign terrorist, criminal, and political entities, including specially designated individuals and nation states.[107] Both FinCEN and OFAC pre-date the formation of TFI.[108]

---

assistance Abroad, GAO-06-632T (Apr. 6, 20016), *available at* http://www.gao.gov/products/GAO-06-632T.

[101] Testimony of Celina Realuyo, Professor of Practice, William J. Perry Center for Hemispheric Defense Studies at National Defense University, *Hearings, supra* note 10 (A Dangerous Nexus: Terrorism, Crime and Corruption).

[102] *Id.*

[103] P.L. 108-447. U.S. Dep't of the Treasury, *Terrorism and Financial Intelligence* (last updated June 28, 2013), http://www.treasury.gov/about/organizational-structure/offices/Pages/Office-of-Terrorism-and-Financial-Intelligence.aspx.

[104] *Id.*

[105] OIA was established by the Intelligence Authorization Act for Fiscal Year 2004 (P.L. 108-177).

[106] The Intelligence Reform and Terrorism Prevention Act of 2004 (P.L. 108-458) authorized the Secretary of the Treasury, or the Secretary's designee, as the lead U.S. government liaison to the Financial Action Task Force.

[107] Authorities for OFAC to designate such entities are derived from executive order and federal statutes, including the International Emergency Economic Powers Act (IEEPA), the Antiterrorism and Effective Death Penalty Act of 1996 (AEDPA), and the Foreign Narcotics Kingpin Designation Act.

[108] *Id.*

FinCEN's mission is to safeguard the financial system, combat money laundering, and promote national security through the collection, analysis, and dissemination of financial intelligence.[109] Then-FinCEN Director Jennifer Shasky Calvery told the Task Force on May 24, 2016, that FinCEN, the official Financial Intelligence Unit (FIU) of the United States, is the lead bureau in efforts to thwart AML and terrorism financing. Ms. Calvery elaborated:

> We disseminate information to our law enforcement partners, intelligence authorities, border police ... [and] relevant FIUs.... [O]ver the past eight months we have received 354 positive responses from 41 foreign FIUs that the financial intelligence we provided either corroborated information related to an ongoing investigation or provided new investigative leads.[110]

The U.S. Counter Terrorist Financing Legal Framework

On September 23, 2001, President George W. Bush issued Executive Order 13224, blocking property and prohibiting transactions with persons who commit, threaten to commit, or support terrorism.[111] In public remarks upon issuing E.O. 13224, President Bush announced:

> Today, we have launched a strike on the financial foundation of the global terror network.... We have developed the international financial equivalent of law enforcement's 'Most Wanted' list. And it puts the financial world on notice.... Money is the lifeblood of terrorist operations. Today, we're asking the world to stop payment.[112]

Days after, the UN Security Council also adopted Resolution 1373 as an additional international measure to combat terrorism.[113] E.O. 13224 and Security Council Resolution 1373 provide the basic framework for efforts to identify and freeze assets of individuals and entities associated with terrorism.

---

[109] *Id.*

[110] *See* testimony of Jennifer Shasky-Calvery, former Director, FinCEN, U.S. Dep't of the Treasury, *Hearings, supra* note 18, (Stopping Terror Finance: A Coordinated Government Effort).

[111] *Blocking Property and Prohibiting Transactions with Persons who Commit, Threaten to Commit, or Support Terrorism*, Exec. Order No. 13,224, 3 C.F.R.786-90 (2001), *available at* https://www.treasury.gov/resource-center/sanctions/Programs/Documents/terror.pdf.

[112] Remarks in the Rose Garden, Washington, D.C., by President George W. Bush, *President Freezes Terrorists' Assets* (Sept. 24, 2001), *available at* http://2001-2009.state.gov/s/ct/rls/rm/2001/5041.htm.

[113] UN Security Council, Resolution 1373 (2001), *available at* http://www.un.org/en/sc/ctc/specialmeetings/2012/docs/United%20Nations%20Security%20Council%20Resolution%201373%20(2001).pdf.

The following month, in October 2001, Congress enacted the USA PATRIOT Act to strengthen the U.S. government's ability to detect, report, and prevent terrorist activities, including potential connections between organized crime, terrorism, and corruption.[114] Among the most notable amendments to the Bank Secrecy Act, which requires U.S. financial institutions to assist U.S. government agencies in detecting and preventing money laundering, is Title III of the USA PATRIOT Act of 2001.[115] This title requires financial institutions to establish, implement, and maintain a program to prevent money laundering, related illicit finance, and terror financing.[116]

USA PATRIOT Act Information Sharing Provisions

Section 311 of the USA PATRIOT Act authorizes the Treasury Secretary to determine whether a foreign country, financial institution, type of account, or class of transactions, is a "primary money laundering concern" and to subsequently impose any one or a combination of "special measures."[117] FinCEN has used Section 311 to alert the U.S. financial system to terrorist financing threats associated with several foreign jurisdictions and foreign financial institutions, including the Islamic Republic of Iran; Lebanese Canadian Bank; the Commercial Bank of Syria, including its subsidiary Syrian Lebanese Commercial Bank; Halawi Exchange Co.; and Kassem Rmeiti & Co.[118]

Section 314 of the USA PATRIOT Act strengthens the U.S. government's ability to share information with financial institutions to aid in law enforcement investigations against terrorist financing threats.[119] Section 314(a) allows law enforcement authorities to share information with financial institutions regarding individuals, entities, and organizations engaged in or reasonably suspected of engaging in terrorist acts, and to determine whether the target of an investigation maintains an account at a particular financial institution.[120] Section 314(b) creates

---

[114] *Uniting and Strengthening America by Providing Appropriate Tools Required to Intercept and Obstruct Terrorism* (USA PATRIOT) *Act* of 2001, P.L. 107-56, 115 Stat. 272.

[115] *The International Money Laundering Abatement and Anti-Terrorism Financing Act of 2001*, P.L. No. 107-56, tit. III, (Oct. 26, 2001), 115 Stat. 296.

[116] 31 USC § 5318(h)(1) (2000 & Supp. IV 2004); *see* Jimmy Gurulé, *Unfunding Terror*, 157 (2008).

[117] The five special measures are enumerated and may require financial institutions to (1) keep special records and file reports on particular transactions; (2) obtain information on the beneficial ownership on any account opened or maintained in the U.S.; (3) identify and obtain information about customers permitted to use or whose transactions are routed through a foreign bank's 'payable-through' account; (4) identify and obtain information about customers permitted to use, or whose transactions are routed through, a foreign bank's 'correspondent' account or (5) prohibit, or impose conditions upon the opening or maintaining in the U.S. of a correspondent account or payable-through account. 31 U.S.C. § 5318A(b)(1)-(5).

[118] A list of Section 311 Special Measures taken by FinCEN is *available at* http://www.fincen.gov/statutes_regs/patriot/section311.html.

[119] *See* note 115, *supra*, P.L. 107-56, §314 (115 Stat. 272).

[120] *See* 31 U.S.C. § 5318.

a "safe harbor" provision allowing for limited bank-to-bank information sharing.[121] The Task Force heard testimony suggesting it may be necessary to refine the "safe harbor" for information sharing to clarify that a bank need not have a "good faith" belief that an actual violation occurred before filing a suspicious activity report (SAR) with FinCEN, and to clarify that there is no civil liability for complying with the BSA.[122]

Section 319(a) enhances law enforcement's ability to impose penalties on and pursue assets of financial institutions overseas, while Section 319(b) provides law enforcement with summons and subpoena authority with respect to foreign banks that have correspondent accounts in the United States.[123] Particularly recently, the government has aggressively sought to incentivize statutory compliance by dramatically increasing the actions taken against institutions found to be deficient in BSA compliance. In December 2012, HSBC, a UK-headquartered financial institution with a substantial U.S. presence, was ordered to pay a total of approximately $1.92 billion in civil money penalties and asset forfeitures for allowing hundreds of millions of dollars in drug proceeds to flow into the U.S. financial system.[124] Furthermore, in a July 2014 settlement with U.S. regulators and law enforcement, BNP Paribas, in addition to paying a total of approximately $8.9 billion in criminal penalties and asset forfeitures, was subjected to a yearlong suspension of certain U.S. dollar-clearing services through its New York branch and other affiliates.[125]

Helping the Developing World Fight Terrorist Financing

Because an effective AML/CFT regime is only as strong as its weakest link, the United States has dedicated substantial resources to helping developing countries develop adequate AML/CFT efforts. Agencies throughout the government have a hand in this assistance, including the Federal Reserve System; the Federal Deposit Insurance Corporation (FDIC); the Criminal Investigations Division of the Internal Revenue Service (IRS); DHS, through the United States Secret Service,

---

[121] *Id.*

[122] Testimony of Chip Poncy, Senior Advisor, Center on Sanctions and Illicit Finance, FDD, *Hearings, supra* note 11 (Evaluating the Security of the U.S. Financial Sector). In a private meeting with Task Force Members on July 8, 2015, a half dozen multinational banks were very pointed about needing a robust safe harbor to share information with one another on illicit activity beyond what they link directly to money laundering and terrorist financing activities, because terrorists are resorting to varying crimes to finance their activities.

[123] *See* 18 U.S.C. § 981(k); 31 U.S.C. § 5318(k)(3).

[124] *See* Deferred Prosecution Agreement at 3, *United States v. HSBC Bank USA, N A. and HSBC Holdings, PLC*, No. 12-CR-763 (S.D.N.Y. Dec. 11, 2012).

[125] *See* U.S. Dep't of Justice, Press Release, *BNP Paribas Agrees to Plead Guilty and to Pay $8.9 Billion for Illegally Processing Financial Transactions for Countries Subject to U.S. Economic Sanctions* (June 30, 2014), *available at* https://www.justice.gov/opa/pr/bnp-paribas-agrees-plead-guilty-and-pay-89-billion-illegally-processing-financial.

Customs and Border Protection (CPB) and Immigrant Customs Enforcement (ICE); the Department of Justice, through the DEA, Asset Forfeiture and Money Laundering Section, and National Security Division; and the State Department's Bureau of International Narcotics and Law Enforcement Affairs, and Bureau of Counterterrorism, and the U.S. Agency for International Development.[126]

According to the State Department's most recent report to Congress on money laundering and financial crimes, the U.S. government provided AML/CFT support to more than 100 countries in 2014 in the form of training, mentoring, and other support for the full range of AML/CFT efforts.[127] While Treasury's OFAC imposes targeted sanctions, and provides global guidance and regulatory standard setting, both OFAC and FinCEN offer training and technical assistance to build the capabilities of national government AML/CFT efforts as well.[128] Treasury's Office of Technical Assistance (OTA), operating with an annual budget of approximately $50 million,[129] also provides a number of different training programs including short- and long-term tours of duty for its experts.

On May 24, 2016, Deputy Assistant Treasury Secretary for Technical Assistance Larry McDonald explained to the Task Force that providing technical assistance to developing and transitional countries is key to combating AML/CFT. During testimony he stated:

> [r]ecipients of technical assistance must be genuinely committed to implementing change and willing to engage in a collaborative learning process and then to apply the lessons learned in day-to-day job functions. An additional critical component is a commitment at the policy and political levels to push for transparency and accountability in public finance when, inevitably, entrenched interests resist. Finally, governments that receive technical assistance must show a commitment to creating and retaining a corps of career professionals. It is disheartening when, with a change of government in our partner countries, OTA's technical level counterparts are replaced and capacity building efforts need to begin anew.[130]

Multilateral organizations also provide technical assistance and training at different levels. In remarks delivered in April 2015, Yury Fedetov—Executive

---

[126] U.S. Dep't of State, *International Narcotics Control Strategy Report, Money Laundering and Financial Crimes* (March 2015), *available at* http://www.state.gov/j/inl/rls/nrcrpt/2016/.
[127] *Id.*
[128] OFAC publishes lists of Specially Designated Nationals, as well as a Consolidated Sanctions list, and others. OFAC enforces these financial sanctions, as well as sanctions taken under Sec. 311 of the USA PATRIOT Act.
[129] Testimony of Larry McDonald, Treasury Deputy Assistant Secretary for Technical Assistance and Afghanistan, *Hearings, supra* 18 (Stopping Terror Finance: A Coordinated Government Effort).
[130] *Id.*

Director of the United Nations Office on Drugs and Crime (UNODC)—commented that:

> [The] most frequently identified technical assistance needs in countering terrorist financing are one, strengthening the effective cooperation between national agencies which are involved directly or indirectly in fighting terrorist financing, and two, enhancing cooperation between regional and international networks.[131]

Both the World Bank and the International Monetary Fund (IMF) have programs aimed at helping countries improve their efforts to combat illicit finance. Mariano Federici—formerly Senior Counsel with the IMF—now serves as President of the Argentine FIU in the administration of the recently elected President Mauricio Marci. In a Task Force hearing held on June 8, 2016, Federici explained previous vulnerabilities in the Argentine financial system, specifically with the FIU and its inability to identify and combat money laundering and terrorist financing.[132] Federici said the FIU was previously "overpopulated with people unfit for the technical profile, who were unable to meet legal requirements to be a member of the FIU" and who had "[n]o understanding of money laundering [or] terrorist financing" and lacked a strategy.[133]

Federici believes these shortcomings allowed "discretionary use" of AML/CFT tools, but emphasized the Argentine FIU has learned from its mistakes.[134] Due in large part to technical assistance provided by the Treasury Department's OTA, however, Federici expressed optimism for the Argentine FIU's developing capabilities and commitment to AML/CFT and other international standards.[135] Still, the international community has yet to clarify the varying roles that state, regional, and international entities should play in coordinating and implementing effective AML/CFT capacity building assistance. As terrorist financing and other illicit financial activity continues to pose risks to the international financial system, some have called for greater AML/CFT cooperation among national and international agencies.[136]

Harmonizing AML/CFT Standards

---

[131] Remarks of Yury Fedetov, *UNODC High-Level Special Event on Strengthening National and International Cooperation in Preventing and Countering Terrorist Financing* (Apr. 14, 2015), *available at* https://www.unodc.org/unodc/en/speeches/2015/cc-terrorismfinancing-140415.html.

[132] Testimony of Mariano Federici, President of Argentina's Financial Intelligence Unit, *Hearings, supra* 19 (The Enemy in our Backyard: Examining Terror Funding Streams from South America).

[133] *Id.*

[134] *Id.*

[135] *Id.*

[136] Emerging Terrorist Financing Risks FATF Report, *supra* note 22.

International legal obligations to combat terror financing are negotiated within the framework of the United Nations.[137] International standards-setting bodies like FATF and the Organization for Economic Cooperation and Development (OECD) also coordinate these efforts.[138] Even though the IMF and the World Bank are responsible for providing technical assistance and capacity building on combating AML and promoting CFT,[139] FATF also has special guidance on AML/CFT capacity building for low-performing countries[140] and FATF conducts regular evaluations of every member country's efforts in this area, which are published along with recommendations for improvement.[141] Specifically, FATF recently issued a revised set of 40 recommendations on international AML/CFT standards,[142] which now fully incorporate FATF's nine "Special Recommendations."[143] These recommendations set out the basic framework to detect and prevent terrorist financing. FATF also encourages and coordinates the activities of nine FATF-Style Regional Bodies,[144] which, together with FATF, constitute an "affiliated global network to combat money laundering and the financing of terrorism."[145] Furthermore, the so-called Egmont Group serves as the "international standard setter" for FIUs more generally, and its guidance

---

[137] Notably, the United Nations Security Council has also issued specific mandates to target individuals and funding streams associated with Al-Qaeda and ISIS. For instance, the Security Council mirrored U.S. policy in 1999 when it adopted Resolution 1267, to require UN member states to impose financial sanctions on the Taliban for providing support and sanctuary to Al-Qaeda.

[138] *See. e.g.,* Organization for Economic Cooperation and Development, *Illicit Financial Flows from Developing Countries: Measuring OECD Responses* (2014), *available at* http://www.oecd.org/publications/measuring-oecd-responses-to-illicit-financial-flows-from-developing-countries-9789264203501-en.htm.

[139] *Id.*

[140] Financial Action Task Force, *Guidance on Capacity Building for Mutual Evaluations and Implementation of the FATF Standards Within Low Capacity Countries,* (Feb. 29, 2008), *available at* http://www.fatf-gafi.org/media/fatf/documents/reports/Capacity%20building%20LCC.pdf.

[141] *Id.*

[142] *See, FATF Recommendations,* (Feb. 2012), available at http://www.fatf-gafi.org/publications/fatfrecommendations/documents/fatf-recommendations.html; *see also FATF 40 Recommendations,* (Oct. 2003), *available at* http://www.fatf-gafi.org/media/fatf/documents/FATF%20Standards%20-%2040%20Recommendations%20rc.pdf.

[143] *See FATF IX Special Recommendations,* (Oct. 2011), *available at* http://www.fatf-gafi.org/publications/fatfrecommendations/documents/ixspecialrecommendations.html.

[144] These nine groups are the Asia/Pacific Group on Money Laundering (APG), the Caribbean Financial Action Task Force (CFATF), the Committee of Experts on the Evaluation of Anti-Money Laundering Measures and the Financing of Terrorism (MONEYVAL), the Eastern and Southern Africa Anti-Money Laundering Group (ESAAMLG), the Eurasian Group on Combating Money Laundering and Financing of Terrorism (EAG), the FATF of Latin America (FAFILAT); the Inter-Governmental Action Group against Money Laundering in West Africa (GIABA); the Middle East and North Africa FATF (MENAFATF); and the Task Force on Money Laundering in Central Africa (GABAC); *See Financial Action Task Force & FATF-Style Regional Bodies,* http://www.apgml.org/fatf-and-fsrb/page.aspx?p=94065425-e6aa-479f-8701-5ca5d07ccfe8.

[145] *See* U.S. Dep't of State, *2016 International Narcotics Control Strategy Report (INCSR),* (Mar. 2016), *available at* http://www.state.gov/j/inl/rls/nrcrpt/2016/vol2/253361.htm.

documents are interlinked with FATF standards.[146] As the U.S. FIU, FinCEN uses this information to leverage law enforcement's work, but also exchanges information as appropriate with the other national FIUs comprising the Egmont Group.[147]

In February 2016, FATF held its most recent plenary session in Paris, focusing in particular on terrorist financing, which was identified as "the top priority" for FATF.[148] At this meeting, FATF members adopted a consolidated counter terrorist financing strategy.[149] Chief among FATF's goals is to "identify and take measures in relation to any country with strategic deficiencies for terrorist financing."[150] As of February 2016, FATF reported that 36 jurisdictions, 40 percent of which lacked legal power to prosecute terrorist financiers or apply targeted financial sanctions in 2015, have taken some remedial actions.[151] However, there reportedly remain 15 jurisdictions that FATF identifies as requiring "urgent action to address their shortcomings, including requesting technical assistance from relevant bodies if necessary."[152]

While international coordinating bodies like FATF set standards on AML/CFT efforts, there is no similar central coordinating body to set a global policy agenda on providing capacity building efforts bilaterally or multilaterally, resulting in redundancies and gaps. Mr. James Adams—a retired Vice President of the West Asia and Pacific Region at the World Bank—explained to the Task Force in a March 1, 2016, hearing the difficulties donors face in their efforts to provide technical assistance to developing countries:

> Often the recipient government does not provide an appropriate environment for either expert staff or the longer-term capacity development programs. Common problems involve resentment of higher salaries of expert staff, the failure to assign local staff to work with experts, the absence of comprehensive monitory plans to ensure that local staff training programs

---

[146] Egmont Group of Financial Intelligence Units, Charter, approved by the Egmont Group Heads of Financial Intelligence Unit, (July 2013), published (Oct. 30, 2013).

[147] The Egmont Group began in 1995 as a small group of 14 national FIUs seeking international cooperation on financial intelligence matters. The State Department describes the Egmont Group as the "international standard setter" for FIUs, whose guidance documents are interlinked with the FATF standards; *See* U.S. Dep't of State, *2016 International Narcotics Control Strategy Report (INCSR)*, 27 (Mar. 2016), *available at* http://www.state.gov/j/inl/rls/nrcrpt/2016/vol2/253361.htm.

[148] Financial Action Task Force, *Outcomes of the Plenary Meeting of the FATF, Paris*, 17-19 (Feb. 19, 2016), *available at* http://www.fatf-gafi.org/publications/fatfgeneral/documents/outcomes-plenary-february-2016.html.

[149] *Id.*

[150] Consolidated FATF Strategy Report, *supra* note 4.

[151] *Id.*

[152] Financial Action Task Force, *Outcomes of the Plenary Meeting of the FATF, Paris*, 17-19 (Feb. 2016), *available at* http://www.fatf-gafi.org/publications/fatfgeneral/documents/outcomes-plenary-february-2016.html.

are put in place, and sometimes the simple refusal to hire the needed expertise.[153]

In the same hearing, Mr. Adams also acknowledged donors often share responsibility for underlying difficulties in providing technical assistance and capacity building in developing countries, stating:

> Donor behavior presents a problem as well. Coordination is problematic … [e]xperts from different countries will compete for attention of senior officials and give conflicting advice; project-based funding will frequently end before adequate capacity is established; key government staff are poached by donors offering better terms than the government does; and often donors push for experts that recipient governments do not feel are required.[154]

A wide range of donor entities are also actively engaged in providing a broad array of AML/CFT technical assistance and training offerings, which are not consistently catalogued or coordinated. It is believed that "improved coordination among donor governments … could make global development assistance more efficient and effective."[155] Donor coordination, which is called "harmonization," has been a major theme of international development cooperation agreements in the last decade, including the 2005 Paris Declaration on Aid Effectiveness, to which the U.S. and other major donors have committed themselves.[156] In his testimony before the Task Force on March 1, 2016, Mr. Adams also expressed his belief that the combination of bureaucratic ineptitude and corruption with weak institutional capabilities and oversight make financial systems in developing countries attractive targets for criminals and terrorists, either for outright theft or as a favorable operating environment. In the hearing, he specified:

> Gaps in banking supervision capacities and weak technical skills make these countries attractive targets. Moreover, governance and corruption issues with government bureaucracies can often undermine even the efforts of honest governments in these areas.[157]

---

[153] Testimony of James W. Adams, former Vice President of the East Asia and Pacific Region at the World Bank, *Hearings, supra* note 15 (Helping the Developing World Fight Terror Finance).
[154] *Id.*
[155] Congressional Research Service, *Foreign Aid: International Donor Coordination of Development Assistance,* (Feb. 2013), *available at* https://www.fas.org/sgp/crs/row/R41185.pd
[156] *Id.*
[157] Testimony of James W. Adams, former Vice President of the East Asia and Pacific Region at the World Bank, *Hearings, supra* note 15 (Helping the Developing World Fight Terror Finance).

In light of these factors, many wonder if the United States' ability to coordinate on counter terrorist financing assistance among international donors is affected by these coordination gaps.[158]

Some observers have also questioned the effectiveness of recent AML/CFT capacity-building efforts more generally. For example, a 2015 OECD report found that while developed countries' compliance with key AML/CFT standards has improved, particularly following international responses to the Al-Qaeda terrorist attacks of September 11, 2001, full compliance with key OECD recommendations and obligations remains low.[159] Compliance is an even greater concern in developing countries, since larger Gross Domestic Product levels and a higher quality of domestic economic and legal institutions generally are accompanied by greater compliance with AML/CFT standards.[160]

That said, FATF has cautioned that aggressive implementation of AML/CFT standards and procedures can have the unintended consequence of impairing or even preventing low-income households from accessing the formal financial sector. Robert M. Kimmitt—former Deputy Treasury Secretary, Under Secretary of State for Political Affairs and National Security Council Executive Secretary and General Counsel—warned of the unintended consequences of aggressive implementation of AML/CFT standards before the Task Force in his testimony on March 1, 2016:

> [A]s we work with U.S. and overseas financial institutions, let us not forget the laws of unintended consequences. If we so harshly regulate banks that they withdraw services from post-conflict and other developing countries that are ideal breeding grounds for terrorists and their financiers, we will drive the work of these financiers into the shadows.... We must expect banks to be held to high standards in this area, but not set the bar so impossibly high that the only rational business decision is to withdraw.[161]

One issue that has proven difficult for the United States to address involves so-called "remittances"—wire transfers from people living in the U.S. to persons,

---

[158] *See, e.g.*, U.S. Gov't Accountability Office, *Agencies Can Improve Efforts to Deliver Counter-Terrorism-Financing Training and Technical assistance Abroad*, GAO-06-632T, (Apr. 6, 2016), *available at* http://www.gao.gov/products/GAO-06-632T.

[159] Organization for Economic Cooperation and Development, *Illicit Financial Flows from Developing Countries: Measuring OECD Responses* (2014), *available at* http://www.oecd.org/publications/measuring-oecd-responses-to-illicit-financial-flows-from-developing-countries-9789264203501-en.htm.

[160] Concepcion Verdugo Yepes, 'Compliance with the AML/CFT International Standard: Lessons from a Cross-Country Analysis," International Monetary Fund, Working Paper 11/177 (July 2011), *available at* https://www.imf.org/external/pubs/ft/wp/2011/wp11177.pdf.

[161] Testimony of Ambassador Robert M. Kimmitt, Senior International Counsel, *Hearings, supra* note 15 (Helping the Developing World Fight Terror Finance).

often family members, overseas, which totaled over $432 billion in 2015.[162] The issue has manifested itself in so-called "bank discontinuance" or "de-risking," phenomena in which financial institutions that fear they may be fined or prosecuted for failing to identify or enabling illicit remittance transfers simply stop offering retail account services to companies providing remittance services.[163] The result is a more difficult and expensive money transfer process for those wanting to transfer money legitimately, and both law enforcement and bank regulators warn that discontinuance eventually will drive legitimate transfers into the illegitimate underground economy.[164] Somalia is often used as a prime example of what can go wrong with remittance "de-risking." Over the past several years, U.S. and international financial institutions have been refusing to process payments to Somalia, which receives an estimated $100 million in remittances from the U.S. annually, mostly "in fear that they could not certify ... whether funds transferred by them might eventually end up in the hands of terrorists...."[165] Sizeable Somali communities in Minneapolis, Minnesota, and Columbus, Ohio, have been particularly affected by what amounts to a de-facto ban on legitimate remittances to the country.[166] As described by Clay Lowery—Vice President at Rock Creek Global Advisors and former Assistant Secretary for International Affairs at the Treasury Department:

> [T]he potential consequences of making remittance flows more difficult and expensive are worthy of our concern – either people who depend on these financial flows for their everyday livelihood will suffer or we will see more and more of these funds chased into the shadows, as desperate people will find less transparent means to move money overseas.[167]

Banking regulators and officials of successive administrations have sought to emphasize that efforts to stop terrorist financing and related financial crimes are not intended to be a "zero tolerance" regime, but instead are intended to be "risk-

---

[162] *See* Martin Weiss, "Remittances: Background and Issues for Congress," Congressional Research Service (CRS) memorandum, (May 9, 2016), *available at* https://www.fas.org/sgp/crs/misc/R43217.pdf.

[163] According to FATF, "de-risking refers to the phenomenon of financial institutions terminating or restricting business relationship with clients or categories of clients to avoid, rather than manage, risk in line with the FATF's risk-based approach." *See* http://www.fatf-gafi.org/topics/fatfrecommendations/documents/rba-and-de-risking.html.

[164] *See, e.g.*, Manuel Orozco and Julia Yansura, "Keeping the Lifeline Open: Remittances and Markets in Somalia," *Oxfam America, African Development Solutions, and the Inter-American Dialogue*, (July 2013), *available at* https://www.oxfamamerica.org/static/media/files/somalia-remittance-report-web.pdf.

[165] *See* Martin Weiss, "Remittances: Background and Issues for Congress," Congressional Research Service memorandum, 12 (May 9, 2016), *available at* https://www.fas.org/sgp/crs/misc/R43217.pdf.

[166] *Id.*

[167] Testimony of Clay Lowery, Vice President at Rock Creek Global Advisors and former Assistant Secretary for International Affairs at the Treasury Department, *Hearings, supra* note 15 (Helping the Developing World Fight Terror Finance).

based."[168] However, banks across the United States have continued to decline retail businesses that present too much risk measured against the potential profit and cost of compliance. So-called "de-risking" has become a particular challenge in the past few years along the southwestern U.S. border with Mexico in Calexico County, California.[169] IMF head Christine Lagarde warned in July 2016 that many emerging markets could also face systemic disruptions if this "de-risking" trend is not reversed, stating:

> [L]arge global banks are under pressure to raise capital, streamline their business models, and re-evaluate their risk exposures. As a result, many of them have been in the process of closing business lines that they consider marginal to their bottom line, or detrimental to their risk profile. So, large banks are withdrawing from smaller countries. This is perhaps most evident in the decline of correspondent banking relationships – a serious concern for those countries that have few avenues for participating in the global payment and settlement systems....[170]

In the wake of this criticism, a group of senior Treasury officials and regulators issued a blog post that said there is "no general expectation" that banks know everything all of their customers or their banking partners' customers are doing— only that they understand the risk presented by the business.[171] A joint Fact Sheet clarifying federal supervision of foreign correspondent banking relationships was released concurrently with the Federal Reserve, FDIC, National Credit Union Administration, and the Office of the Comptroller of the Currency.[172]

A further challenge is that any country's efforts to combat terrorist financing is embedded in a deep and wide national framework of polices and institutions with

---

[168] *See* Emily Glazer and Aruna Viswanatha, "U.S. Defends its Curbs on Money Laundering," WALL ST. J., (Aug. 30, 2016), *available at* http://www.wsj.com/articles/u-s-banking-regulators-seek-to-dispel-certain-myths-on-anti-money-laundering-rules-1472583839.

[169] *Id*. Chairman Hensarling was also cc'd on letter to the FDIC and DOJ expressing "strong concern regarding the closure of 75 percent of the local banks in Calexico, California... " *See* letter from Ryan E. Kelley, Chairman, Imperial County Board of Supervisors, to the Hon. Loretta Lynch, Attorney General, DOJ, and the Hon. Martin Gruenberg, Chairman, FDIC (Apr. 27, 2015) [this letter is on file with the Committee].

[170] *See* Remarks of Christine Lagarde at the Federal Reserve Bank of New York, *Relations in Banking-Making it Work for Everyone*, (July 18, 2016) *available at* http://www.imf.org/en/News/Articles/2016/07/15/13/45/SP071816-Relations-in-Banking-Making-It-Work-For-Everyone.

[171] Nathan Sheets, Adam Szubin and Amias Gerety, "Complementary Goals- Protecting the Financial System form Abuse and Expanding Access to the Financial System," (Aug. 30, 2016), *available at* https://www.treasury.gov/connect/blog/Pages/Complementary-Goals---Protecting-the-Financial-System-from-Abuse-and-Expanding-Access-to-the-Financial-System.aspx?_ga=1.179506916.116319694.1472842293.

[172] U.S. Dep't of the Treasury et al, *Joint Fact Sheet on Foreign Correspondent Banking: Approach to BSA/AML and OFAC Sanctions Supervision and Enforcement* (Aug. 30, 2016), *available at* http://www.ots.treas.gov/topics/compliance-bsa/foreign-correspondent-banking-fact-sheet.pdf.

diverse priorities (e.g., criminal justice, financial regulation and supervision, tax, government and public administration, etc.). Even in developed countries, policymakers choose to consider how best to help governments create whole-of-government AML/CFT policies and strategies, and this becomes more difficult in countries with less-strong government functions. William Wechsler—a Senior Fellow at the Center for American Progress—summarized the unique challenges faced when attempting to implement FATF's international standards in developing countries. In his testimony to the Task Force on March 1, 2016, he said:

> [S]pecific programs to build partnership capacity to combat terrorist financing should be integrated in a wider strategy to build associated capabilities. It does relatively little good to draft model anti-money laundering laws and regulations if the host country has little ability to enforce those laws. Helping to build another county's police force isn't as useful if there is no effective judiciary. And even if there are judges willing to convict terrorists and their financiers ... there needs to be prisons to keep them.[173]

---

[173] Testimony of William Wechsler, Senior Fellow, Center for American Progress, *Hearings, supra* note 15 (Helping the Developing World Fight Terror Finance).

Evaluating the Security of the Financial Sector

Methods of Moving Terrorist Proceeds

The three most common methods terrorists use to move money are (1) the physical movement of cash; (2) the movement of funds through the banking system and non-bank financial institutions; and (3) the misuse of the international trade system.[174] In a recent Treasury Department analysis, the physical movement of cash accounted for 28 percent of terrorism conviction cases since 2011, while movement directly through banks constituted 22 percent.[175] One of the most prevalent ways terrorists move funds through the banking system is by direct deposits at financial institutions.[176] Terrorists make use of non-bank financial institutions mainly through money service businesses (MSB)[177] or alternative remittance systems that oftentimes resemble the ancient, informal "hawala" money transfer system.[178] While the use of trade-based money laundering—the process of moving value through trade transactions to legitimize the illicit origins of criminal proceeds—is thought to be less used by terrorists, it is another common way of moving illicit value in general and one of the least understood, as discussed in detail at the Task Force's February 3, 2016, hearing.[179] According to John Cassara—former intelligence officer and Treasury Special Agent—although the scale of trade-based money laundering has never been "systematically examined," one study found that almost $220 billion of illicit value was moved out of the U.S. in the form of value transfer in 2013 alone.[180]

---

[174] Terrorist Financing FATF Report, *supra* note 21 at 21.

[175] The Treasury Department conducted an analysis on terrorism and terrorism-related convictions between 2001 and 2014. Using publicly available documents (indictments, sentencing memoranda, law enforcement press releases, media reports, etc.) the cases were examined more closely in order to determine key financial components. In the 229 cases surveyed, 96 included information on the financial component to the investigation, either raising or moving the funds. These cases were then further analyzed to determine what specific method or channel was used to raise or move funds. *See* Treasury TF Risk Assessment, *supra* note 2.

[176] *Id*.

[177] Banks and Money Service Businesses accounted for over 90 percent of all financial institution SAR filings with the subject line "terrorist financing." *See* Financial Crimes Enforcement Network Suspicious Activity Report (SAR) Stats; *See* Treasury TF Risk Assessment at 46, *supra* note 2.

[178] "Hawala" is an alternative remittance system that allows the transfer of funds both domestically and internationally without using financial institutions.

[179] *Hearings, supra* note 14 (Trading with the Enemy: Trade-Based Money Laundering is the Growth Industry in Terror Finance).

[180] This analysis was given to John Cassara by Dr. John Zdanowicz, President, International Trade Alert, Inc., on June 30, 2015, via email; Testimony of John Cassara, former intelligence officer and Treasury Special Agent, *Hearings, supra* note 14 (Trading with the Enemy: Trade-Based Money Laundering is the Growth Industry in Terror Finance).

The products and services provided by financial institutions are an especially attractive means for terrorist groups seeking to move funds globally because of the speed and ease with which they can move funds within the international financial system and the appearance of legitimacy that attaches to such transactions.[181] The perpetrators of the September 11, 2001, terrorist attacks opened personal checking accounts, deposited and withdrew cash, conducted international wire transfers, used travelers checks, and accumulated transactions on conventional credit cards.[182] As much of this activity was not spotted until after the attack, many of the AML/CFT improvements in the USA PATRIOT Act were directly aimed at addressing those blind spots, or at improving use of data to which the government had access but which it used poorly if at all.

The extent to which terrorists use the formal banking sector is up to debate among experts. For instance, Howard Shatz—a senior economist at the RAND Corporation—argues that ISIS is not using the formal financial system, but rather storing its money internally and relying on an informal system of couriers and *hawaladars*—people who operate hawalas—to move it around.[183] However, given the significant amounts of money the group is bringing in through several means, other experts, like Jimmy Gurulé—former Under Secretary for Enforcement at the Treasury Department—believe that ISIS is covertly using the formal banking system, especially through banks in Iraq, Qatar, and Kuwait.[184] During a November 2014 Financial Services Committee hearing on ISIS financing, Gurulé testified:

> [ISIS] money has to be entering into the financial system at some point, and I think we need to do a better job…. [T]he Department of the Treasury, needs to be doing a better job or intensify its efforts … to identify the financial institutions that are knowingly receiving and transferring ISIS-related funds.[185]

At some point some portion of the money terrorist organizations use to fund their operations must enter the formal financial system, so it is paramount that U.S. financial institutions have the necessary tools in place to identify such activity so they do not become inadvertent conduits or enablers of the next terror attack.

---

[181] Terrorist Financing FATF Report, *supra* note 21.

[182] *See The 9/11 Commission Report*, 170 (2004), *available at* http://govinfo.library.unt.edu/911/report/911Report.pdf.

[183] Howard Shatz, Senior Economist at RAND Corporation, briefing with Committee staff on October 2, 2014.

[184] *Terrorist Financing and the Islamic State: Hearing before the H. Comm. on Fin. Serv.*, 113th Cong. at 54, (Nov. 13, 2014), *available at* http://financialservices.house.gov/calendar/eventsingle.aspx?EventID=398424.

[185] *Id.*

Additionally, according to the Treasury Department, the U.S. faces a "residual" risk of exposure due to the size and scope of international transactions that flow through the U.S. financial system, including through the large network of foreign bank subsidiary branches operating in the United States.[186] Specifically, Treasury says the misuse of correspondent banking makes it particularly challenging to identify and root out terrorist financing.[187] While U.S. financial institutions are required to conduct due diligence on "higher risk" foreign correspondents and are prohibited from maintaining correspondent accounts for foreign "shell banks" that have no physical presence in the U.S., there have been egregious instances of U.S. banks not adequately managing potential terrorist financing risks posed by their relationships with foreign financial institutions.[188]

BSA/AML and U.S. Sanctions programs

The combination of a strong AML/CFT legal framework and effective supervision has succeeded in making it more difficult for terrorists to access the U.S. financial system, often forcing support networks to resort to costlier or riskier means of meeting their operational needs.[189]

While Treasury's FinCEN is responsible for the administration and enforcement of BSA regulations, the responsibility of examining financial institutions for the thoroughness of their AML/CFT efforts is delegated to several financial regulators.[190] The current BSA regulatory regime requires financial institutions to develop a system of internal controls to ensure ongoing compliance and requires independent testing for the adequacy of the efforts.[191] In addition, these institutions must file various forms with FinCEN that are aimed at allowing the government to either spot crimes before they occur, or trace their origins after they are discovered: namely, currency transaction reports (CTR) for large cash transactions exceeding $10,000 and SARs to identify certain "high-risk" merchants or transactions, including combinations of transactions which are often grouped to

---

[186] Treasury TF Risk Assessment, *supra* note 2.

[187] *Id*. 49-50

[188] *U.S. Vulnerabilities to Money Laundering, Drugs, and Terrorist Financing: HSBC Case History: Hearing before the S. Permanent Subcomm. on Investigations*, 225, 228, 111th Cong. (July 17, 2012), *available at* http://www.hsgac.senate.gov/subcommittees/investigations/hearings/us-vulnerabilities-to-money-laundering-drugs-and-terrorist-financing-hsbc-case-history.

[189] *See* David Cohen, Under Secretary for Terrorism and Financial Intelligence, Dep't of the Treasury, Remarks before the Center for a New American Security, *Confronting New Threats in Terrorist Financing*, (Mar. 4, 2014) *available at* https://www.treasury.gov/press-center/press-releases/Pages/jl2308.aspx.

[190] 31 C.F.R. § 103.56. Federal banking regulators include the Board of Governors of the Federal Reserve System, FDIC, NCUA and the OCC. The other regulators are the Securities and Exchange Commission (SEC), the Commodity Futures Trading Commission (CFTC) and the IRS.

[191] *Id*.

avoid the filing of a CTR, an activity known as "structuring."[192] According to Task Force testimony from then-FinCEN Director Jennifer Shasky Calvery on May 24, 2016, FinCEN receives approximately 55,000 new financial institution filings each day from both reporting streams.[193] To meet growing requirements for information on terrorist financing, FinCEN stood up an "intelligence product line" called the Flash Report in 2014 that allows for electronic data filing.[194]

The consensus that emerged from the Task Force hearings was that there is a need for greater information sharing throughout the financial system and among government agencies, as well as increased integration of government databases.[195] Others have concluded that FinCEN and the federal financial regulators must do a better job of coordinating bank examination information that might involve multiple agencies.[196] For comparison sake, relevant trade data is "scattered" between agencies and private sector entities, which may be hampering efforts to stop trade-based money laundering.[197] Dr. Nikos Passas of Northeastern University testified to the importance of ensuring that "government data are gathered and analyzed in one place," ideally FinCEN[198]; and Farley Mesko—co-founder and CEO of Sayari Analytics—also testified to the importance of properly including "open source data and better integration with the private sector" to combat TBML.[199]

OFAC is the principal administer and enforcer of a vigorous sanctions regime against terrorist financing, drug smuggling, human rights abuses and a variety of other Congressionally specified activities, in collaboration with the regulatory, law enforcement, and intelligence communities.[200] Violators of U.S. economic sanctions

---

[192] Testimony of Jennifer Shasky Calvery, former Director, FinCEN, U.S. Dep't of the Treasury, *Hearings, supra* note 18 (Stopping Terror Finance: A Coordinated Government Effort). See, *e.g.*, 12 C.F.R. § 21.21 (national banks); 12 C.F.R. § 208.61 (state member banks); 12 C.F.R. § 326.8 (nonmember banks); 12 C.F.R. § 748.2 (credit unions). The Securities and Exchange Commission (SEC) and Commodity Futures Trading Commission (CFTC) also impost similar requirements on the financial institutions they supervise. *See* FINRA Rule 3310 (securities broker-dealers); and National Futures Association Rule 2-9(c) (commodities brokers and futures commission merchants).

[193] Testimony of Jennifer Shasky Calvery, former Director, FinCEN, U.S. Dep't of the Treasury, *Hearings, supra* note 18 (Stopping Terror Finance: A Coordinated Government Effort).

[194] *Id.*

[195] *Hearings, supra* note 15 (Helping the Developing World Fight Terror Finance); *Hearings, supra* note 13 (Could America Do More? An examination of U.S. Efforts to Stop the Financing of Terror).

[196] *See, e.g.*, U.S. Gov't Accountability Office, *Federal Agencies Should Take Action to Further Improve Coordination and Information-Sharing Efforts*, (Feb. 2009), *available at* http://www.gao.gov/products/GAO-09-227.

[197] Testimony of Dr. Nikos Passas, *Hearings, supra* note 14 (Trading with the Enemy: Trade-Based Money Laundering is the Growth Industry in Terror Finance).

[198] *Id.*

[199] Testimony of Farley Mesko, CEO, Sayari Analytics, *Hearings, supra* note 14 (Trading with the Enemy: Trade-Based Money Laundering is the Growth Industry in Terror Finance).

[200] Remarks of David Cohen, Under Secretary for Terrorism and Financial Intelligence, Dep't of the Treasury, *U.S. Vulnerabilities to Money Laundering, Drugs, and Terrorist Financing: HSBC Case History: Hearing before the S. Comm. on Homeland Security and Governmental Affairs Permanent*

can be subject to a range of administrative, civil, and criminal penalties.[201] In a recent assessment conducted at the request of the Task Force, GAO concluded that financial institutions have been fined $5.2 billion for BSA/AML violations and about $6.8 billion for violations of U.S. sanctions program requirements since 2009.[202]

Bulk Cash Smuggling

Cash smuggling has become increasingly attractive for terrorist networks because of its "anonymity, portability, liquidity and lack of audit trail."[203] According to the 9/11 Commission, for instance, Al-Qaeda regularly recruited couriers internally within the organization to physically transport cash.[204] An analysis by the Treasury Department indicates that 18 terrorist finance-related prosecutions in the U.S. against various FTOs have involved the use of cash to transfer funds to terrorist organizations since 2001.[205] Additionally, the use of unregulated *hawala* transfers is very common—they were reportedly used to facilitate the May 2010 attempted car bombing in Times Square.[206]

According to Treasury, cash smuggling will continue to be used as a means to move funds by a variety of terrorist organizations, including the remains of Al-Qaeda and its affiliates, ISIS, Al-Shabaab, Hezbollah, and FARC.[207] The U.S. government, particularly law enforcement agencies, proactively investigates and prosecutes instances of bulk cash smuggling. For example, ICE and CBP have established special programs and initiatives to target bulk cash smuggling across

---

Subcommittee on Investigations, (July 17, 2012), *available at* http://www.hsgac.senate.gov/download/?id=55d94bbb-cbee-4a35-89ca-5493a12d73dd.

[201] *Id.*

[202] U.S. Gov't Accountability Office, *Fines, Penalties, and Forfeitures for Violations of Financial Crimes and Sanctions Requirements*, GAO-16-297, (March 2016), *available at* http://www.gao.gov/products/GAO-16-297.

[203] Treasury TF Risk Assessment, *supra* note 2.

[204] *See* supra note 181; *The 9/11 Commission Report*, (2004), *available at* http://govinfo.library.unt.edu/911/report/911Report.pdf.

[205] This analysis was conducted by Treasury on terrorism and terrorism-related convictions between 2001 and 2014. Using publicly available documents (indictments, sentencing memoranda, law enforcement press releases, media reports, etc.), the cases were examined more closely in order to determine key financial components. Of the 229 cases surveyed, 96 included information on the financial component to the investigation, either raising or moving the funds. *See* Treasury TF Risk Assessment, *supra* note 2, at 26.

[206] *See* U.S. Dep't of Justice, *Pakistani Man Sentenced on Unlicensed Money Transmitting Charges and Immigration Fraud*, (Apr. 12, 2011), *available at* https://archives.fbi.gov/archives/boston/press-releases/2011/pakistani-man-sentenced-on-unlicensed-money-transmitting-charges-and-immigration-fraud; and U.S. Dep't of the Treasury, FinCEN, *Informal Value Transfer Systems*, Advisory, FIN-2010-A011, (Sept. 1, 2010), *available at* https://www.ffiec.gov/bsa_aml_infobase/documents/FinCEN_DOCs/FIN-2012-A001.pdf.

[207] Treasury TF Risk Assessment, *supra* note 2.

U.S. borders.[208] DOJ and other prosecutorial authorities have also levied criminal penalties for failing to file Reports of International Transportation of Currency or Monetary Instruments (CMIR), which are designed to capture the cross-border transfer of currency in excess of $10,000, similar to CTR requirements.[209]

Trade Based Money Laundering

Ranking Member Maxine Waters described trade-based money laundering at a February 3, 2016, hearing on the topic as one of "the most widespread, pernicious and least understood forms of money laundering."[210] For instance, in two schemes involving Lebanon-based Hezbollah, the Lebanese Canadian Bank (LCB) facilitated the laundering of South American drug proceeds through the Lebanese financial system via trade-based schemes involving used cars and consumer goods.[211] Despite a mostly successful "takedown strategy" engineered by the DEA in 2010, and a subsequent designation of the Lebanese Canadian Bank under Section 311 of the PATRIOT Act that led to its ultimate demise, David Asher—a member of the Board of Advisors at the Center on Sanctions and Illicit Finance at FDD—testified at May 21, 2015, Task Force hearing that "Hezbollah's trade based laundering scheme has only expanded..." since that time.[212] Furthermore, in a June 2015 risk assessment, the Treasury Department concluded that trade-based money laundering is not a dominant method for terrorist financing;[213] however, witnesses at a February 2016, Task Force hearing including John Cassara—a former U.S. intelligence officer and Treasury special agent—disagreed, saying that compared to other forms of terrorist financing, trade based money laundering "is a major

---

[208] *See* U.S. Dep't of Homeland Security, *Disrupt Terrorist Financing*, (last published July 13, 2015), *available at* http://www.dhs.gov/topic/disrupt-terrorist-financing.

[209] *See* 31 U.S.C. § 5332.

[210] *See* Remarks of the Hon. Maxine Waters, Ranking Member, H. Fin. Serv. Cmte., *Hearing, supra* note 14 (Trading with the Enemy: Trade-Based Money Laundering is the Growth Industry in Terror Finance).

[211] Asia/Pacific Group on Money Laundering (APG), *APG Typology Report on Trade Based Money Laundering*, (July 20, 2012) *available at* http://www.apgml.org/methods-and-trends/documents/default.aspx?s=date&c=2f18e690-1838-4310-b16a-8112ffa857b1; Jo Becker, "Beirut Bank Seen As Hub of Hezbollah's Finances," N.Y. TIMES, (Dec.13, 2011); Sebastian Rotella, "Government Says Hezbollah Profits from U.S. Cocaine Market Via Link to Mexican Cartel," PROPUBLICA, (Dec. 13, 2011); "Prosecutors Say Hezbollah Laundered Millions of Dollars into U.S.," AP, (Dec. 15, 2011), http://www.foxnews.com/us/2011/12/15/prosecutors-say-hezbollah-laundered-millions-dollars-into-us.html; Devlin Barrett, "U.S. Intensifies Bid to Defund Hezbollah," WALL ST. J., (Dec. 16, 2015).

[212] Testimony of Dr. David Asher, Board Member, CSIF, Foundation for Defense of Democracies, *Hearings, supra* note 10 (A Dangerous Nexus: Terrorism, Crime and Corruption).

[213] Treasury TF Risk Assessment, *supra* note 2.

problem" in certain areas of the world, adding that there is a vast potential for terrorist groups to exploit the international trade system.[214]

Mr. Cassara told the Task Force that, while the "magnitude of TBML has never been systematically examined," one academic study of the 2013 U.S. trade data found $220 billion of illicit value was moved out of the United States (six percent of trade), and about $340 billion was moved into the country using suspect trade transactions (about nine percent of U.S. trade).[215] To remedy the situation, witnesses encouraged the establishment and reinvigoration of Trade Transparency Units (TTUs) to examine trade anomalies in domestic and foreign trade data.[216] The U.S. established the first TTU in 2004 through DHS, and, according to the State Department, the eight international TTUs currently in existence—mostly in South America—plan to develop an international network of TTUs, similar to the Egmont Group of FIUs.[217] Louis Bock—a former Agent with the former United States Customs Service—recommended in testimony to the Task Force that the U.S. TTU be housed at FinCEN given Treasury's "great job" with FIUs and its existing international agreements with revenue agencies.[218]

Strengthening Company Formation Procedure

Like other criminals, terrorists have created and exploited "shell companies" and accounts offshore in jurisdictions with less-stringent regulation and a less vigilant law enforcement presence to both disguise and finance their activities.[219]

Shell companies are business entities whose ambiguous ownership structure masks the identities of the people who ultimately control or profit from the companies—the so-called "beneficial owners."[220] While the mere existence of offshore accounts is not necessarily indicative of illicit activity, unscrupulous actors

---

[214] Testimony of John Cassara, Former Intelligence Officer and Treasury Special Agent, *Hearings, supra* note 14 (Trading with the Enemy: Trade-Based Money Laundering is the Growth Industry in Terror Finance).

[215] *Id.*

[216] *Id.*

[217] During testimony, Louis Bock, a retired senior special agent at the U.S. Customs Service, raised concerns that "the existing DHS TTU's attention is focused 90 percent on South America," which "does little to attack current evolving terrorist threats..." He encouraged a broader focus of TTU resources as "[t]he real money flowing to ISIS involves trade from the Middle East, Europe and including Turkey." *Id.* at 9; *See also* U.S. Department of State, *INCSR*, Vol. 2, (March 2015), *available at* http://www.state.gov/j/inl/rls/nrcrpt/2015/.

[218] Testimony of John Cassara, Former Intelligence Officer and Treasury Special Agent, *Hearings, supra* note 14 (Trading with the Enemy: Trade-Based Money Laundering is the Growth Industry in Terror Finance).

[219] Diana L. Ohlbaum, "Terrorism, Inc. How Shell Companies Aid Terrorism, Crime and Corruption," *Open Society Foundations* (Oct.2013), *available at* http://www.opensocietyfoundations.org/briefing-papers/terrorism-inc-how-shell-companies-aid-terrorism-crime-and-corruption.

[220] *Id.*

may seek to exploit the anonymity provided by such accounts. Companies with untraceable ownership have been described as "the vehicle of choice for money launderers, bribe givers and takers, sanctions busters, tax evaders and financers of terrorism,"[221] since information on the "beneficial owners" of U.S.-formed shell companies is often unavailable to law enforcement.[222]

Many, but not all, G20 countries have business-formation processes that require disclosure of beneficial ownership to government agencies.[223] However, in the United States, incorporation is performed at the state level and there is currently no similar process in place to gather and update information on corporate or limited liability company (LLC) formation if states do not require it—and many states fall into this category.[224] Given the current company formation structure, the U.S. has become a preferred destination for illicit actors from around the world, who often set up companies but do no business in the U.S., to avoid even the necessity of minimal disclosure to the IRS.[225]

For example, the son of Equatorial Guinea's dictator, Teodoro Obiang, purchased a $30 million mansion in Malibu, California, and a private jet using shell companies based in California and the British Virgin Islands, according to a report by the NGO Global Witness, an organization which has long pushed for public disclosure of corporate beneficiaries.[226] Hezbollah has also financed its activities in part by using shell companies in North Carolina to smuggle cigarettes to finance terrorism;[227] and Russian arms trafficker Viktor Bout used at least a dozen shell companies in Delaware, Texas, and Florida to operate his global arms smuggling

---

[221] *See* "Launderers Anonymous: A Study Highlights How Easy It Is to Set Up Untraceable Companies," ECONOMIST (Sept. 22, 2012), *available at* http://www.economist.com/node/21563286.
[222] U.S. Senate, Caucus on International Narcotics Control, *The Buck Stops Here: Improving U.S. Anti-Money Laundering Practices* (Apr. 25, 2013), *available at* http://www.drugcaucus.senate.gov/sites/default/files/Money%20Laundering%20Report%20-%20Final.pdf; Leslie Wayne, "How Delaware Thrives as a Corporate Tax Haven," *The New York Times* (June 30, 2012), *available at* http://www.nytimes.com/2012/07/01/business/how-delaware-thrives-as-a-corporate-tax-haven.html?_r=0.
[223] According to Transparency International, 15 of the G20 countries have weak or average beneficial ownership transparency legal frameworks in place, and two countries have yet to even adopt a legal definition of beneficial ownership. *See* "Were G20 corruption promise nothing more than a photo-op? (Nov. 12, 2015), *available at* http://www.transparency.org/whatwedo/pub/just_for_show_g20_promises.
[224] *Id.*
[225] *See* World Bank and UNODC, Stolen Asset Recovery Initiative, *The Puppet Masters,* World Bank Publications (Oct. 24, 2011), *available at* http://star.worldbank.org/star/publication/puppet-masters
[226] Global Witness, *Anonymous Companies: How Hidden Company Ownership is a Major Barrier in the Fight Against Poverty and What to Do About It,* (Dec. 2013), *available at* file:///F:/Terrorist%20Financing/Hearing%20%233/Anonymous%20Companies%20Global%20Witness%20briefing.pdf.
[227] Dennis M. Lormel, "It's Time to Pry Criminals Out of Their Shell (Companies)," CLEVELAND PLAIN DEALER (Aug. 16, 2013), *available at* http://www.cleveland.com/opinion/index.ssf/2013/08/its_time_to_pry_criminals_out.html.

operation.[228] Shell companies have also been used to facilitate bribes to Russian officials, defraud the E.U., and evade Iranian sanctions.[229] Recent press accounts have documented anonymous cash purchases of high-end real estate in New York City and Miami, Florida, asserting that such purchases are part of complex schemes to hide or move illicit funds,[230] and FinCEN has recently taken note of this concern by issuing Geographic Targeting Orders (GTO) requiring U.S. title insurance companies to identify the people behind companies paying "all cash" in certain high-end real estate transactions.[231]

FATF,[232] the World Bank, and the Stolen Asset Recovery Initiative of the United Nations Office on Drugs and Crime[233] have explored the misuse of corporate vehicles for illicit purposes.[234] A recent example that illustrates this potential for abuse is the so-called Panama Papers incident.[235] In April 2016, the International Consortium of Investigative Journalists (ICIJ) disclosed the existence of 11.5 million files of leaked financial documents and attorney-client communications related to transactions in more than 214,000 offshore companies handled by the Panamanian law firm Mossack Fonseca.[236] These leaked documents revealed the use of shell companies by several well-known public figures as well as by alleged drug traffickers from Latin America.[237]

---

[228] *Id.*

[229] Global Witness, *Anonymous Companies: How Hidden Company Ownership is a Major Barrier in the Fight Against Poverty and What to Do About It*, (Dec. 2013), *available at* file:///F:/Terrorist%20Financing/Hearing%20%233/Anonymous%20Companies%20Global%20Witness%20briefing.pdf.

[230] *See Anonymous, Inc.*, Steve Kroft reporting, 60 Minutes, (Jan. 31, 2016), *available at* http://www.cbsnews.com/news/anonymous-inc-60-minutes-steve-kroft-investigation/.

[231] *See, e.g.*, U.S. Dep't of Treasury, *FinCEN Expands Reach of Real Estate 'Geographic Targeting Orders' Beyond Manhattan and Miami*, (July 27, 2016), *available at* https://www.fincen.gov/news_room/nr/html/20160727.html.; *FinCEN Takes Aim at Real Estate Secrecy in Manhattan and Miami*, (Jan. 13, 2016), *available at* https://www.fincen.gov/news_room/nr/html/20160113.html.

[232] FATF (2006) and FATF & CFATF (2010).

[233] *See* World Bank and UNODC, Stolen Asset Recovery Initiative, *The Puppet Masters,* World Bank Publications (2011), *available at* http://www.fatf-gafi.org/media/fatf/documents/reports/Guidance-transparency-beneficial-ownership.pdf.

[234] *See* Financial Action Task Force Report, *Transparency and Beneficial Ownership*, (Oct. 2014), *available at* http://www.fatf-gafi.org/media/fatf/documents/reports/Guidance-transparency-beneficial-ownership.pdf.

[235] *See, e.g.*, "Giant Leak of Offshore Financial Records Exposes Global Array of Crime and Corruption," *International Consortium of Investigative Journalists*, (Apr.3, 2016), *available at* https://panamapapers.icij.org/20160403-panama-papers-global-overview.html; Elyssa Pachico, "Panama Papers Highlight How LatAm's Elites Hide Wealth," *InSight Crime*, (Apr.4, 2016) , *available at* http://www.insightcrime.org/news-analysis/panama-papers-highlight-how-latam-s-elites-hide-wealth.

[236] *Id.*

[237] *Id.*

On May 5, 2016, Treasury released a final "Consumer Due Diligence" (CDD) rule, which added new regulations requiring financial institutions to know and verify the personal information of "beneficial owners," defined as any individual who owns 25 percent or more of the equity interest in a legal entity, or an individual with "significant responsibility" to control the entity.[238] The move was the culmination of a lengthy process that began with the issuance of an Advance Notice of Proposed Rulemaking on customer due diligence in March 2012, and a subsequent proposed rule in August 2014.[239]

The issue of anonymous beneficial ownership as a problem for law enforcement has also been the subject of discussion in nearly every hearing held by the Task Force. For instance, at a June 24, 2015, hearing, Manhattan District Attorney Cyrus Vance Jr. opined that having a "simple requirement to identify beneficial owners on state incorporation forms would vastly improve the capacity of American law enforcement to attack terrorism finance and disrupt terror plots."[240] Chip Poncy—former Director of Treasury's Office of Strategic Policy for Terrorist Financing and Financial Crime—echoed this concern:

> This [C]ommittee can strengthen U.S. leadership in overcoming [terrorist financing and money laundering] … [adopting] legislation to require the disclosure and maintenance of meaningful beneficial ownership information in our company formation processes. Such legislation is required to address the chronic abuse of legal entities that mask the identities and illicit financing activities of the full scope of criminal and illicit financing activities … [and supporting] the issuance of Treasury's proposed rule on customer due diligence, consistent with that of standards. Such action is required to address the systemic challenges posed by customer due diligence practices that fall below global standards here in the United States and particularly with respect to beneficial ownership.[241]

---

[238] *See* Treasury Announces Key Regulations and Legislation to Counter Money Laundering and Corruption, Combat Tax Evasion, (May 5, 2016), *available at* https://www.treasury.gov/press-center/press-releases/Pages/jl0451.aspx.

[239] *See* F.R. Vol. 79, No. 149, FinCEN, Customer Due Diligence Requirements for Financial Institutions (Aug. 5, 2014), *available at* https://www.fincen.gov/statutes_regs/files/CDD-NPRM-Final.pdf; *See, e.g.*, Mary Beth Goodman, "Beneficial Ownership Rules Would Drag Criminals into Daylight," AB (Feb.18, 2015), *available at* http://www.americanbanker.com/bankthink/beneficial-ownership-rules-would-drag-criminals-into-daylight-1072763-1.html.

[240] *Hearings, supra* note 11 (Evaluating the Security of the U.S. Financial Sector).

[241] *Id.*

Recommendations

During the second session of the 114th Congress, Task Force leaders introduced legislation that sought to address several issues identified in the Task Force's hearings. Chairman Fitzpatrick, Ranking Member Lynch and Vice Chairman Pittenger expect the bipartisanship on addressing terrorist financing to continue in the new Congress, with the overarching goal of improving efforts to block or impede illicit finance by increasing cooperation between agencies, between the government and the private sector, and between governments—both in the G20 and in the developing world. Inherent in these information sharing efforts is the understanding that the financial services industry has been a willing partner, but that providing information is burdensome and expensive, and that collecting information on any financial transaction is intrusive to the privacy of consumers, so it is imperative to use that information as effectively and carefully as possible.

That said, in the Task Force's view, the most achievable near-term goals revolve around increasing law enforcement's access to information already in the possession of the government but not readily accessible; requiring the executive branch to develop and constantly refine a whole-of-government strategy towards fighting illicit finance; and modestly refining some existing information sharing statutes to clarify Congressional intent.

Near Term

Task Force leaders introduced several bipartisan bills before the Task Force expired on July 5, 2016:

- Task Force Chairman Michael Fitzpatrick sponsored **H.R. 5594**, the "*National Strategy for Combating Terrorist, Underground, and Other Illicit Financing Act*," co-sponsored by Reps. Kyrsten Sinema (D-AZ) and Nydia Velazquez (D-NY). The bill would require the President, acting through the Treasury Secretary, to develop and publish an annual whole-of-government strategy to combat money laundering and terrorist financing. The proposal builds on a narrower requirement for a biannual report outlined in a 1998 law sponsored by Rep. Velazquez[242]; the requirement expired and the latest version was prepared in 2007. H.R. 5594 seeks to ensure better intra-governmental coordination and give Congress a road map for resource allocation or the addition of necessary new authorities to keep ahead of innovations by criminals or terrorists. In the post-9/11 period it became clear that various agencies were not coordinating their efforts well, which led to blind spots that allowed the attackers to operate in the U.S. undetected. While many of those issues were addressed, new personalities, new challenges and the natural inclination of

---

[242] H.R. 1756: Money Laundering and Financial Crimes Strategy Act of 1998, (105th Congress).

bureaucracies to protect their turf have reintroduced inefficiencies. Chairman Fitzpatrick's view was that the exercise of creating this strategy, similar to an existing requirement that the government have a unified strategy to fight drug trafficking, would help improve cooperation and illuminate areas where Congress may need to intervene. The bill passed the House on July 11, 2016, by voice vote.

- Ranking Member Stephen Lynch introduced **H.R. 5602**, co-sponsored by Rep. Peter King of New York. The bill would amend an existing statute that allows the Treasury Secretary to require increased reporting on specific high-risk transactions in specific geographic areas for a limited amount of time to help increase surveillance of suspected illicit finance. The increased surveillance is known as a "Geographic Targeting Order." Current statute allows these orders to be issued for the reporting of cash or "monetary instruments," but the Treasury Department believes the definition may not cover all the ways that illicit value is or can be transferred in the wake of massive technology innovations in financial services. The bill would therefore allow the more complete collection of information on "funds" involved in such transactions. Treasury has effectively used GTOs in the past to target a number of illicit activities. Early in 2016 the Treasury Secretary issued, and then expanded, requirements to scrutinize high-dollar-value all-cash purchases of high-end real estate in New York, Miami, and later in parts of Texas and California, believing such transactions might be evidence of money laundering or the outgrowth of other illicit activity. The bill passed the House July 11, 2016, by a vote of 356-47.

- Vice Chairman Robert Pittenger introduced **H.R. 5607**, the "*Enhancing Treasury's Anti-Terror Tools Act*," co-sponsored by Rep. Lynch. The bill as introduced had seven policy sections each aimed at enhancing Treasury's anti-illicit finance tools by addressing issues that had come up repeatedly in Task Force hearings.

  o Two sections from the introduced version of this bill were removed before consideration: the first, which would make the Treasury Secretary a fulltime member of the National Security Council, grew out of concerns that the Secretary is only an "invited" member to the nation's top security policy group despite Treasury's prominent roles in U.S. efforts to stop illicit finance, and a second would unify the many different streams of import and export data that are reported to the government but often not easily available to the various departments that would use them for anti-crime or revenue-collection purposes.

o The remaining sections passed the House on July 11, 2016, by a vote of 362-45. One seeks a study of the way Treasury is represented in embassies overseas. Task Force Members heard repeatedly that, despite the urgency of counter terrorist financing efforts, fewer than a dozen and a half Treasury personnel are assigned to cover all overseas embassies. Other sections of the legislation urge the Secretary of the Treasury to work with his counterpart finance ministers to better integrate their intelligence communities into their AML/CFT efforts in the same way Treasury's Office of Intelligence and Analysis is tightly integrated with FinCEN; direct the Secretary to report to Congress on a potential pilot program aimed at improving the safe flow of legitimate remittances and on whether the Office of Terrorism and Financial Intelligence ought to be formally made a separate bureau similar to the FBI's status as a separate bureau of the Justice Department; and mirror Rep. Lynch's effort to clarify that GTOs should cover all funds and not merely a subset of all potential value transfers.

o Ranking Member Lynch introduced **H.R. 5603**, the "*Kleptocracy Asset Recovery Ac*t," co-sponsored by Rep. Keith Rothfus (R-PA). The bill seeks to establish a reward program aimed at helping the U.S. identify, freeze and, if appropriate, repatriate assets linked to foreign government corruption or the proceeds of such corruption that are often hidden behind complex financial structures, in an effort to help intensify the global fight against corruption, which is often an enabler of terrorism.

o Vice Chairman Pittenger introduced **H.R. 5606**, the "*Anti-Terrorism Information Sharing Is Truth Act*," co-sponsored by Ranking Member Maxine Waters. The bill seeks to refine "safe harbors" for the sharing of anti-terror information, reaffirming Congressional intent in existing statute that encourages the government to share terror methodologies with banks to help them better recognize such activity, and to encourage more appropriate bank-to-bank sharing of such information. It also reaffirms a "safe harbor" from potential civil liability that financial institutions might incur by complying with existing statutory requirements to report suspicious activities. The bill was considered under suspension of the rules on July 11, 2016, but failed to achieve the necessary approval of two-thirds of Members who voted, 229-177.

On its last day in session in the 114th Congress, the U.S. Senate Committee on Banking, Housing, and Urban Affairs took up H.R. 5602 and it was adopted with a bipartisan amendment from Chairman Richard Shelby and Ranking Member Sherrod Brown. This version of the bill contained the exact text of H.R. 5602, essentially all of H.R. 5594, and three sections form H.R. 5607. That version was approved by unanimous consent in the Senate but as the House had adjourned by the time the legislation returned, it was not considered and thus not enacted.

Longer Term

The Task Force believes that in the longer term—beginning early in the 115th Congress—a number of the issues raised during its previous hearings will need continued Congressional attention. Among them are:

- *Better interagency coordination, resource allocation, and de-confliction.* While FinCEN, OFAC, and TFI have had budget increases nearly every year for the past decade, those increases have been modest when compared with the heavier workload they have experienced—the explosive growth of terrorist threats, the globalization of the narcotics trade and transnational crime, and the dramatic increase in the use of sanctions as a diplomatic tool—and the Task Force believes a thorough examination of resource levels is appropriate. Members of the Task Force and witnesses at hearings regularly questioned whether budgets for such efforts are adequate. Additionally, while government efforts to fight financial crime have been significantly enhanced, the inefficiencies of large bureaucracies and jurisdictional tensions can serve to blunt such tools. Accordingly, the Task Force believes that consideration needs to be given to ways to recruit and retain the best analysts and investigators of financial crime because the private sector often seems to use government service in this area in the same way a baseball team uses its farm system as a training ground for its most successful players. While that means good, well-trained people are working in the private sector, it can leave the government scrambling for talent or constantly disrupted by turnover at all levels.

- *Better use of and access to information that can identify illicit finance.* The fact that in the second decade of the 21st century various government agencies involved in law enforcement and regulatory oversight of the import and export of goods do not have single-source, real-time access to all related data is inexplicable and an inefficient use of existing information. FinCEN's model of collecting reports on suspected or possibly illicit finance and then making both the data and analysis of it available throughout the government (and as appropriate to state and local law enforcement) provides a useful model for solving this problem. Additionally, while a corporate registration system that allows bad actors in some instances to conceal ownership or control is a significant AML/CFT vulnerability, it is difficult to put banks in the position of having to determine such ownership or control when in many instances even law enforcement agents with warrants cannot breach such anonymity. Several plausible solutions for getting such information to law enforcement without interfering with otherwise legal business practices have been proposed and likely will be considered in the 115th Congress. One concept that the Task Force believes is worthy of further consideration is a pilot program that would form a "utility-like" entity intended to reduce financial institutions' burden of performing "know your customer" verification. Finally, while FinCEN's Bank Secrecy Act Advisory Group—consisting of law enforcement, banks and regulators—has improved the information flow between the government and banks regarding the government's expectations for combating financial crimes and criminal methodologies, more needs to be done in this area. The government and banks have managed to construct a much needed and essentially real-time, secure facility for information-sharing to stop cyber-attacks, and this model seems like a useful one for countering terror finance. Additionally, although Congress ago passed a law encouraging bank-to-bank sharing of information that could aid in countering financial crimes without fear of liability a decade and a half, the Treasury Department's regulations enabling that cooperation are written in such a way that banks are reluctant to share information that could potentially stop a variety of such crimes. Particularly because the banks themselves have sought clarification of Congressional intent, the Task Force believes work in this area is imperative.

- *Adding more overseas Treasury attachés.* While it may not be necessary to have a Treasury attaché in every embassy, the Task Force believes that having fewer than a dozen and a half attachés around the world is insufficient given the current terror threat, the explosion of financial crime, and the increasing interconnectedness of global economies and financial systems. This proposal would imply funding challenges, but determining the proper distribution of attachés would be the first stop toward addressing the issue.

- *Continued attention to helping developing countries fight illicit finance.* Witnesses at a number of Task Force hearings testified that more attention to the effort of helping developing countries improve governance, financial law enforcement, regulatory, trade and even imprisonment mechanisms would benefit both the citizens of those countries and help G20 countries by reducing lax environments that criminals and terrorists alike can exploit. Witnesses told the Task Force that even within the U.S., department-to-department coordination of technical assistance efforts is uneven, leading to gaps and duplication, and that coordination among major donor countries of their bilateral technical assistance, and of that aid with technical assistance provided by multilaterals, is next to non-existent. Several witnesses suggested that while it would be difficult to erect and maintain an international coordination and de-confliction mechanism similar to FATF—and that previous efforts to do so have not succeeded—any effort on this front should be helpful in improving assistance delivery to those countries that could best use it.

- *A greater domestic and international focus on stopping trade-based money laundering*. The Task Force heard from numerous witnesses that inefficiently organized, patchwork import/export regulation and law enforcement can allow exploitation even in G20 countries, facilitating the transfer of assets, goods, and perhaps weapons, and resulting in extraordinary loss of revenue. In developing countries, the threat is even greater: witnesses told the Task Force that an efficient capture of reasonable import and export duties in many countries would give them the resources to improve governance in general, strengthen law enforcement that could curtail crime, and make the country less hospitable for terrorists. Increased funds also potentially would be available for public health, education and infrastructure development. Witnesses told the Task Force that a well-developed system of Trade Transparency Units around the world similar to that of financial intelligence units would allow governments to exchange information to ensure that shipments actually contain what they were claimed to contain, and that the value is not misrepresented. The Task Force heard that formation of an Egmont Group-like international body to work towards harmonizing trade transparency internationally could help impede the free flow of not just illicit funds, but of stolen cultural items and potentially of weapons.

- *Development of a harmonized regulatory and examination procedure for nonbank financial institutions—primarily money service businesses but also emerging value transfer technologies—to squeeze out illicit finance and provide banks the comfort necessary for them to again widely offer MSBs retail account services.* The fact that nonbank regulation and examination is spread between the federal government—which devotes far less time to the effort than it does to bank regulation—and states, which have widely differing standards for the work, means that there is ample opportunity for arbitraging to the lowest level of regulation and examination and thus a potential that nonbanks may be used to channel illicit funding. That situation not only penalizes the good actors who put in the effort to run legitimate systems, but makes banks leery of offering retail banking services to any player in the sector. In turn, that penalizes American citizens who want to send money home to family members in developing countries, forcing remittances toward illicit funds-transfer channels where it can commingle with terror funds or the proceeds of drug crime or human trafficking, and can impede the development of new and innovative value transfer technologies. While it is unlikely the federal government can erect a regulatory and examination framework similar to that for banks, the Task Force heard extensive testimony that harmonizing state and federal standards would be a good first step and might help prevent emerging value transfer technologies form becoming a new Wild West of funds transfers.

- *Development of a whole-of-government strategy to combat terror finance and other forms of financial crimes.* While the government produces studies of the terror finance threat and of money laundering methodologies, absent a requirement for a regularly updated unified strategy, departments and agencies pursue their efforts in ways that can lead to duplication of effort, gaps and general inefficiency. Given the motivation that criminals and terrorists have to innovate past existing detection and interdiction regimes and the fact they do not need to clear new methodologies through bureaucracies, they often are nimble at developing new channels through which to funnel bad assets. A constantly updated strategy will have the added benefit of increasing intra-government networking and awareness of emerging tools that could be used to stop the flow of illicit funds.

- **_Beneficial ownership of corporate entities._** FATF's 2016 Mutual Evaluation of United States efforts to fight the various forms of illicit finance, released at the end of 2016, found that "lack of timely access to adequate, accurate and current beneficial ownership … information remains one the of the fundamental gaps in the U.S. context."[243] It should be noted that moves by FinCEN in the spring of 2016 to focus bank's AML efforts more closely on identifying beneficial owners of accounts or transactions were intended to address this issue, but are viewed by some as inadequate. Since the FinCEN requirements were not fully in place during the bulk of FATF's evaluation period, it is unclear the extent to which they affected the evaluation.

- **_Re-animation of the interagency Terrorist Financing Working Group._** TFWG was created in 2001 and was tasked with coordinating the interagency delivery of training and technical assistance to combat terrorist financing. The group has been dormant at least four years for a variety of reasons, but should be reestablished as soon as possible.

---

[243] _See_ Financial Action Task Force Report, _United States' Measures to Combat Money Laundering and Terrorist Financing,_ (Dec. 2016), _available at_ http://www.fatf-gafi.org/publications/mutualevaluations/documents/mer-united-states-2016.html.

Conclusion

The threat of terrorism to the United States, its financial sector, and the world is unlikely to disappear anytime soon. Terrorist groups and their sympathizers are constantly evolving the methods they use to raise and move funds to carry out acts of violence and destruction. Although only some of these actors directly employ the formal financial sector, all funds connected to terrorism or proceeds of crime more generally, come into contact with financial institutions at some point. To effectively counter the financing of terrorism, experts like former Treasury Under Secretary for Enforcement Jimmy Gurulé believe the U.S. government must continue to evaluate and evolve the effectiveness of measures to curtail terror financing to protect national security and save innocent lives.

Throughout its two years in operation, the Financial Services Committee's Task Force to Investigate Terrorism Financing has engaged in a systematic review of the nature of the terrorist finance threat, with a goal of determining how the federal government can work internally and externally to identify and impede the flow of terror funds and how the financial sector and international bodies can best offer assistance in this effort. It is the hope of its Members that the Task Force's legislative proposals and long term recommendations can develop a map for future Congressional oversight and action to more effectively combat terror finance.

Appendix A: Further Reading[1]

April 22, 2015, Task Force to Investigate Terrorism Financing Hearing titled "A Survey of Global Terrorism and Terrorist Financing"

Executive Summary

The threat of terrorism is continually evolving, with an increasing number of groups around the world threatening the United States and its allies. Many of these groups are utilizing diverse methods to generate and move funds to support their activities and organizations. This hearing will focus on the major terror groups currently operating across the globe to obtain an overview of the terrorist threat and methods of terror financing.

Headquartered in Syria, the Islamic State (also known as ISIL, ISIS, IS, and Daesh) has become one of the world's most violent and dangerous terror groups. The group is also exceedingly well financed relative to other terrorist organizations. In 2014, the Islamic State generated approximately $1 million per day. These funds were raised predominantly through the sale of oil smuggled into Syria and Turkey. The group has also utilized other funding streams to include taxation and extortion, the sale of antiquities, and kidnapping for ransom.

In Africa, Islamist extremist groups Boko Haram and Al-Shabaab both seek to create an Islamic state in Nigeria and Somalia respectively. Primarily through the kidnapping and extortion of local Nigerians and foreigners, Boko Haram is estimated to have an annual net revenue of $10 million. With thousands of fighters under its control, it is believed to be the largest jihadi group to pledge allegiance to the Islamic State. Al-Shabaab has also utilized kidnapping and extortion in addition to relying heavily on its illicit charcoal and sugar trade to generate revenue. In 2012, Al-Shabaab aligned itself with al-Qaeda when it pledged its loyalty to the group.

Based in Lebanon, the Shiite Muslim terror group Hezbollah has been linked with South American drug trafficking organizations operating out of the tri-border region. This criminal partnership has generated millions of dollars in revenue for the group to fund their operations in the Middle East. Further, there is a growing concern that terrorist groups could use Latin American criminal organizations to infiltrate the United States.

In Europe, the al-Qaeda affiliate, al-Qaeda in the Arabian Peninsula (AQAP), actively trained and funded French citizens to perpetrate the January 9, 2015,

---

[1] All memoranda in this Appendix were prepared by the Congressional Research Service (CRS) at the Task Force's request.

attack against *Charlie Hebdo,* a Paris-based satirical newsweekly that had published cartoon depictions of the Prophet Muhammad.

Although no terrorist organization has successfully carried out a direct terrorist attack since 9/11, the rise in violence by home-grown Islamic extremists and the growing threat from abroad make it crucial for the federal government to use every tool at its disposal to stop and destroy the terror threat.

An Overview of Terror Groups and Terrorist Financing by Region
The Middle East
The Islamic State (ISIL) – Iraq[2]

<u>Background</u>

The Islamic State organization is the successor to al-Qaeda in Iraq (AQI). Established in 2004, AQI pledged loyalty to al-Qaeda and targeted U.S. and coalition forces in Iraq. In 2006, AQI changed its name to the Islamic State of Iraq (ISI). Following the outbreak of unrest in Syria in 2011, ISI leader Abu Bakr al Baghdadi tasked Muhammad al Jawlani with establishing Al Nusrah Front (ANF) in Syria to fight the Assad government.[3] ISI provided Jawlani with funding, manpower, and guidance, although ANF did not publicly acknowledge its ties to al-Qaeda. In April 2013, Baghdadi unilaterally announced a merger of ISI and ANF, under the name Islamic State in Iraq and the Levant (ISIL or ISIS). ANF and al-Qaeda leadership both rejected the merger, and al-Qaeda leader Ayman al Zawahiri ordered Baghdadi to confine his operations to Iraq. Baghdadi refused, and ISI began fighting in Syria under the name ISIL, eventually coming into direct confrontation with ANF and other Syrian opposition forces. In February 2014, Zawahiri publicly severed ties with ISIL, citing the group's brutal tactics, infighting with other Sunni groups, and refusal to cede Syria operations to ANF. In June 2014 Baghdadi declared the establishment of an Islamic caliphate and changed ISIL's name to the Islamic State.

Headquartered in the eastern Syrian city of Raqqah, the Islamic State operates primarily in northeastern Syria and northwestern Iraq. Through an extended military campaign against both government and opposition forces, the group gradually gained control over a roughly contiguous area along the Tigris and Euphrates rivers spanning hundreds of miles. In February 2015 congressional testimony, U.S. Director for National Intelligence James Clapper reconfirmed the

---

[2] The section entitled "The Islamic State (ISIL) - Iraq" is derived nearly verbatim from Carla E. Humud et. al, "Islamic State Financing and U.S. Policy Approaches," *CRS Report R43980* (April 10, 2015), *available at* http://www.crs.gov/pdfloader/R43980.

[3] *Id. see* fn. 3, "Senior Administration Officials on Terrorist Designations of the al-Nusrah Front as an Alias for al-Qaeda in Iraq," Special Briefing via teleconference, December 11, 2012.

intelligence community's estimate that the Islamic State can muster "somewhere in the range between 20,000 and 32,000 fighters" but noted that there has been "substantial attrition" and the group has been turning to conscription in some areas. IS militants in 2014 beheaded three Americans captured in Syria; a fourth U.S. citizen was also killed while held by the group. The Islamic State has encouraged followers to conduct lone-wolf attacks in Europe and the United States.

The Islamic State's Sources of Revenue

According to congressional testimony by Patrick Johnston of the RAND Corporation in late 2014, the key difference between the financial activities of the Islamic State's predecessors and its current financial profile is not the types of revenue sources, but the scale of activities.[4] Between August 2008 and January 2009, ISI's master financial ledgers in Mosul reportedly showed the group generating slightly less than $1 million in fundraising per month. In 2014, the Islamic State was able to generate the same amount—or more—per *day*. The Islamic State is also believed to be the richest terrorist organization in history, controlling vast amounts of territory, including oil fields and refineries, in both Syria and Iraq.[5] This section surveys specific IS revenue sources, some of which were initially cultivated by AQI and ISI.

Syrian Oil and the Islamic State

Much of the physical and economic damage to the Syrian oil sector took place between March 2011 and June 2014, when IS forces expanded their control of oil-producing regions in northeast Syria. Selling IS oil is technically difficult because the group has no traditional export facilities or access to the open market. As a result, the group must ship its oil by truck to the Turkish border where oil brokers and traders buy the oil and make cash payments, or payments in kind of petroleum products. Because the Syrian government considers IS oil to be stolen contraband and because international sanctions limit the markets the oil can legally enter, IS oil trades at a steeply discounted price. It has been reported that IS oil might have been selling for as little as $18 per barrel at the Turkish border, when Brent, a world price reference crude oil was selling for about $107 per barrel.[6]

---

[4] Patrick B. Johnston (RAND Corporation), testimony on "Countering ISIL's Financing" before the U.S. House Committee on Financial Services, November 13, 2014.

[5] *See e.g.*, Martin Chulov, "How an arrest in Iraq revealed ISIS's $2 billion jihadist network," *The Guardian* (June 15, 2014); Helen Lock, "How ISIS became the wealthiest terror group in history," *The Independent* (September 15, 2014), *available at* http://www.independent.co.uk/news/world/middle-east/how-isis-became-the-wealthiest-terror-group- in-history-9732750.html; Shawna Ohm, "ISIS: World's scariest terrorist group also the richest," *Yahoo Finance* (August 12, 20014), *available at* http://finance.yahoo.com/news/isis-the-world-s- richest-terrorist-organization--knights-151427465.html.

[6] *See* Ma'ad Fayad, *ISIS in Control of 60 Percent of Syrian Oil*, ASHARQ AL-AWSAT, July 11, 2014, *available at* http://www.aawsat.net/2014/07/article 55334174.

Iraqi Oil and the Islamic State

The Islamic State has been in control of a number of relatively small oil fields in northern Iraq, selling volumes of oil through Turkey in essentially the same manner as their sales of Syrian oil. While IS forces are not in control of a modern operating oil refinery, the group has refined oil in crude, small, mobile refineries with capacities of about 300 to 500 barrels per day of petroleum products. Petroleum products may also be easier to sell to Turkish brokers because they can enter retail markets directly, avoiding the documentation attendant with processing at a legitimate refinery.

Antiquities

Some analysts believe that the second largest source of revenue for the Islamic State is the sale of antiquities looted from areas under the group's control.[7] This includes items stolen from museums, storage depots, or private collections, as well as those newly excavated from among the hundreds of archeological sites in the area. One archeologist from the Iraqi government's Department of Antiquities stated that a third of Iraq's archaeological sites are now under IS control.[8] Items from these sites are sold in neighboring states or smuggled into Europe. Some U.S. estimates have placed the total volume of illicit trade at more than $100 million a year.[9]

Taxes, Extortion, and Asset Seizure

In a February 2015 report, the Financial Action Task Force (FATF), an international body focused on combatting money laundering and terrorism financing, found that the Islamic State finances itself largely through extortion rackets in its areas of operation. The report notes, "while ISIL frames its activities as 'taxation' or 'charitable giving,' it in fact runs a sophisticated protection racket where involuntary 'donations' purchase momentary safety or temporary continuity

---

[7] *See, e.g.*, Testimony of Matthew Levitt, Director of the Stein Program on Counterterrorism and Intelligence, Washington Institute for Near East Policy, *Terrorist Financing and the Islamic State: Hearing before the H. Comm. on Financial Services*, 113th Cong. (Nov. 13, 2014).

[8] Janine Di Giovanni, Leah McGrath Goodman, and Damien Sharkov, "How Does ISIS Fund Its Reign of Terror?," *Newsweek* (November 6, 2014), *available at* http://www.newsweek.com/2014/11/14/how-does-isis-fund-its-reign-terror-282607.html.

[9] Joe Parkinson, Ayla Albayrak and Duncan Mavin, "Syrian 'Monuments Men' Race to Protect Antiquities as Looting Bankrolls Terror," *The Wall Street Journal* (February 10, 2015), *available at* http://www.wsj.com/articles/syrian-monuments-men-race-to-protect-antiquities-as-looting-bankrolls-terror-1423615241.

of business."[10] Another study estimates that the Islamic State generates up to $360 million per year though taxation and extortion.[11]

The U.S. Treasury Department estimates that the Islamic State in 2014 gained access to at least a half billion dollars in cash by seizing control of state-owned bank branches in the Iraqi provinces of Ninevah, Al-Anbar, Salah Din, and Kirkuk.[12] The Islamic State approached private Iraqi banks differently, choosing instead to levy a tax of 5% on all customer cash withdrawals.[13]

Kidnapping for Ransom[14]

The Islamic State has generated significant income through the use of kidnapping for ransom. The United Nations estimates that the Islamic State collected $35-$45 million in ransom fees in 2014 alone—a higher annual yield than both al-Qaeda in the Arabian Peninsula (an estimated $20 million in ransom between 2011 and 2013) and al-Qaeda in the Islamic Maghreb (an estimated $75 million since 2010).[15]   A 2014 UN report on the Islamic State and the al-Qaeda-affiliated Nusrah Front states that the victims are mostly local residents, but also include a smaller number of foreign aid workers and journalists. However, the report also assesses that the group's high level of fundraising from kidnappings for ransom is not likely to be sustainable.

External Support

The Islamic State receives financial support from individuals in Gulf State and European countries, but observers generally agree that these amounts are modest in comparison to what the group generates internally. Analysts estimate that the Islamic State in 2013-14 accumulated up to $40 million from donors in

---

[10] FATF Report, *Financing of the Terrorist Organization Islamic State in Iraq and the Levant (ISIL)*, February 2015.

[11] Jean-Charles Brisard and Damien Martinez, *Islamic State: The Economy-Based Terrorist Funding*, October 2014.

[12] Jennifer L. Fowler, Deputy Assistant Secretary of Terrorist Financing and Financial Crimes, Treasury Department. Statement submitted for the conference, "Taking the Fight to ISIL: Operationalizing CT Lines of Effort Against the Islamic State Group," Washington Institute for Near East Policy, February 2, 2015.

[13] FATF Report, *supra* note 8.

[14] While it is U.S. policy to not pay concessions to individuals or groups holding official or private U.S. citizens hostage, other countries are not similarly constrained. *See* U.S. Department of State Foreign Affairs Manual, 7 FAM 1823 (July 26, 2006); Greg Botelho, "Q&A: ISIS Threat to japan Sheds Light on Harsh Realities of Kidnappings, Ransom," *CNN* (January 20, 2015), *available at* http://www.cnn.com/2015/01/20/world/ransom-hostages/.

[15] Statement by Ms. Yotsana Lalji, 1267 Al-Qaida Monitoring Team, November 24, 2014. Some of these figures appear to be based on estimates from unnamed Member States (see S/2014/770, paras.50-51 at http://www.un.org/ga/search/view_doc.asp?symbol=S/2014/770). Other estimates are higher—see, for example, "Paying Ransoms, Europe Bankrolls Qaeda Terror," *New York Times*, July 29, 2014.

Saudi Arabia, Qatar, and Kuwait. While the United States has worked with partner states in the Gulf to pass legislation curbing the flow of funds to the areas, implementation remains irregular. In October 2014, David Cohen, then-Under Secretary of the Treasury for Terrorism and Financial Intelligence, stated that Kuwait and Qatar were still "permissive jurisdictions" for terrorism financing.[16]

Africa

Boko Haram (Nigeria)

<u>Background</u>

Boko Haram was founded in 2002 in Maiduguri, Nigeria, by cleric Mohammed Yusuf.[17] Loosely translated from the region's Hausa language, Boko Haram means "Western education is forbidden."[18] The group's official name is Jama'atu Ahlis Sunna Lidda'awati wal-Jihad, which in Arabic means "People Committed to the Propagation of the Prophet's Teachings and Jihad."[19] The group seeks to establish an Islamic state in Nigeria, including the implementation of Sharia criminal courts across the country.[20] Boko Haram has attacked Nigeria's police and army, politicians, schools, religious buildings, public institutions, and civilians with increasing regularity since 2009.[21] More than ten thousand people have been killed in Boko Haram-related violence, and 1.5 million have been displaced.[22] Some experts view the group as an armed revolt against government corruption, abusive security forces, and widening regional economic disparity.[23] The U.S. State Department designated Boko Haram as a "Foreign Terrorist Organization" on November 13, 2013.[24]

At its inception, the group did not intend to overthrow the Nigerian government. This changed in July 2009 when Boko Haram members refused to obey a law requiring motorcycle riders to wear helmets because in their view doing so would be un-Islamic.[25] The arrest of several of its members incited a riot with

---

[16] Remarks by Treasury Under Secretary for Terrorism and Financial Intelligence David Cohen at the Carnegie Endowment for International Peace, "Attacking ISIL's Financial Foundation," October 23, 2014.

[17] Mohammed Aly Sergie, "Boko Haram," *Council on Foreign Relations Backgrounders* (March 13, 2015), *available at* http://www.cfr.org/nigeria/boko-haram/p25739.

[18] Farouk Chothia, "Who Are Nigeria's Boko Haram Islamists?" *BBC News* (January 21, 2015), *available at* http://www.bbc.com/news/world-africa-13809501.

[19] *Id.*

[20] Sergie, *supra* note 16.

[21] *Id.*

[22] *Id.*

[23] *Id.*

[24] *See* Media Note, Office of the Spokesperson, Terrorist Designations of Boko Haram and Ansaru (November 13, 2013), http://www.state.gov/r/pa/prs/ps/2013/11/217509.htm.

[25] John Ford, "The Origins of Boko Haram," *The National Interest* (June 6, 2014), *available at*

http://nationalinterest.org/feature/the-origins-boko-haram-10609?page=2.

Nigerian police resulting in 800 deaths.[26] Yusuf was subsequently arrested and shot and killed outside police headquarters.[27] After Abubakar Shekau, Yusuf's former second-in-command, assumed the leadership of Boko Haram, the group's activities turned increasingly violent.[28] Under Shekau, Boko Haram has engaged in terrorist tactics that have included a suicide attack on a United Nations building in Abuja in 2011, the killings of dozens of students, the burning of villages, establishing ties to regional terror groups, and the abduction of over 200 schoolgirls in April 2014.[29] On March 7, 2015, Shekau pledged allegiance to ISIL.[30] Five days later, ISIL accepted the pledge via audiotape and described it as an expansion of the group's caliphate to West Africa.[31]

How Boko Haram is Funded

To fund its operations, Boko Haram deploys a system of couriers to move cash inside Nigeria and across the border from neighboring African states.[32] Boko Haram's annual net income has been estimated at $10 million.[33] These funds have been raised primarily through kidnapping and extortion.[34] Some U.S. officials have estimated that the group was paid as much as $1 million for the release of a wealthy Nigerian.[35] Foreigners have fetched higher ransoms – in February 2013, Boko Haram was paid $3 million for the release of a French family of seven kidnapped in northern Cameroon.[36]

The group has also smuggled drugs to raise funds. In 2012, the Drug Enforcement Administration indicated that the group was becoming increasingly involved in cocaine trafficking to raise money for its activities, or was being bankrolled by the traffickers in exchange for support. [37]

---

[26] *Id.*
[27] Sergie, *supra* note 16.
[28] Ford, *supra* note 25.
[29] Sergie, *supra* note 16.
[30] Rukmini Callimachi, "Boko Haram Generates Uncertainty With Pledge of Allegiance to Islamic State," *The New York Times* (March 7, 2015), *available at* http://www.nytimes.com/2015/03/08/world/africa/boko-haram-is-said-to-pledge-allegiance-to-islamic-state.html.
[31] "IS Welcomes Boko Haram Allegiance," *AFP* (March 12, 2015), *available at* http://news.yahoo.com/accepts-allegiance-nigeria-jihadists-boko-haram-201513146.html.
[32] Phil Stewart and Lesley Wroughton, "How Boko Haram is Beating U.S. Efforts to Choke Its Financing," *Reuters* (July 1, 2014), *available at* http://www.reuters.com/article/2014/07/01/us-usa-nigeria-bokoharam-insight-idUSKBN0F636920140701.
[33] Farouk, Chothia, "Boko Haram Crisis: How Have Nigeria's Militants Become So Strong?," BBC News (January 26, 2015), *available at* http://www.bbc.com/news/world-africa-30933860.
[34] *Id.*
[35] *Id.*
[36] Chothia, *supra* note 17.
[37] Ntaryike Divine, Jr., "Drug Trafficking Rising in Central Africa, Warns Interpol," *Voice of America* (September 8, 2012), *available at* http://www.voanews.com/content/drug-trafficking-rising-in-central-africa-warns-interpol/1504026.html.

The U.S. Treasury Department also has evidence that al-Qaeda has financially supported Boko Haram.[38] The amount of this support, however, is dwarfed by the millions of dollars the group makes through its kidnapping and ransom activities. One U.S. estimate of financial transfers from AQIM was in the low hundreds of thousands of dollars.[39]

Al-Shabaab (Somalia)

Background

Al-Shabaab ("the Youth" in Arabic) is an Islamist extremist group bent on the creation of a fundamentalist Islamic state in Somalia. Its origins date back to the political upheaval that took place after the overthrow of the military dictator Mohammed Siad Barre in 1991.[40] Starting in the late 1990s, as part of local efforts, neighborhood Sharia courts were established to instill law and order.[41] The courts soon became power centers with their own militias and religious ideologies.[42] In mid-2004, 11 of the courts merged to form the Islamic Courts Union (ICU) led by Sheikh Ahmed.[43] In June 2006, the ICU defeated the warlords who controlled Mogadishu for the past decade and began to impose a degree of order.[44] With Al-Shabaab acting as its youth militia, fundamentalist elements of the ICU used this opportunity to impose their version of strict Islamic law.[45]

At the request of Somalia's transitional government, Ethiopia invaded Somalia in December 2006 and ousted the ICU from Mogadishu.[46] Al-Shabaab retreated to the south of the country where it began organizing guerilla assaults on Ethiopian forces.[47] Rob Wise, a counterterrorism expert at the Center for Strategic and International Studies, believes that the Ethiopian occupation of Somalia is responsible for "transforming [Al-Shabaab] from a small, relatively unimportant part of a more moderate Islamic movement into the most powerful and radical armed faction in the country."[48] On February 26, 2008, the U.S. State Department

---

[38] Stewart and Wroughton, *supra* note 31.

[39] *Id.*

[40] Rob Wise, "Al Shabaab," *AQAM Future Studies Project Case Study Series* (July 2011), *available at* http://csis.org/files/publication/110715_Wise_AlShabaab_AQAM%20Futures%20Case%20Study_WEB.pdf.

[41] *Id.*

[42] *Id.*

[43] *Id.*

[44] *Id.*

[45] *Id.*

[46] Jonathan Masters and Mohammed Aly Sergie, "Al-Shabaab," *Council on Foreign Relations Backgrounders* (March 5, 2015), *available at* http://www.cfr.org/somalia/al-shabab/p18650.

[47] *Id.*

[48] *Id.*

designated Al-Shabaab a "Foreign Terrorist Organization."[49] In February, 2012, the group formally pledged its loyalty to al-Qaeda leader Ayman al-Zawahiri.[50]

While initially focusing on targets in Somalia, Al-Shabaab has expanded its violence into Kenya and Uganda.[51] The group has focused its atrocities against Kenya due to the country's joint actions with the Africa Union in Somalia.[52] On September 21, 2013, the group claimed responsibility for killing over 67 persons at the Westgate Premier shopping mall in Nairobi, Kenya.[53]   Most recently, on April 2, 2015, Al-Shabaab gunmen targeted Garissa University College in Kenya and killed over 147 persons.[54]

How Al-Shabaab is Funded[55]

Counterterrorism experts say Al-Shabaab has benefited from several different sources of income over the years, including revenue from other terrorist groups, state sponsors, the Somali diaspora, charities, piracy, kidnapping, and the extortion of local businesses. The governments of Eritrea, Iran, Saudi Arabia, Syria, Qatar, and Yemen have been cited as financiers—although most officially deny these claims.

Domestically, the group built an extensive racketeering operation in Kismayo after seizing control of the southern port city and its economy in 2008. The trade of charcoal, in particular, is essential to the city's commerce. A Kenya-led assault liberated Kismayo from Al-Shabaab control in October 2012—a victory that many experts say strategically crippled the jihadi group.

However, an October 2014 UN Security Council report says Al-Shabaab's illicit charcoal trading hasn't been interrupted by "the military offensive against the group" and continues in Kismayo and nearby Barawe. Charcoal exports are a component of a trade that includes al-Shabaab's importation of sugar, much of which then makes its way into Kenya illegally. Roughly ten thousand bags

---

[49] *See* Office of the Coordinator for Counterterrorism, Designation of Al-Shabaab as a Foreign Terrorist Organization (February 26, 2008), http://www.state.gov/j/ct/rls/other/des/102446.htm.
[50] Wire Staff, "Al-Shabaab Joining al Qaeda, Monitor Group Says," *CNN* (February 10, 2012), *available at* http://www.cnn.com/2012/02/09/world/africa/somalia-shabaab-qaeda/index.html.
[51] Adam Taylor, "What's Behind the Return of Al-Shabaab, The Terror Group That Killed at Least 147 People in Kenya?" *The Washington Post* (April 3, 2015), *available at* http://www.washingtonpost.com/blogs/worldviews/wp/2015/04/03/whats-behind-the-return-of-al-shabab-the-terror-group-that-killed-at-least-147-people-in-kenya/.
[52] *Id.*
[53] *Id.*
[54] Edith Honan, "Al Shabaab Kills at Least 147 at Kenyan University; Siege Ends," *Reuters*, (April 2, 2015), *available at* http://www.reuters.com/article/2015/04/02/us-kenya-security-college-idUSKBN0MT0CK20150402.
[55] The section entitled "How Al-Shabaab is Funded" is derived nearly verbatim from Masters and Sergie, *supra* note 45.

of contraband sugar worth hundreds of thousands of dollars may be smuggled into Kenya every day, according to the UN. In April 2013, Kenyan officials complained that Al-Shabaab operatives were attempting to infiltrate the country's sugar trade.

South America

Hezbollah (in the tri-border region)

Background

Hezbollah ("Party of God" in Arabic) is a Shiite Muslim political party that came into existence after Israel entered and subsequently occupied Lebanon in In response to Israel's efforts to expel Palestinian militants in southern Lebanon, a group of disenfranchised Shiites joined together in support of an Iranian-style clerical regime.[57] This group issued its founding manifesto as Hezbollah in 1985.[58] Their mission statement included the following tenets: loyalty to Iran's leader, Ayatollah Khomeni; establishment of an Islamic regime; expulsion of the United States, France, and Israel from Lebanon; and the destruction of Israel.[59] The State Department designated Hezbollah a Foreign Terrorist Organization on October 8, 1997.[60]

Drug Trafficking Revenue

Since 2010, Hezbollah has been linked with South American drug trafficking organizations operating out of the tri-border region (Argentina, Brazil, and Paraguay).[61] Hezbollah has used the proceeds from trafficking cocaine into Europe and the Middle East to finance its operations.[62] During a recent hearing before the Senate Homeland Security and Government Affairs Committee, Lieutenant General Kenneth E. Tovo, U.S. Southern Command, made the following comments about Hezbollah:

---

[56] Jonathan Masters and Zachary Laub, "Hezbollah (a.k.a. Hizbollah, Hizbu'llah)" *Council on Foreign Relations Backgrounders* (January 3, 2014), *available at* http://www.cfr.org/lebanon/hezbollah-k-hizbollah-hizbullah/p9155.

[57] *Id.*

[58] *Id.*

[59] *Id.*

[60] *See* U.S. State Department Bureau of Counterterrorism, Foreign Terrorist Organizations (August 10, 1997), http://www.state.gov/j/ct/rls/other/des/123085.htm.

[61] Clare Ribando Seelke et. al, "Latin America and the Caribbean: Illicit Drug Trafficking and U.S. Counterdrug Programs," *CRS Report R41215* (April 30, 2010), *available at* http://assets.opencrs.com/rpts/R41215_20100430.pdf.

[62] Edwin Mora, "State Dep't: Hezbollah Raising Funds Through Drug Cartels in South America But 'No Credible Information' of Terrorist Operations There," *CNS News* (June 9, 2010), *available at* http://cnsnews.com/news/article/state-dept-hezbollah-raising-funds-through-drug-cartels-south-america-no-credible.

[O]n a broader scale, we know that some of these [terrorist] organizations do receive financial benefit from the drug trade — a topic of much discussion amongst the intel community about how much cooperation and convergence, as we call it, there really is . . . There is dispute about that, but I think it's fair to say that there is a good amount of profit that Lebanese Hezbollah makes off of illicit trafficking writ large on at least the order of tens of millions and much of it is funneled through the money laundering system and fuels their operations back in the Middle East.[63]

In a March 12, 2015 statement to Congress, General John F. Kelly of U.S. Southern Command expressed similar concerns:

[T]he terrorist group Lebanese Hezbollah—which has long viewed the region as a potential attack venue against Israeli or other Western targets—has supporters and sympathizers in Lebanese diaspora communities in Latin America, some of whom are involved in lucrative illicit activities like money laundering and trafficking in counterfeit goods and drugs. These clan-based criminal networks exploit corruption and lax law enforcement in places like the Tri-Border Area of Brazil, Paraguay, and Argentina and the Colón Free Trade Zone in Panama and generate revenue, an unknown amount of which is transferred to Lebanese Hezbollah.[64]

General Kelly also mentioned that Iran has established more than 80 "cultural centers" in a region (Latin America) with an extremely small Muslim population.[65] He emphasized that, as the foremost state sponsor of terrorism, Iran's involvement in the region is a matter of concern.[66]

Europe
Al-Qaeda in the Arab Peninsula – AQAP (Charlie Hebdo Attack - France)

On January 7, 2015, Said and Cherif Kouachi entered the offices of the French satirical newspaper *Charlie Hebdo* in Paris and killed 11 employees and a French National Police Officer in retaliation for a cartoon depicting the Prophet Mohammed. It was later determined that Said Kouachi visited Yemen in 2011 to

---

[63] *See* Testimony of Lt. Gen. Kenneth E. Tovo, U.S. Southern Command, *Securing the Border: Understanding and Addressing the Root Causes of Central American Migration to the United States: Hearing before the S. Comm. On Homeland Security and Governmental Affairs,* 114th Cong. (March 10, 2015).
[64] *See* Posture Statement of General John F. Kelly, United States Southern Command, before the 114th Congress Senate Armed Services Committee (March 12, 2015).
[65] *Id. at 7.*
[66] *Id.*

train with the group al-Qaeda in the Arab Peninsula (AQAP).[67] In addition, before they carried out the attack on *Charlie Hebdo,* the Kouachi brothers called a local television station and said they had been financed by AQAP.[68]

Based in Yemen, AQAP is a militant Islamist group that was formed in 2009 through the union of the Saudi and Yemeni branches of al-Qaeda.[69] The group initially targeted only local, U.S., and Western Interests in the Arabian Peninsula, but has now adopted a global strategy.[70] Top U.S. security officials hold AQAP to be the greatest threat to the American homeland.[71]

According to U.S. officials, AQAP follows the funding streams of other al-Qaeda affiliates.[72] This includes sources such as bank robberies, drug proceeds, and phony charities.[73] According to U.S. Treasury officials, kidnapping for ransom continues to generate **tens of millions of dollars** in revenues for AQAP and other al-Qaeda groups.[74] A classified December 2009 memo from then-Secretary of State Hillary Clinton indicated that donors in Saudi Arabia were "the most significant source" of **funding to Sunni terrorist groups**, including al-Qaeda.[75]

---

[67] Mark Hosenball, "Said Kouachi, Suspect in Charlie Hebdo Attack, Trained in Yemen: Reports," Huffington Post (January 08, 2015), *available at* http://www.huffingtonpost.com/2015/01/08/said-kouachi-yemen_n_6439300.html.

[68] James Gordon Meek, "Al-Qaeda Gave Charlie Hebdo Killers $20K," *ABC News* (January 14, 2015), *available at* http://abcnews.go.com/International/al-qaeda-laid-plan-charlie-hebdo-massacre-video/story?id=28213640.

[69] CFR.org Staff, "Al-Qaeda in the Arabian Peninsula (AQAP)," *Council on Foreign Relations Backgrounders* (March 19, 2015), *available at http://www.cfr.org/yemen/al-qaeda-arabian-peninsula-aqap/p9369,*

[70] *See* National Counterterrorism Center, Counterterrorism Guide, *available at* http://www.nctc.gov/site/groups/aqap.html.

[71] Lee Ferran, "What is AQAP, the Terror Group Claiming Charlie Hebdo Attack?," *ABC News* (January 14, 2015), *available at* http://abcnews.go.com/International/aqap-terror-group-claiming-charlie-hebdo-attack/story?id=28223532.

[72] CFR.org Staff, *supra* note 68.

[73] *Id.*

[74] *Id.*

[75] *Id.*

May 21, 2015, Task Force to Investigate Terrorism Financing hearing titled "A Dangerous Nexus: Terrorism, Crime, and Corruption"

Introduction

Various observers have asserted that transnational terrorism, crime, and corruption interact in varied and significant ways, to the detriment of U.S. national security. In congressional testimony from February 2015, the Director of National Intelligence (DNI) James Clapper identified terrorism and transnational organized crime as among the top eight global threats to U.S. national security.[1] According to DNI Clapper, both terrorist and transnational criminal groups thrive in highly insecure regions of the world, with terrorist groups contributing to regional instability and internal conflict, while transnational organized crime groups exploit these environments for financial gain and corruptive influence. The February 2015 *National Security Strategy* echoes this theory of how terrorism, crime, and corruption represent mutually reinforcing and interconnected threats: "[D]iffuse networks of al-Qa'ida, ISIL [Islamic State of Iraq and the Levant or IS], and affiliated groups threaten U.S. citizens, interests, allies, and partners. Violent extremists exploit upheaval across the Middle East and North Africa. Fragile and conflict-affected states incubate and spawn... illicit weapons and drug smugglers.... Too often, failures in governance and endemic corruption hold back the potential of rising regions."[2]

Shifting Perspectives?

Although observers recognize that terrorist and criminal actors have long represented distinct entities with unique strategic objectives and motivations, U.S. officials have increasingly adopted an understanding that multiple illicit actors at times converge in particular regions, cooperate for various purposes, and, in combination, contribute to greater insecurity.[3] This perspective is largely based on recent U.S. experiences of responding to conflict and instability across the globe, including:

- Afghanistan and Pakistan, where extremists, including the Taliban and other insurgency-associated armed groups, also profit from a booming illicit opium

---

[1] James Clapper, Director of the Office of National Intelligence, *Worldwide Threat Assessment of the U.S. Intelligence Community,* statement for the record, U.S. Senate, Committee on Armed Services, February 26, 2015.

[2] White House, Administration of President Barack Obama, *National Security Strategy*, February 6, 2015.

[3] See also Phil Williams, "Lawlessness and Disorder: An Emerging Paradigm for the 21st Century," in *Convergence: Illicit Networks and National Security in the Age of Globalization*, Michael Miklaucic and Jacqueline Brewer, eds., April 2013.

trade that is largely facilitated by corrupt officials;[4]

- Latin America, where terrorists, including the Foreign Terrorist Organization-designated (FTO) Revolutionary Armed Forces of Colombia (FARC) and the Shining Path in Peru control the majority of the world's illicit cocaine cultivation and production, and cooperate with corrupt government officials in countries such as Venezuela, other international terrorist groups, as well as transnational criminal groups that smuggle a wide range of contraband into the United States;[5]

- Libya, where political instability since the fall of Muammar Gaddafi's regime in 2011 has attracted Al Qaeda-affiliated groups and IS-aligned extremists that profit and contributed to a significant uptick in criminal consolidation of power and the flow of illicit weapons, migrants, and goods throughout the region;[6]

- West Africa, where entrenched kleptocratic regimes such as Guinea-Bissau and a confluence of illicit actors have contributed to the region's emergence as a major narcotics transit point and connected terrorist-affiliated migrant-, cigarette-, and weapons-smugglers with age-old nomadic trade routes through the Sahel, where groups such as Al Qaeda in the Islamic Maghreb (AQIM) operate.[7]

This new perspective, at times contested, represents a possible departure from the historical assumption that terrorist and criminal groups would avoid interaction, viewing each other as a liability. In theory, the unique organizational purposes of the two distinct groups, in which terrorists are primarily motivated by ideology and criminals by profit, contributed to the perception that a confluence of the two threats would be rare. According to this viewpoint, terrorist groups would be ideologically resistant to participating in illicit activities and economies that could undermine their popular support and possibly lead to greater scrutiny by the international security community. Moreover, both entities would be wary of compromising internal security by establishing relationships with potentially unreliable outside actors and attracting heightened attention from authorities. In some instances, terrorist groups may, over time, develop capabilities that lessen their reliance on external criminal services. In other instances, criminal groups may develop terrorist-type tactics or attempt to integrate, sometimes forcefully, into a terrorist group's organization to secure influence and access to resources.

---

[4] U.N. Office on Drugs and Crime, *The Global Afghan Opium Trade: A Threat Assessment*, July 29, 2011; U.N. Office on Drugs and Crime, *Crime and Insurgency: The Transnational Threat of Afghan Opium*, October 21, 2009.

[5] Vanda Felbab-Brown, *Shooting Up: Counterinsurgency and the War on Drugs*, 2010.

[6] U.N. Security Council Panel of Experts on Libya, *Final Report*, S/2015/128, February 23, 2015.

[7] U.N. Office on Drugs and Crime, *Transnational Organized Crime in West Africa: A Threat Assessment*, February 25, 2013.

Beyond individual anecdotes and case studies, a 2014 network analysis by the Combating Terrorism Center at West Point suggests that criminal and terrorist groups may be highly interconnected.[8] Using a commercially available data set covering a range of illicit activities, including terrorism, drug trafficking, organized crime, human smuggling, and corruption, researchers conducted a network analysis of more than 2,700 individuals operating in 3,600 places and linked by 15,000 relationships that spanned 122 countries. In total, the network analysis found more than 1,000 country-to-country relationships (see **Figure 1**). According to the analysis, 98% of the individuals in the data set were separated by a maximum of two degrees of association. The study further found that criminals and terrorists interacted. According to the study, 46% of the connections associated with terrorist actors were linked to non-terrorist actors. Conversely, 35% of the connections associated with non-terrorist actors were linked to terrorists.

Figure 1. Transnational Relationships of Illicit Actors

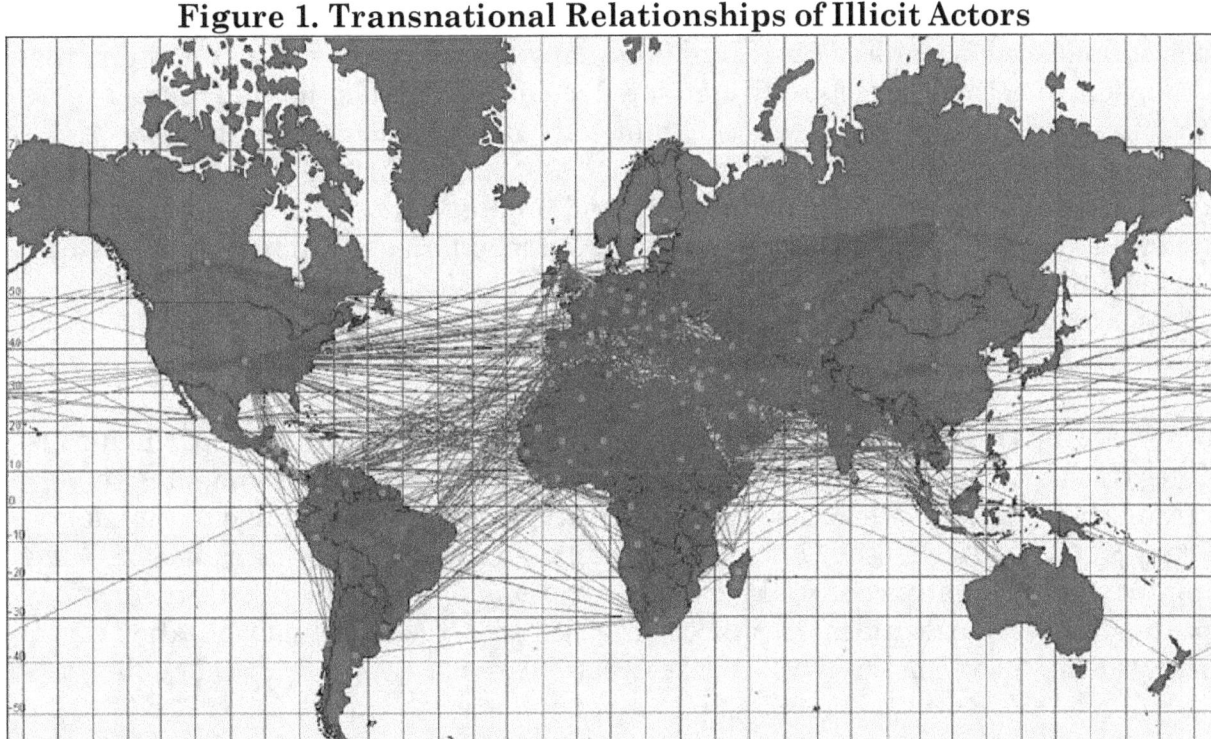

Source: Scott Helfstein and John Solomon, *Risky Business: The Global Threat Network and the Politics of Contraband*, Combating Terrorism Center at West Point, May 2014, p. 47.

Notes: As noted above, researchers at the Combating Terrorism Center at West Point used commercially available data on illicit actors from World-Check to map a network of more than 2,700 individuals. The above figure, published in *Risky Business: The Global Threat Network and the Politics of Contraband*, summarizes country-to-country connections within the network. It provides visual evidence of

---

[8] Scott Helfstein and John Solomon, *Risky Business: The Global Threat Network and the Politics of Contraband*, Combating Terrorism Center at West Point, May 2014.

the transnational scope of the network, but simplifies the relationships by looking only at bilateral relationships rather than the strength of the connections.

Motivations, Patterns, and Interactions

Unclassified, publicly available reports describe crime-terrorism interactions as varying significantly in scope and changing over time, as membership, resources, and ideological views evolve.[9] In some cases, crime-terrorism relationships are primarily transactional in nature, based on partnerships of convenience and complementary business ties. Reasons for such transactional relationships could include a need for illicit financial or smuggling expertise to move and hide money, people, and weapons.

In other cases, terrorist groups may pursue criminal activities primarily for fundraising purposes. Since the end of the Cold War and corresponding declines in traditional state-sponsored sources of funding, some observers suggest that terrorist groups have become increasingly motivated to generate funds through criminal activity to sustain organizational capabilities.[10] Heightened international counterterrorism measures in the past decade may have further motivated terrorist groups to seek alternative, more underground funding options. The universe of potential crime-for-profit activities is vast. Common forms of criminal fundraising include drug trafficking, kidnapping for ransom, and local extortion and theft. Increasingly, cybercrime and cyber-related activities are said to be an area of interest for criminal and terrorist groups alike.

Groups may also transition along an apparent crime-terrorism continuum.[11] Over time, ideologically motivated groups that initially avoid involvement with criminal activities may become increasingly attracted by the lucrative nature of criminal activities. In other instances, criminal groups may become radicalized and apply their criminal expertise to conduct operations that not only result in illicit profits but also further ideologically oriented goals. Crucial in the facilitation of many crime-terrorism interactions are corrupt actors in the private and public

---

[9] Louise Shelley and John Picarelli, "Methods Not Motives: Implications of the Convergence of International Organized Crime and Terrorism," *Police Practice and Research*, Vol. 3, No. 4, 2002; John Picarelli, "Osama bin Corleone? Vito the Jackal? Framing Threat Convergence Through an Examination of Transnational Organized Crime and International Terrorism," *Terrorism and Political Violence*, Vol. 24, No. 2, 2012.
[10] U.S. Department of Defense, Office of the Undersecretary of Defense for Acquisition and Technology, Defense Science Board, *1997 Summer Study Task Force on DOD Responses to Transnational Threats*, Vol. 1, final report, October 1997; White House, Administration of President William Clinton, *International Crime Threat Assessment*, December 2000; Steven Hutchinson and Pat O'Malley, "A Crime-Terror Nexus? Thinking on Some of the Links Between Terrorism and Criminality," *Studies in Conflict & Terrorism*, Vol. 30, No. 12, December 2007.
[11] Tamara Makarenko, "The Crime-Terror Continuum: Tracing the Interplay between Transnational Organized Crime and Terrorism," *Global Crime*, Vol. 6, No. 1, February 2004.

sectors, including so-called "gatekeepers," local and regional "fixers," and "shadow facilitators."[12]

Money Laundering

Illicit support activities may include money laundering techniques to obfuscate the origins and recipients of funds through front companies, charities, shell corporations, and other third-party business structures. The movement and storage of money may also involve bulk cash smuggling and cash couriers; the exploitation of informal remittance mechanisms, international trade systems, and the formal international banking sector; as well as the use of unregulated diamonds, gold, and other minerals and commodities for stored value. Multiple financial actions by the Treasury Department in recent years have highlighted the ability of Hezbollah, a terrorist group with reputedly sophisticated financial expertise, to exploit the international financial system and move and store illicit assets.[13]

Human Smuggling

Illicit support activities may include the clandestine movement of people and the use of false identities to facilitate international travel of known illicit actors without detection. Such activities may involve the use of vendors of fraudulent identity and travel documents and criminal groups with local expertise in exploiting porous borders. The State Department's 2013 *Country Reports on Terrorism*, published in April 2014, identified Panama's Darien region as a "significant pathway for human smuggling with potential counterterrorism implications."[14] The Panamanian National Border Service reported that 30% of all irregular migrants detected were from African, Middle Eastern, and South Asian countries—and that some portion of this smuggling was facilitated by FARC members operating along the Panamanian-Colombian border. In another example cited by the State Department, terrorist groups exploited the services of organized criminal groups operating in South Africa with an expertise in passport forgery to "assume false identities and enable them to move freely throughout Africa."[15]

Arms Trafficking

---

[12] Doug Farah, *Fixers, Super Fixers and Shadow Facilitators: How Networks Connect*, International Assessment and Strategy Center, April 23, 2012.

[13] The Treasury Department's Financial Crimes Enforcement Network (FinCEN) has applied special measures, pursuant to Section 311 of the USA PATRIOT Act (31 U.S.C. 5318A), to several financial institutions due in part to allegations of Hezbollah-related financial activity. See for example FinCEN-prepared findings, published in the *Federal Register*, on Lebanese Canadian Bank SAL (February 2, 2011), Kassem Rmeiti & Co. foreign Exchange (April 23, 2013), Halawi Exchange Co. (April 23, 2013), and FBME Bank Ltd. (July 15, 2014).

[14] U.S. Department of State, *Country Reports on Terrorism 2013*, April 2014.

[15] Ibid.

Illicit support activities may include the movement and acquisition of arms, ammunition, and military materiel central to the operations of both criminal and terrorist groups. In one example, the RAND Corporation reported that the Liberation Tigers of Tamil Eelam (LTTE) have maintained a cadre of criminal intermediaries for procuring and smuggling weapons.[16] Such affiliations between arms brokers and LTTE appear to have been purposefully indirect in order to maintain sufficient distance between criminal activities and the leaders of the Tamil Tigers. In a more recent example, the UN Security Council's Panel of Experts on Libya has found that illicit arms transfers have proliferated outside the country since the fall of Gaddafi in 2011, reaching and reinforcing the military capacity of terrorist groups operating in countries such as Algeria, Chad, Egypt, Mali, Niger, Syria, Sudan, and Tunisia.[17]

Corruption

Through bribery, financial inducements, and other forms of coercion, including the credible threat of violence, both criminal and terrorist elements can take advantage of corrupt actors to facilitate their operations and reduce the likelihood of detection and capture. Corrupt actors may range from border guards, financial regulators, justice sector officials, high-level policymakers and political figures, to private bankers, small business owners, and industry magnates. Government protection may take several forms, such as selectively ignoring evidence of illicit activity perpetrated by certain groups; actively providing intelligence and other support to illicit actors; or the wholesale ceding of authority and legitimacy to an illicit group. The Treasury Department has sought to reveal these interactions through targeted financial sanctions designations against senior military, intelligence, and parliamentary figures in Venezuela, who reportedly supported the FARC's drug and arms trafficking activities.[18] In Afghanistan, the U.S. Drug Enforcement Agency (DEA), Treasury Department, and Defense Department led an interagency, forward deployed entity called the Afghanistan Threat Finance Cell (ATFC) specifically geared for targeting illicit financial networks linked to terrorism, the Taliban, drug trafficking, and corruption.

Drug Trafficking

Terrorist and insurgent groups are associated with major drug-producing countries, such as Afghanistan, Burma, Colombia, Morocco, and Peru, as well as

---

[16] Angel Rabasa et al., "The Convergence of Terrorism, Insurgency, and Crime," in *Beyond al-Qaeda, Part 2: The Outer Rings of the Terrorist Universe*, RAND Corporation, 2006.

[17] U.N. Security Council Panel of Experts on Libya, *Final Report*, S/2015/128, February 23, 2015.

[18] U.S. Department of the Treasury, "Treasury Designates Four Venezuelan Officials for Providing Arms and Security to the FARC," press release, September 8, 2011.

countries through which key drug transit routes pass.[19] In drug-producing countries, the narcotics trade has the potential to provide terrorist groups with an added bonus: recruits and sympathizers among impoverished, neglected, and isolated farmers who cannot only cultivate drug crops but also popularize and reinforce anti-government movements. According to the DEA, 22 of 59 FTOs at the end of FY2014 were linked to drug trafficking.[20] Although the United Nations Office on Drugs and Crime conservatively estimated that the global value of the drug trade in 2003 was worth $322 billion at the retail level, terrorist groups likely receive a small fraction of that total.[21] Nevertheless, profits from drug cultivation, production, and trafficking have been sufficient to transform previously ideologically motivated terrorist groups into more criminally oriented actors, including the FARC and National Liberation Army in Colombia, the Shining Path in Peru, and the Kurdistan Workers' Party in Turkey.

Kidnapping for Ransom

A form of hostage taking, kidnapping for ransom (KFR) is a popular means of collecting illicit profits for both organized crime as well as terrorist groups. KFR is often perceived as a crime of low risk, low cost, and high reward. The State Department's 2013 *Country Reports on Terrorism* named KFR "the most frequent and profitable source of illicit financing" for terrorist groups.[22] A July 2014 *New York Times* article reported that at least $125 million in ransom money had been paid to terrorist groups affiliated with Al Qaeda since 2008—including more than $90 million to Al Qaeda in the Islamic Maghreb, nearly $30 million to Al Qaeda in the Arabian Peninsula (AQAP), and $5 million to Al Shabaab.[23] Among these ransom payments, according to the Treasury Department, was a €30 million transfer in October 2013 to AQIM for the release of four French hostages who worked for the French government-owned firm Areva and a $5 million transfer to Al Shabaab for the release of two Spanish hostages.[24] The Islamic State is reported to have netted between $35 and $45 million in ransom payments in 2014.[25]

Extortion and Local Crimes

---

[19] Vanda Felbab-Brown, *Shooting Up: Counterinsurgency and the War on Drugs*, 2010.

[20] U.S. Drug Enforcement Administration, *FY2016 Performance Budget Congressional Submission*, 2015.

[21] U.N. Office on Drugs and Crime, *2005 World Drug Report*, Vol. 1, June 2005.

[22] U.S. Department of State, *Country Reports on Terrorism 2013*, April 2014.

[23] Rukmini Callimachi, "Paying Ransoms, Europe Bankrolls Qaeda Terror," *New York Times*, July 29, 2014.

[24] David Cohen, Under Secretary for Terrorism and Financial Intelligence, remarks at the Center for a New American Security on "Confronting New Threats in Terrorist Financing," March 4, 2014.

[25] U.N. Security Council Al-Qaida Sanctions Committee, *Sixteenth Report of the Analytical Support and Sanctions Monitoring Team Submitted Pursuant to Resolution 2161 (2014) concerning Al-Qaida and Associated Individuals and Entities*, S/2014/770, October 29, 2014.

Multiple reports identify local extortion and theft as a key source of revenue for numerous terrorist organizations. Terrorists may levy "taxes" for various reasons at key roadway crossings, ports of entry, and areas under their control. Local resources, ranging from antiquities to rare wildlife, have been exploited for profit by groups such as the Islamic State and the Lord's Resistance Army. According to the State Department, the National Liberation Army has extorted oil and gas companies in Colombia while Tehrik-i-Taliban Pakistan has engaged in truck robbery. [26] Numerous reports also indicate that the Islamic State, Boko Haram, and Abu Sayyaf have robbed and taken control of bank branches in the areas where these groups operate. Al Shabaab has reportedly profited from the illegal charcoal trade.[27]

U.S. Policy Responses

Policy responses to the interaction of international crime, terrorism, and corruption are inherently complex and often case-specific. Responses have variously included action through diplomacy, foreign assistance, financial tools, intelligence collection and analysis, military support, border security, and law enforcement investigations. There is no formal budget or planning process that describes the full extent to which the U.S. government is responding to nexus threats. Yet, many observers have argued that a key tool to combat the confluence of crime, terrorism, and corruption is to follow the overlapping money trails.[28]

Since the September 11 attacks, Congress has enacted several landmark bills that provide the U.S. government greater authority and additional tools to counter the convergence of illicit threats, including organized crime and terrorism. Less than six weeks after the attack, Congress enacted the USA PATRIOT Act (P.L. 107-56) to strengthen the U.S. government's ability to detect, report, and prevent terrorist activities, including potential connections between organized crime, terrorism, and corruption. Subsequent congressional efforts to enhance U.S. efforts to combat threat finance included the establishment within the Treasury Department of the Office of Terrorism and Financial Intelligence (TFI) (P.L. 108-447), which leverages a combination of financial policy, enforcement, and intelligence capabilities to fulfill its mission of protecting the financial system "against illicit use and combating rogue nations, terrorist facilitators, weapons of

---

[26] U.S. Department of State, *Country Reports on Terrorism 2013*, April 2014.
[27] U.N. Environment Programme, *The Environmental Crime Crisis: Threats to Sustainable Development from Illegal Exploitation and Trade in Wildlife and Forest Resources*, rapid response assessment, 2014.
[28] Danielle Camner and Celina Realuyo, "Threat Finance: A Critical Enabler for Illicit Networks," in *Convergence: Illicit Networks and National Security in the Age of Globalization*, Michael Miklaucic and Jacqueline Brewer, eds., April 2013.

mass destruction (WMD) proliferators, money launderers, drug kingpins, and other national security threats."[29]

Bureaus and offices within TFI include the Office of Terrorist Financing and Financial Crimes (TFFC), the Financial Crimes Enforcement Network (FinCEN), the Office of Foreign Assets Control (OFAC), and the Office of Intelligence and Analysis (OIA)—each of which contributes to U.S. efforts to combat threats related to crime, terrorism, and corruption.

- FinCEN, for example, has administered a procedure, authorized pursuant to the USA PATRIOT Act and popularly known as Section 311, to apply enhanced regulatory requirements, called "special measures," against designated jurisdictions, financial institutions, or international transactions deemed to be of "primary money laundering concern." Among the jurisdictional factors that can be considered when applying Section 311 measures are "evidence that organized criminal groups, international terrorists, or both, have transacted business in that jurisdiction as well as "the extent to which that jurisdiction is characterized by high levels of official or institutional corruption."

- OFAC administers multiple sanctions programs to block transactions and freeze assets within U.S. jurisdiction of specified foreign terrorist, criminal, and political entities, including specially designated individuals and nation states. Authorities for OFAC to designate such entities are derived from executive order and federal statutes, including the International Emergency Economic Powers Act (IEEPA), the Antiterrorism and Effective Death Penalty Act of 1996 (AEDPA), and the Foreign Narcotics Kingpin Designation Act.

- TFFC is the policy development and outreach office for TFI, which, among other priorities, leads the U.S. delegation to the Financial Action Task Force (FATF).[30] FATF is an intergovernmental body that develops and promotes international financial regulatory standards and has produced risk-based guidelines for identifying and preventing illicit actors, including criminals, terrorists, and corrupt officials, from exploiting financial institutions.

- OIA, which was established by the Intelligence Authorization Act for Fiscal Year 2004 (P.L. 108-177), contributes all-source financial threat assessments

---

[29] U.S. Department of the Treasury, *Terrorism and Financial Intelligence*, http://www.treasury.gov/about/organizational-structure/offices/Pages/Office-of-Terrorism-and-Financial-Intelligence.aspx.
[30] The Intelligence Reform and Terrorism Prevention Act of 2004 (P.L. 108-458) authorized the Secretary of the Treasury, or the Secretary's designee, as the lead U.S. government official to the Financial Action Task Force.

and products as a formal member of the U.S. Intelligence Community. Its analysts have been central in interagency efforts such as the Afghanistan Threat Finance Cell (ATFC) as well as its predecessor the Iraq Threat Finance Cell (ITFC).

Continuing a policy approach that was invigorated by the response to 9/11, the February 2015 *National Security Strategy* appears to endorse ongoing efforts to combat crime-terrorism nexus threats through financial enforcement and regulatory policy tools. It states that targeted economic sanctions "will remain an effective tool for imposing costs on irresponsible actors and helping to dismantle criminal and terrorist networks."[31] The strategy notes that the U.S. government aims to work within the FATF, the G-20, and other international fora "to promote financial transparency and prevent the global financial system from being abused by transnational criminal and terrorist organizations to engage in, or launder the proceeds of illegal activity."

As the United States continues to grapple with the implications of a global environment in which multiple and often overlapping illicit actors pose threats to national security, some may question the U.S. government's choice and application of policy responses when new illustrations of the crime-terrorism nexus emerge. As terrorists, criminals, and corrupt officials continue to exploit opportunities to move funds and hide their financial tracks, others may question the effectiveness or limits of such policy responses.

---

[31] White House, Administration of President Barack Obama, *National Security Strategy*, February 6, 2015.

June 24, 2015, Task Force to Investigate Terrorism Financing hearing entitled "Evaluating the Security of the U.S. Financial Sector"

Introduction

Terrorist groups and actors are constantly seeking to exploit the U.S. financial system to fund their operations and launder their revenue. The growth and complexity of the international financial system has also enabled illicit actors to place and move money, hide assets, and conduct transactions anywhere in the world, exposing financial centers to exploitation and abuse. These actors seek to circumvent anti-money laundering and counter-terrorist financing measures by, among other things, taking advantage of the unsettled area of beneficial ownership to form shell corporations. Moreover, the U.S. has seen terrorist groups use banks to place and transfer funds, along with cash transportation provided by cash couriers.

The U.S. financial services sector has also been recognized as a prime target for sophisticated and organized cyber attacks.   The increase in the frequency and breadth of attacks on banks can be attributed to banks holding not only money but also sensitive personally identifiable information and clients' intellectual property. In light of this trend, the financial sector is considered to be one of the most experienced industries at dealing with cyber attacks.

Beneficial Ownership

Background

Terrorists and criminals have created and used shell companies to both disguise and finance their activities.[1] Shell companies are business entities whose ambiguous or deceptive ownership structures hide the identities of the people who ultimately control or profit from the companies – the "beneficial owners."[2] Such untraceable shell companies have few, if any, employees and can be used to hide illegal businesses or facilitate illegal activity, such as tax evasion and Ponzi schemes that can rob billions from unsuspecting citizens.[3] They have been described as "the vehicle of choice for money launderers, bribe givers and takers, sanctions busters, tax evaders and financers of terrorism,"[4] because they are an

---

[1] Diana L. Ohlbaum, "Terrorism, Inc. How Shell Companies Aid Terrorism, Crime and Corruption," *Open Society Foundations* (October 2013), *available at* http://www.opensocietyfoundations.org/briefing-papers/terrorism-inc-how-shell-companies-aid-terrorism-crime-and-corruption.

[2] *Id.*

[3] *Id.*

[4] *See* "Launderers Anonymous: A Study Highlights How Easy It Is to Set Up Untraceable Companies," *the Economist* (September 22, 2012), *available at* http://www.economist.com/node/21563286.

ideal mechanism for international money launderers since information on their beneficial owners is often unavailable to law enforcement.[5] Currently, there is no process in place to keep an updated list of the names of the beneficial owners of corporations or limited liability companies (LLCs) formed pursuant to state laws.[6]

The U.S. is a preferred destination for illicit actors from around the world to set up companies for the purpose of moving or hiding dirty money.[7] For example, the son of Equatorial Guinea's dictator, Teodoro Obiang, purchased a $30 million mansion in Malibu and a jet using shell companies based in California and the British Virgin Islands;[8] Hezbollah financed its activities in part by using shell companies in North Carolina to smuggle cigarettes to finance terrorism;[9] and Russian arms trafficker Viktor Bout used at least a dozen shell companies in Delaware, Texas, and Florida to operate his global arms smuggling operation.[10] Shell companies have also been used to bribe Russian officials, defraud the E.U., and evade Iranian sanctions.[11]

The international community has also examined the misuse of corporate vehicles for illicit purposes. In particular, the FATF,[12] the World Bank, and the United Nations Office of Drugs and Crime Stolen Asset Recovery Initiative[13] have explored the misuse of corporate vehicles for illicit purposes. In general, these studies found the lack of sufficient, accurate and timely beneficial ownership information facilitated money laundering and terrorist financing by disguising: (1) the identity of known or suspected criminals, (2) the true purpose of an account or

---

[5] U.S. Senate, Caucus on International Narcotics Control, *The Buck Stops Here: Improving U.S. Anti-Money Laundering Practices* (April 25, 2013), *available at* http://www.drugcaucus.senate.gov/sites/default/files/Money%20Laundering%20Report%20-%20Final.pdf; Leslie Wayne, "How Delaware Thrives as a Corporate Tax Haven," *The New York Times* (June 30, 2012), *available at* http://www.nytimes.com/2012/07/01/business/how-delaware-thrives-as-a-corporate-tax-haven.html?_r=0.

[6] *Id.*

[7] *See* World Bank and UNODC Stolen Asset Recovery Initiative, *The Puppet Masters,* World Bank (2011).

[8] Anonymous Companies: How Hidden Company Ownership is a Major Barrier in the Fight Against Poverty and What to Do About It, Global Witness (December 2013), *available at* *file:///F:/Terrorist%20Financing/Hearing%20%233/Anonymous%20Companies%20Global%20Witness%20briefing.pdf.*

[9] Dennis M. Lormel, "It's Time to Pry Criminals Out of Their Shell (Companies)," *Cleveland Plain Dealer* (August 16, 2013, *available at* http://www.cleveland.com/opinion/index.ssf/2013/08/its_time_to_pry_criminals_out.html.

[10] *Id.*

[11] *See* Anonymous Companies, *supra,* note 10.

[12] FATF (2206) and FATF & CFATF (2010).

[13] *See* World Bank and UNODC Stolen Asset Recovery Initiative, *supra,* note 7.

property held by a corporate vehicle, and (3) the source or use of funds or property associated with a corporate vehicle.[14]

Congressional Action on Beneficial Ownership

Since May 2008, Congress has addressed the issue of beneficial ownership through bipartisan legislation known as the "Incorporation Transparency and Law Enforcement Act." This bill would have required the disclosure of beneficial owners at the time of incorporation, and would have made such information available to only law enforcement. A version of this bipartisan bill has been introduced in every successive session of Congress through 2013. The latest Senate version of the bill[15] would require states to add a single additional question to their existing incorporation forms to provide the names of the beneficial owners of corporations being formed.[16] The National Association of Secretaries of State has opposed this legislation due to concerns over implementation costs.[17]

The Administration's Beneficial Ownership Action Plan

In June 2013, the G8 in Lough Erne, Northern Ireland met and agreed to an action plan to prevent the misuse of shell companies and similar legal arrangements. The action plan required companies to maintain their beneficial ownership information and that the information should be available to law enforcement and other competent authorities.[18] Additionally, countries were to consider making such information available to financial institutions and other regulated businesses.[19] Trust information should be collected and available, the principles explained, but only to law enforcement.[20] These principles were largely reiterated by the Financial Action Task Force (FATF)—the body setting international anti-money laundering standards—in their Guidance on Transparency and Beneficial Ownership in October 2014 and by the G20 in their High Level Principles on Beneficial Ownership in November 2014.[21]

---

[14] *See* Financial Action Task Force Report, *Transparency and Beneficial Ownership*, October 2014, *available at* http://www.fatf-gafi.org/media/fatf/documents/reports/Guidance-transparency-beneficial-ownership.pdf.

[15] *See* Statement of Senator Carl Levin (D-Mich), On Introduction of the Incorporation and Law Enforcement Assistant Act (August 1, 2013).

[16] Incorporation Transparency and Law Enforcement Act, S. 1465, 113th Cong. (2013).

[17] *See* National Association of Secretaries of State, *NASS Company Formation Task Force*, http://www.nass.org/nass-initiatives/nass-company-formation-task-force/

[18] Liz Confalone, "A Brief, Recent History of Beneficial Ownership Transparency on the Global Agenda," *Global Financial Integrity* (December 5, 2014), *available at* http://www.gfintegrity.org/brief-recent-history-beneficial-ownership-transparency-global-agenda/. [19] *Id.*

[20] *Id.*

[21] *Id.*

On June 18, 2013, the Administration announced the "National Action Plan on Preventing the Misuse of Companies and Legal Arrangements" where it defined beneficial ownership as a "natural person who, directly or indirectly, exercises substantial control over a covered legal entity or has a substantial economic interest in, or receives substantial economic benefit from, such legal entity, subject to several exceptions." [22] The plan would also ensure law enforcement authorities, including tax authorities, would be able to access beneficial ownership information upon appropriate request through a central registry at the state level.[23]

In March 2014, the Administration announced a legislative proposal intended to help law enforcement investigate the use of shell companies established solely for illegal activity.[24] The proposal would require all companies formed in any state to obtain a federal tax employee identification number. [25] This would be achieved by requiring the IRS to collect the beneficial owner information of all legal entities organized in any state.[26] The IRS would also be allowed to share this information with law enforcement officials to identify and investigate persons who form and misuse U.S. corporate structures to launder criminal proceeds and finance terrorism through the banking system.[27] The proposal has not received congressional sponsorship.

Actions by the Treasury Department

The Treasury's Financial Crimes Enforcement Network (FinCEN) issued an Advance Notice of Proposed Rulemaking on customer due diligence by financial institutions in March 2012. On July 30, 2014, FinCEN issued a Notice of Proposed Rulemaking (NPRM) that added a new element requiring financial institutions to know and verify the identities of the beneficial owners, or the real people who own, control and profit from the companies planning to use their services.[28] This rule was intended to increase financial transparency and further the U.S.'s commitment in the G-8 Action Plan for Transparency of Company Ownership and Control.[29]

---

[22] *See* The White House Office of the Press Secretary, *United States G-8 Action Plan for Transparency of Company Ownership and Control* (June 18, 2013), *available at* https://www.whitehouse.gov/the-press-office/2013/06/18/united-states-g-8-action-plan-transparency-company-ownership-and-control.

[23] *Id.*

[24] The White House Blog, Beneficial Ownership Legislation Proposal (April, 4, 2014), *available at* https://www.whitehouse.gov/blog/2014/04/04/beneficial-ownership-legislation-proposal.

[25] *Id.*

[26] *Id.*

[27] *Id.*

[28] *See* Samuel Rubenfeld, *Proposed Rule to Force Banks to Identify Beneficial Owners, The Wall Street Journal* (July 30, 2014), *available at* http://blogs.wsj.com/riskandcompliance/2014/07/30/u-s-treasury-proposes-rule-forcing-banks-to-identify-beneficial-owners/.

[29] The U.S. Treasury Press Center, *Treasury Issues Proposed Rules to Enhance Financial Transparency* (July 30, 2014), *available at* http://www.treasury.gov/press-center/press-releases/Pages/jl2595.aspx.

Under the proposed rule, a financial institution would require any person opening an account to fill out a form identifying him or herself, the legal entity for which the person is opening the account, and any beneficial owners associated with the legal entity.[30] The proposal defines "beneficial owner" as any individual who owns 25% or more of the equity interest in the legal entity, or an individual with "significant responsibility" to control the entity.[31] The person opening the account would furnish on the form a beneficial owner's name, address, date of birth and social security (or passport) number.[32] Concerns about these proposals have been raised by groups such as the American Bankers Association and the Bankers Association for Finance and Trade. In particular, these groups have argued that the proposals would impose an undue burden and expense on banks.[33] FinCEN has received and is currently reviewing approximately 130 comments on the NPRM.

Moving and Placing Funds: Vulnerabilities and Risks[34]

The growth and increasing sophistication of the international financial system in recent years has enabled illicit actors to place and move money, hide assets, and conduct transactions anywhere in the world, exposing financial centers to exploitation and abuse in an unprecedented way. The United States has seen a wide variety of terrorist groups, including al Qaeda (AQ) and its affiliates, Al-Shabaab, Hamas and Hizballah, use banks[35] to place and transfer funds, along with cash transportation provided by cash couriers.

The AML/CFT controls required by the U.S. regulatory framework aid financial institutions in identifying risk, provide valuable information to law enforcement, and inform U.S. national security policy. These required measures include the establishment of AML programs and reporting and record keeping requirements to provide useful information to law enforcement and national security authorities for the purpose of combating the full range of illicit finance threats. An AML program must include, at a minimum, a system of internal

---

[30] *Id.*

[31] *Id.*

[32] *Id.*

[33] Mary Beth Goodman, "Beneficial Ownership Rules Would Drag Criminals into Daylight," *American Banker* (February 18, 2015), *available at* http://www.americanbanker.com/bankthink/beneficial-ownership-rules-would-drag-criminals-into-daylight-1072763-1.html.

[34] The section entitled "Moving and Placing Funds: Vulnerabilities and Risks" is derived nearly verbatim from the U.S. Department of the Treasury, *National Terrorist Financing Risk Assessment*, (June 2015), *available* at http://www.treasury.gov/resource-center/terrorist-illicit-finance/Documents/National%20Terrorist%20Financing%20Risk%20Assessment%20%E2%80%93%2006-12-2015.pdf.

[35] Under the BSA, as implemented by 31 C.F.R. § 1010.100, the term "bank" includes each agent, agency, branch or office within the U.S. of commercial banks, savings and loan associations, thrift institutions, credit unions, and foreign banks. The term "bank" is used throughout this document generically to refer to these financial institutions.

controls to ensure ongoing compliance, independent testing, designation of an individual responsible for managing BSA compliance and training for appropriate personnel.[36] An effective AML/CFT regime also includes enhanced due diligence procedures for those customers that present a high risk for money laundering or terrorist financing (TF), as well as for the provision of foreign correspondent accounts and private banking services.[37] However, when these safeguards are not effectively implemented or stringently enforced, money launderers, terrorist financiers and other illicit actors are able to abuse the U.S. financial system.

The combination of a strong AML/CFT legal framework and effective supervision has succeeded in making it more difficult for terrorists and their facilitators to access the U.S. financial system, often forcing support networks to resort to costlier and/or riskier means of meeting their operational needs.[38]

Broadly speaking, based on an analysis of U.S. law enforcement investigations and prosecutions relating to TF, two methods of moving money to terrorists and terrorist organizations have been predominate in the convictions and cases pending since 2001: the physical movement of cash and the movement of funds through the banking system.[39] Funds moved through the banking system were placed into the banking system by directly depositing cash at a bank. The physical movement of cash accounted for 28 percent of these cases while movement directly through banks constituted 22 percent.

Banks

Banks are an attractive means for terrorist groups seeking to move funds globally because of the speed and ease at which they can move funds within the international financial system.[40] Through their global networks and inter-bank

---

[36] *See, e.g.,* 12 C.F.R. § 21.21 (national banks); 12 C.F.R. § 208.61 (state member banks); 12 C.F.R. § 326.8 (nonmember banks); 12 C.F.R. § 748.2 (credit unions); FINRA Rule 3310 (securities broker-dealers); and National Futures Association Rule 2-9(c) (commodities brokers and futures commission merchants). *See also* Federal Financial Institutions Examination Council (FFIEC) BSA/AML Examination Manual (2014), pp. 28-29. Available at https://www.ffiec.gov/bsa_aml_infobase/documents/BSA_AML_Man_2014.pdf.
[37] *See id.* at 112-118 & 125-129. *See also* Joint Guidance on Obtaining and Retaining Beneficial Ownership Information, FIN– 2010–G001, March 5, 2010.
[38] *See* David Cohen, Under Secretary for Terrorism and Financial Intelligence, Department of the Treasury, Remarks before the Center for a New American Security, "Confronting New Threats in Terrorist Financing," March 4, 2014.
[39] An analysis was conducted by Treasury on terrorism and terrorism-related convictions between 2001 and 2014. Using publicly available documents (indictments, sentencing memoranda, law enforcement press releases, media reports, etc.) the cases were examined more closely in order to determine key financial components. In the 229 cases surveyed, 96 included information on the financial component to the investigation, either raising or moving the funds. These cases were then further analyzed to determine what specific method or channel was used to raise or move funds.
[40] *See* FATF, Terrorist Financing, p. 21, February 2008.

relationships, U.S. banks can instantly transfer funds for their customers almost anywhere in the world. Additionally, because of the importance of the United States to global financial markets activity, many foreign banks have established subsidiary branches or agencies in the United States to gain access to U.S.-based customers and to serve their own local customers' needs in the United States.

In light of this vulnerability, the U.S. government has implemented an AML/CFT regulatory framework that includes robust implementation of targeted financial sanctions, which has made it more difficult for terrorists and their support networks to access the U.S. financial system. This framework aids financial institutions in identifying and managing risk, provides valuable information to law enforcement, and creates the foundation of financial transparency required to apply targeted financial measures against the various national security threats that seek to operate within the U.S. financial system.[41]

OFAC administers and enforces a vigorous sanctions regime in collaboration with the regulatory, law enforcement, and intelligence communities. Violators of U.S. economic sanctions can be subject to a range of administrative, civil and criminal penalties. The federal banking agencies[42] conduct regular examinations of banks to ensure compliance with BSA/AML programs, including ensuring that such institutions have an effective BSA/AML and OFAC compliance program that: identifies higher-risk areas, provides for appropriate internal controls for screening and reporting, establishes independent testing for compliance, designates an employee or employees as responsible for OFAC compliance, and creates training programs for appropriate personnel.[43] The SEC and CFTC impose similar requirements on financial institutions they supervise.

The enactment of the USA PATRIOT Act following the September 11, 2001 terrorist attacks enhanced the efforts of the U.S. government to prevent the U.S. financial system from being used to facilitate TF. For example, under Section 311 of the USA PATRIOT Act, the Secretary of the Treasury is authorized to find a foreign jurisdiction, foreign financial institution, class of international transactions, or type of account to be of primary money laundering concern, and to subsequently impose any one or a combination of special measures that U.S. financial institutions must take to protect the U.S. financial system, including from risks associated with

---

[41] David Cohen, Under Secretary for Terrorism and Financial Intelligence, Department of the Treasury, Testimony before the Senate Committee on Homeland Security and Governmental Affairs Permanent Subcommittee on Investigations, "U.S. Vulnerabilities to Money Laundering, Drugs, and Terrorist Financing: HSBC Case History," July 17, 2012. Available at http://www.hsgac.senate.gov/download/?id=55d94bbb-cbee-4a35-89ca-5493a12d73dd.

[42] For the purposes of the National TF Risk Assessment, the relevant federal banking agencies are the FRB, FDIC, NCUA and OCC.

[43] The Federal Financial Institutions Examination Council (FFIEC) BSA/AML Examination Manual includes specific portions on compliance with OFAC's targeted financial sanctions regime. See FFIEC BSA/AML Manual 2014, pp. 145-154.

TF.[44] These special measures range from enhanced due diligence, recordkeeping, and reporting requirements, up to and including, prohibition against establishing or maintaining any correspondent account or payable through account for or on behalf of a foreign financial institution, if the account involves a jurisdiction, financial institution, class of transaction, or type of account that is of primary money laundering concern. Treasury, through FinCEN, has utilized Section 311 to alert the U.S. financial system to TF threats associated with several foreign jurisdictions and foreign financial institutions, including: the Islamic Republic of Iran; LCB; the Commercial Bank of Syria (CBS) (including its subsidiary Syrian Lebanese Commercial Bank); Halawi Exchange Co.; and Kassem Rmeiti & Co.[45] In finding that CBS was a financial institution of primary money laundering concern, FinCEN noted that "numerous transactions that may be indicative of terrorist financing and money laundering have been observed transiting CBS," including "several transactions through accounts at CBS that reference a reputed financier for Osama bin Laden."[46]

In addition to Section 311, Sections 314(a) and 319 of the USA PATRIOT Act strengthened the U.S. government's ability to take specific regulatory actions to advance law enforcement investigations against TF threats. Section 314(a) allows law enforcement authorities to share information with financial institutions regarding individuals, entities, and organizations engaged in or reasonably suspected of engaging in terrorist acts and to determine whether the target of an investigation maintains an account at a particular financial institution.[47] Section 319(a) enhances law enforcement's ability to pursue assets overseas, while Section 319(b) provides law enforcement with summons and subpoena authority with respect to foreign banks that have correspondent accounts in the United States.[48]

Punitive measures and, for egregious cases, financial penalties, have been applied to banks determined to be out of compliance. For example, in December 2012, HSBC, a UK-headquartered financial institution with a substantial U.S. presence, was ordered to pay a total of approximately $1.9 billion in civil money penalties and asset forfeitures for various violations of U.S. AML and economic sanctions laws and regulations.[49] Furthermore, in a July 2014 settlement with U.S.

---

[44] *See* 31 U.S.C. § 5318A.

[45] A list of Section 311 Special Measures taken by FinCEN is available at http://www.fincen.gov/statutes_regs/patriot/section311.html.

[46] FinCEN, Imposition of a Special Measure Against Commercial Bank of Syria, Including Its Subsidiary, Syrian Lebanese Commercial Bank, as a Financial Institution of Primary Money Laundering Concern, Notice of Proposed Rulemaking, 69 Fed. Reg. 28098, 28100, May 18, 2004.

[47] *See* 31 U.S.C. § 5318.

[48] *See* 18 U.S.C. § 981(k); 31 U.S.C. § 5318(k)(3).

[49] *See* OCC EA 2012-261, AA-EC-2012-140, December 4, 2012 and FRB Docket Nos. 12-062-CMP-FB, 12-062-CMPHC,and 12-062-B-FB, 2-4, December 11, 2012; FinCEN, *In the Matter of HSBC Bank USA, N.A. Mclean, Virginia*, No. 2012-02, December 10, 2012; *see also* Senate Permanent Subcommittee on Investigations, U.S. Vulnerabilities to Money Laundering, Drugs, and Terrorist Financing: HSBC Case History, at 210, July 16, 2012.

regulators and law enforcement, BNP Paribas, in addition to having to pay a total of approximately $8.9 billion in criminal penalties and asset forfeitures, was subjected to a one-year long suspension of certain U.S. dollar-clearing services through its New York branch and other affiliates for business lines on which the misconduct centered.[50] FinCEN has also imposed civil money penalties against U.S. branches of foreign banks for failing to implement adequate due diligence procedures and internal controls that effectively managed the risk arising from the provision of foreign correspondent accounts or dollar-clearing services to financial institutions located in jurisdictions deemed a high-risk for money laundering and TF.[51]

Misuse of Foreign Correspondent Banking

The regulatory and enforcement actions taken by the U.S. government and the subsequent substantial financial and organizational investments by U.S.-based financial institutions have improved AML/CFT compliance among financial institutions.[52] However, the international financial system is interconnected and foreign financial institutions maintain correspondent accounts at and receive services from U.S. financial institutions in order to access the U.S. financial system. These relationships allow financial institutions worldwide to facilitate cross border transactions in the currency of choice. They also enable financial institutions to conduct business and provide services to clients in foreign countries without the expense and burden of establishing a foreign presence. However, some correspondent banking relationships are inherently higher-risk, in large part due to the challenges of "intermediation," where multiple intermediary financial institutions may be involved in a single funds transfer transaction. The complexity and volume of transactions that flow through U.S. correspondent accounts, coupled with the varying (often limited) recordkeeping requirements of funds transfer systems in different countries, increase the likelihood that funds associated with illicit finance, including TF, may flow through these accounts and into the U.S. financial system. These relationships could potentially indirectly expose a U.S. financial institution to risk, including TF, if the foreign financial institution does not effectively implement AML/CFT controls.

To help mitigate against this risk, certain U.S. financial institutions are required to conduct due diligence on their foreign correspondents to ensure that the foreign correspondent's controls are adequate to manage the risk to the U.S.

---

[50] *See* Department of Justice, Press Release, "BNP Paribas Agrees to Plead Guilty and to Pay $8.9 Billion for Illegally Processing Financial Transactions for Countries Subject to U.S. Economic Sanctions," June 30, 2014.

[51] See FinCEN, In the Matter of Doha Bank, New York Branch, New York, New York, No. 2009-1, April 20 2009; FinCEN, In the Matter of The Federal Branch of Arab Bank, PLC, New York, New York, No. 2005-2, August 17, 2005.

[52] For example, in its deferred prosecution agreement with the DOJ, HSBC noted that it had increased AML compliance spending nine –fold and AML staffing ten-fold between 2009 and 2011. *See* HSBC Bank USA, N.A. and HSBC Holdings plc DPA, ¶ 5, December 11, 2012.

financial institution associated with this relationship.[53] These U.S. financial institutions are also required to conduct enhanced due diligence on certain higher risk foreign correspondents which requires (1) enhanced scrutiny, (2) determining whether the foreign correspondent maintains nested accounts for other foreign banks, and (3) the collection of beneficial owner information regarding foreign correspondents that are not publicly traded.[54] In addition to these requirements for foreign correspondents, U.S. financial institutions are also prohibited from maintaining correspondent accounts for foreign "shell banks" (*i.e.*, foreign banks with no physical presence in any country).[55]

Despite these requirements, there have been isolated and particularly egregious instances of U.S. banks not adequately managing potential TF risks posed by their relationships with foreign financial institutions. In one case, the U.S. subsidiary of a foreign parent bank was found to have failed to collect or maintain customer due diligence information on non-U.S. banking affiliates of the foreign parent bank for which it maintained correspondent accounts.[56] This resulted in transactions flowing to and from the United States without appropriate monitoring and alerts to identify movements of funds.[57] A significant number of non-U.S. financial institutions and their customers gained indirect access to the U.S. financial system without appropriate safeguards.[58] These customers included foreign banks that were publicly associated with terrorist organizations or terrorist financing.[59]

Cash Smuggling

As robust implementation of AML/CFT controls across financial institutions has raised the costs, risks and difficulty for TF networks operating within the financial system, cash smuggling has become an increasingly attractive way for foreign terrorists to transfer funds. The use of cash is attractive to criminals mainly because of its anonymity, portability, liquidity and lack of audit trail.

According to the surveyed cases, since 2007, 18 TF-related prosecutions in the United States have in some way involved the use of cash to transfer funds to terrorist organizations. These cases have involved various FTOs, including core AQ, AQ in Iraq (the predecessor organization to ISIL), AQAP, Al-Shabaab, Hizballah, and FARC. There have been several notable cases in which U.S.-based individuals

---

[53] *See* 31 C.F.R. § 1010.610(a); FFIEC BSA/AML Manual, pp. 177-80.
[54] *See* 31 C.F.R. § 1010.610(b).
[55] *See* 31 C.F.R. § 1010.630.
[56] *See* FinCEN, In the Matter of HSBC Bank USA, N.A. Mclean, Virginia, No. 2012-02, December 10, 2012.
[57] *Id.*
[58] *Id.*
[59] *See* Senate Permanent Subcommittee on Investigations, U.S. Vulnerabilities to Money Laundering, Drugs, and Terrorist Financing: HSBC Case History, at 225, 228, July 16, 2012.

sought to smuggle cash for the benefit of Hizballah by concealing it in vehicles. On May 21, 2012, an individual was sentenced to more than six years in prison for conspiring to send hundreds of thousands of dollars to Hizballah.[60] His wife and co-conspirator previously pleaded guilty to one count of conspiracy to provide material support and resources to an FTO. During multiple meetings with an FBI confidential source, the two defendants discussed ways to secretly send money to Hizballah leaders in Lebanon.[61] The two defendants, after discussing multiple options to transfer the funds, ultimately agreed to send approximately $500,000 by concealing it inside a car, which they planned to send to Lebanon via a container ship, demonstrates how terrorist supporters were compelled to resort to cash smuggling – a less efficient means of funds transfer – in an effort to avoid U.S. controls.[62]

Similarly, on July 31, 2012, a Virginia resident pled guilty to attempted money laundering for placing what he believed to be $100,000 belonging to Hizballah inside a Jeep in 2010 and directing it to be shipped to Beirut; his arrest was the result of an FBI-orchestrated sting operation.[63] In a similar case, two Iraqi nationals pleaded guilty to TF-related charges resulting from an FBI-led sting operation.[64] From September 2010 through May 2011, one Iraqi participated in ten separate operations to send weapons and money that he believed was destined for terrorists in Iraq. In January 2011, he recruited the second defendant to assist in these material support operations. Over the course of the conspiracy, the individual believed he had sent $375,000 cash alone and $565,000 cash with the help of the second defendant. The primary means of smuggling the cash was in a hidden compartment of a tractor-trailer which would then be sent on to Iraq.[65]

These case studies demonstrate that cash couriers are being used to transfer funds to terrorist organizations. The U.S. government, particularly LEAs, proactively investigates and prosecutes such cases of abuse in order to effectively mitigate the vulnerability. For example, DHS, through ICE and CBP, has established special programs and initiatives to target bulk cash smuggling across U.S. borders.[66] DOJ and other prosecutorial authorities have levied criminal

---

[60] FBI, Press Release, "Ohio Man Sentenced to 75 Months in Prison for Scheme to Send Money to Hizballah," May 21, 2012. Available at http://www.fbi.gov/cleveland/press-releases/2012/ohio-man-sentenced-to-75-months-inprison-for-scheme-to-send-money-to-hizballah.

[61] *See United States v. Hor and Amera Akl*, No. 3:10-cr-00251-JGC, (N.D. Ohio, filed June 7, 2010).

[62] *Id.*

[63] *See United States v. Mufid Kamal Mrad*, Case No. 1:12mj363 (Affidavit) (E.D. Va. May 30, 2012); *see also* FBI, Press Release, "Vienna Man Pleads Guilty to Attempted Money Laundering," July 31, 2012.

[64] *United States v. Alwan et al*, Case No. 1:11-cr-00013 (Indictment) (W.D. Ky. 2011); Department of Justice, Press Release, "Iraqi National Pleads Guilty to 12-count Terrorism Indictment in Kentucky," August 21, 2012.

[65] *Id.*

[66] *See* Department of Homeland Security, Disrupt Terrorist Financing. Available at http://www.dhs.gov/topic/disrupt-terrorist-financing.

penalties for failing to report the cross-border transfer of currency in excess of $10,000.[67] Additionally, as detailed in the National ML Risk Assessment, the misuse of cash is limited by transaction record keeping and reporting requirements that require financial institutions to verify a customer's identity and retain records of certain information prior to issuing or selling payment instruments when purchased with currency in amounts between $3,000 and $10,000.[68] For cash transactions above $10,000, whether a single transaction or a series of related transactions with a customer in a single business day, financial institutions are required to file a CTR with FinCEN.[69] Other non-financial businesses must report cash transactions of more than $10,000 to the IRS and FinCEN.[70]

Cyber Security of the U.S. Financial Sector

Introduction

In its latest Worldwide Threat Assessment, the U.S. Intelligence Community stated "[c]yber threats to US national and economic security are increasing in frequency, scale, sophistication, and severity of impact."[71] The U.S. financial services sector in particular has been identified as a prime target for sophisticated and organized cyber attacks.[72] The increase in the frequency and breadth of attacks on banks can be attributed to banks holding not only money but also sensitive personally identifiable information and clients' intellectual property.[73] In light of this trend, the financial sector is considered to be one of the most experienced industries at dealing with cyber attacks.[74] The Financial Services Information Sharing and Analysis Center (or FS-ISAC) is the primary industry forum for collaboration on critical security threats facing the global financial services sector and has grown increasingly operational.[75]

Nation-states are commonly considered to be the most significant cyber threat, due to their resources and sophistication. The financial services sector in particular is at an increased risk, relative to other sectors, of sustaining

---

[67] *See* 31 U.S.C. § 5332.

[68] *See* 31 C.F.R. § 1010.415.

[69] *See* 31 U.S.C. § 5313.

[70] *See* 31 U.S.C. § 5331 and 26 U.S.C. § 6050I.

[71] Worldwide Threat Assessment: hearing Before the Senate Armed Services Committee, 114th Cong. (2015), http://www.dni.gov/files/documents/Unclassified_2015_ATA_SFR_-_SASC_FINAL.pdf.

[72] *See A Global Perspective on Cyber Threats: Hearing Before the House Committee on Financial Services, Subcommittee on Oversight and Investigations*, 144th Cong. (2015) (Statement of Michael Madon, Board of Advisors Member, Center on Sanctions and Illicit Finance, FDD, at 2).

[73] *Id.*

[74] Hannah Kuchler, "US Financial Industry Launches Platform to Thwart Cyber Attacks," *Financial Times* (September 24, 2014), *available at* http://www.ft.com/intl/cms/s/0/080092b2-437a-11e4-8a43-00144feabdc0.html#axzz3dGyfOmYz.

[75] *See* Madon, *supra* note 96.

cyberattacks by state actors.[76] In 2014, Russian hackers with connections to the Russian government, conducted one of the largest data breaches of a U.S. corporation when they compromised JP Morgan's servers and exposed the information of 83 million households and businesses.[77] In 2012, over the course of nine months, the Cyber Fighters of Izz ad-din Al Qassam, an activist group sponsored by Iran, targeted major U.S. banks with the largest distributed denial of service (DDoS) attack in history.[78] In 2013, North Korea launched an attack against the South Korean banking system, known as operation "Dark Seoul" that destroyed the information kept on an estimated 48,000 computers.[79]

Terrorist Organizations[80]

While terrorist groups are presently less sophisticated cyber-actors than either nation-states or most cybercrime syndicates, they nevertheless are becoming increasingly proficient in the cyber sphere and have an avowed interest in developing their capabilities. It is no surprise that terrorists are interested in cyberattacks since they are an especially effective method of asymmetrical attack. Cyberterrorism will likely never completely replace traditional terrorist attacks like bombings, but experts believe cyberattacks can be especially effective if used as a force-multiplier alongside them.[81] The risk from cyberterrorism attacks is particularly elevated for the financial sector. As a critical infrastructure and the heart of the U.S. economy, an attack on the financial sector would have an extremely high-impact. Moreover, the financial industry consists of many highly visible symbols of Western capitalism, which are appealing targets for terrorists.

Al Qaeda has expressed interest in "electronic jihad" as a means of disrupting the American economy, and Al Quaeda prisoners have revealed the group's intent to use cyberattacks.[82] Al Quaeda has probed the electronic infrastructure for ways to disrupt or disable critical infrastructure such as electric power, telephone

---

[76] *See* Briefing by the Congressional Research Service, May 28, 2015.

[77] Matthew Goldstein, Nicole Perlroth, and David E. Sanger, "Hackers' Attack Cracked 10 Financial Firms in Major Assault," *The New York Times* (October 3, 2014), *available at* http://dealbook.nytimes.com/2014/10/03/hackers-attack-cracked-10-banks-in-major-assault/?_php=true&_type=blogs&_r=1.

[78] Joseph Menn, "Cyber Attacks Against Banks More Severe Than Most Realize," *Reuters* (May 18, 2013), *available at* http://www.reuters.com/article/2013/05/18/us-cyber-summit-banks-idUSBRE94G0ZP20130518.

[79] *See* K.J. Kwon, "Smoking gun: South Korea uncovers northern rival's hacking codes," April 23, 2015, *available at* http://edition.cnn.com/2015/04/22/asia/koreas-cyber-hacking/index.html?eref=edition.

[80] Prepared Memo for *A Global Overview of Cybersecurity Threats*, 114th Cong. (2015)

[81] Suleymon Ozeren, "Cyberterrorism and International Cooperation," *Responses to Cyber Terrorism*, 72-73 (IOS Press 2008).

[82] *See* Thomas M. Chen, "Cyberterrorism After Stuxnet," *in Terrorism: Commentary on Security Documents, vol. 138, The Resurgent Terrorist Threat*, 16-17 (Douglas C. Lovelace Jr., ed. 2015) (article originally published in the United States Army War College Press, June 2014).

communications, and water supplies.[83] ISIS, too, has announced a "cyber caliphate," though it has so far launched only low-impact website-defacement attacks.[84]

The Syrian Electronic Army (SEA), a group of computer hackers who support Syrian President Bashar Al-Assad, is known for targeting groups unsympathetic to the Assad regime. The SEA's early activity consisted of spamming sites with pro-Assad comments and escalated to large scale DDoS attacks.[85] The SEA is perhaps most noted for claiming responsibility for hacking the Associated Press' Twitter account where it posted "Breaking: Two Explosions in the White House and Barack Obama is injured."[86] This act of cyber vandalism caused the Dow Jones Industrial Average to drop 150 points from 14697.15 to 14548.58.[87] While the market corrected itself within minutes, the fake tweet is estimated to have erased $136 billion in equity market value.[88]

Although it is widely believed that terrorists do not yet have the capabilities to launch destructive or even disruptive cyberattacks, the means of doing so are becoming increasingly cheap and accessible. It costs less than a thousand dollars to purchase a botnet capable of disruptive DDOS attacks, and renting the same system costs only a few dollars an hour.[89] While the capabilities to mount destructive attacks and cyberterrorism are more expensive to mount, the price is dropping. Moreover, terrorists can easily hire the services of sophisticated cyber mercenaries at any time. "Guns-for-hire" who offer their hacking services on the black market can be highly sophisticated; for example, "Hidden Lynx" is a group of hackers-for-hire believed to be behind successful cyberattacks on over 100 organizations including U.S. defense contractors and investment banks.[90]

---

[83] *See* Chen, at 16-17.

[84] Emma Graham-Harrison, "Could Isis's 'cyber caliphate' unleash a deadly attack on key targets?" The Observer, April 12, 2015, *available at* http://www.theguardian.com/world/2015/apr/12/isis-cyber-caliphate-hacking-technology-arms-race.

[85] Andrea Peterson, "The Post Just Got Hacked by the Syrian Electronic Army. Here's Who They Are," *The Washington Post* (August 15, 2013), *available at* http://www.washingtonpost.com/blogs/the-switch/wp/2013/08/15/the-post-just-got-hacked-by-the-syrian-electronic-army-heres-who-they-are/.

[86] Max Fisher, "Syrian Hackers Claim AP Hack That Tipped Stock Market by $136 Billion. Is it Terrorism?" *The Washington Post* (April 23, 2013), *available at* http://www.washingtonpost.com/blogs/worldviews/wp/2013/04/23/syrian-hackers-claim-ap-hack-that-tipped-stock-market-by-136-billion-is-it-terrorism/

[87] *Id.*

[88] *Id.*

[89] Nick Clayton, "Where to Rent a Botnet for $2 an Hour or Buy one for $700," Wall Street Journal, November 5, 2012; http://blogs.wsj.com/tech-europe/2012/11/05/where-to-rent-a-botnet-for-2-an-hour-or-buy-one-for-700/.

[90] *See* Thomas M. Chen, "Cyberterrorism After Stuxnet," *in Terrorism: Commentary on Security Documents, vol. 138, The Resurgent Terrorist Threat,* 19 (Douglas C. Lovelace Jr., ed. 2015) (article originally published in the United States Army War College Press, June 2014).

Looking further down the road, terrorists could begin to draw cyber-capabilities from nation-states just as they draw other types of support from nation-states. As nation-states friendly to terrorist organizations improve their cyber-capabilities, the risk of terrorists gaining access to sophisticated cyber-weapons or beneficial information increases.[91] For example, Iran is a major exporter of terrorism, and its Islamic Revolutionary Guard Corps is known to have provided Hezbollah with (non-cyber) training.[92] Iran could begin providing terrorists cyber-training, or simply offer them a map of any vulnerabilities it has found in U.S. cyber-defenses.[93] While it does not appear to have happened yet, depending on the political situation and its willingness to share information, a nation-state could expand its proxies and partners from hacktivists and criminals to terrorist groups, and thereby catapult terrorists' cyber sophistication to lethal new levels.

---

[91] *See* Thomas M. Chen, "Cyberterrorism After Stuxnet," *in Terrorism: Commentary on Security Documents, vol. 138, The Resurgent Terrorist Threat*, 19 (Douglas C. Lovelace Jr., ed. 2015) (article originally published in the United States Army War College Press, June 2014).

[92] *See* The Future of Homeland Security: Evolving and Emerging Threats: Hearing Before the Senate Committee on Homeland Security & Governmental Affairs 112th Cong., 2012, at 4 (Statement of Frank J. Cilluffo) *available at* http://www.hsgac.senate.gov/hearings/the-future-of-homeland-security-evolving-and-emerging-threats .

[93] *C.f.* Briefing by Illan Berman for the Majority staff of the House Financial Services Committee, May 27, 2015.

July 22, 2015, Task Force to Investigate Terrorism Financing hearing entitled "The Iran Nuclear Deal and its Impact on Terrorism Financing"

Iran and the "P5+1" negotiating powers – the United States, France, Britain, Germany, Russia, and China – engaged in negotiations and finalized a comprehensive nuclear agreement known as a Joint Comprehensive Plan of Action (referred to as JCPA or JCPOA) on July 14, 2015. The JCPA entails substantial commitments by Iran to adhere to strict new limitations on its nuclear program, in exchange for broad sanctions relief. Some U.S. sanctions have been suspended since January 2014 under an interim nuclear accord known as a Joint Plan of Action (JPA or JCPOA).

There are many layers of sanctions imposed on Iran by the United States and its allies, as well as by the United Nations Security Council. The core of the U.S. sanctions regime has been to impose sanctions on foreign entities that conduct certain transactions with Iran. Broad international compliance with these U.S. sanctions has been pivotal to the effectiveness of the sanctions. For the purposes of this memorandum, the term "sanctions" refers to the collective sanctions imposed by the United States, its allies, and the U.N. Security Council.

Sanctions have taken a toll on Iran's economy, by all accounts, as indicated below.

- *Gross Domestic Product (GDP) Decline.* Treasury Secretary Jacob Lew told a Washington D.C. think-tank on April 29, 2015 that Iran's GDP shrank by 9% in the two years ending in March 2014, and is now 15%-20% smaller than it would have been had post-2010 sanctions not been imposed.[1] The sanctions relief of the JPA enabled Iran to achieve slight growth of about 1%-1.5% for all of 2014, according to the International Monetary Fund. The number of nonperforming loans held by Iranian banks increased to about 15%-30%,[2] and the unemployment rate, according to outside observers, is about 20%, although the Iranian government reports the rate at 13%.[3]

- *Reduction in Oil Exports and Oil Production.* Sanctions drove Iran's crude oil sales down about 60% from 2.5 million barrels per day (mbd) in 2011, reducing Iran's revenue from crude oil from $100 billion in 2011 to about $25 billion in 2014, although the 2014 figures are due in part to the sharp drop in oil prices in the second half of that year. The JPA caps Iran's crude oil

---

[1] Department of the Treasury. Remarks of Secretary Jacob J. Lew at the Washington Institute for Near East Policy 30th Anniversary Gala. April 29, 2015.

[2] "Iran's Pivotal Moment." http://www.euromoney.com. September, 2014.

[3] http://www.worldbank.org/en/country/iran/overview

exports at about 1.1 mbd.[4] When the JPA began implementation, Iran's oil production stood at about 2.6-2.8 mbd down from nearly 4.0 mbd at the end of 2011.[5] Iran has avoided dramatic production cuts by storing millions of barrels of unsold crude oil on tankers in the Persian Gulf and in storage tanks on shore. However, according to Treasury Secretary Lew, it is not certain that Iran could quickly return its exports to pre-2012 levels even if sanctions were suspended, because Iran's infrastructure needs substantial modernization.

- *Inaccessibility of Hard Currency.* Not only have Iran's oil exports fallen by volume, but Iran cannot access the great bulk of the hard currency it is paid for its oil (other than the $700 million per month agreed under the JPA). The total Iranian hard currency reserves held in foreign banks are estimated to be about $150 billion.[6] Of that amount, about 75% reportedly is held in foreign banks that are abiding by sanctions and refuse to transfer the funds to Iran's Central Bank.

- *Currency Decline and Inflation Effects.* Sanctions caused the value of the Iranian *rial* on unofficial markets to decline about 56% from January 2012 until January 2014. The drop in value of the currency caused inflation to accelerate during that period to a reported 50% to 70%—a higher figure than the approximately 40% figure acknowledged by Iran's Central Bank. The sanctions relief of the JPA has contributed to a stabilization of Iran's currency and associated reduction of the inflation rate to below 20%.[7]

- *Drop in Industrial Production.* Iran's economy is industrializing, but the manufacturing sector remains dependent on imported parts. Many Iranian manufacturers have been unable to obtain credit and must pre-pay to obtain parts from abroad, often through time-consuming and circuitous mechanisms. This difficulty is particularly acute in the automotive sector, which is Iran's largest industry aside from its energy sector. Iran's production of automobiles fell by about 60% from 2011 to 2013.[8] The JPA has benefitted the auto sector because it eased sanctions on that sector, but press reports say that manufacturing overall has rebounded only modestly since the JPA implementation began.

---

[4] "Why Higher Iran Oil Exports Are Not Roiling Nuclear Deal." *Reuters*, June 13, 2014.
[5] Rick Gladstone, "Data on Iran Dims Outlook for Economy," *New York Times*, October 13, 2012.
[6] Jeffrey Goldberg interview with President Barack Obama. *The Atlantic,* May 31, 2015.
[7]   http://www.tradingeconomics.com/iran/inflation-cpi
[8] Nahid Kalbasi. "Have International Sanctions Crippled Iran's Auto Industry." Washington Institute for Near Policy, June 3, 2015.

The sanctions relief to be provided under the JCPA far exceeds the "limited, temporary, targeted, and reversible" easing of sanctions under the JPA. The JPA's sanctions relief has been as follows:[9]

- Iran's existing oil customers were not required to reduce their oil purchases from Iran "significantly" from the levels they were when the JPA went into effect. To avoid penalizing these oil buyers while the JPA is in effect, the Administration exercised waiver authority under Section 1245(d)(1) of the National Defense Authorization Act for FY2012 (P.L. 112-81) and Section 1244c(1) of the Iran Freedom and Counter-Proliferation Act (IFCA: Title XII, subtitle D, of the National Defense Authorization Act for FY2013, P.L. 112-239). The European Union amended its regulations to allow shipping insurers to provide insurance for ships carrying oil from Iran.[10]

- Iran was able to receive $700 million per month in hard currency from oil sales and $65 million per month to make tuition payments for Iranian students abroad (paid directly to the educational institutions). The waiver authority under Section 1245(d)(1) of the FY2012 NDAA enables Iran's Central Bank to receive these proceeds directly.

- The JPA permitted Iran to resume sales of petrochemicals and trading in gold and other precious metals, and to resume transactions with foreign firms involved in Iran's automotive manufacturing sector. To enable these transactions, the Administration suspended application of Executive Orders 13622 and 13645, several provisions of U.S.-Iran trade regulations, and several sections of IFCA.

- The parties to the JPA pledged to facilitate humanitarian transactions that are already allowed by U.S. and partner country laws, such as sales of medicine to Iran, but which many banks refuse to finance. The United States also committed to license safety-related repairs and inspections inside Iran for certain Iranian airlines.

- The JPA required that the P5+1 "not impose new nuclear-related sanctions," if Iran abides by its commitments under this deal, to the extent permissible within their political systems.[11]

---

[9] The Administration sanctions suspensions and waivers are detailed at http://www.state.gov/p/nea/rls/220049.htm.

[10] Daniel Fineren. "Iran Nuclear Deal Shipping Insurance Element May Help Oil Sales." Reuters, November 24, 2013.

[11] White House Office of the Press Secretary. "Fact Sheet: First Step Understandings Regarding the Islamic Republic of Iran's Nuclear Program." November 23, 2013.

Sanctions Easing Under the JCPA[12]

According to the text of the JCPA, the following sanctions are to be eased:[13]

- Many U.S., virtually all EU, and most U.N. sanctions will be suspended after the International Atomic Energy Agency (IAEA) has verified that Iran has taken certain key nuclear-related steps that are stipulated in an Annex of the JCPA (primarily reducing the size and scope of its enrichment of uranium).

- The U.S. sanctions that are to be suspended are primarily those that sanction foreign entities and countries for conducting specified transactions with Iran (so-called "secondary sanctions"). U.S. sanctions that generally prohibit U.S. firms from conducting transactions with Iran were not altered under the JPA. However, the JCPA does commit the United States to licensing the sale to Iran of commercial aircraft, and the importation of Iranian luxury goods such as carpets, caviar, and some fruits and nuts.[14]

- The U.S. sanctions to be suspended are mostly those imposed since U.N. Security Council Resolution 1929 was enacted in June 2010.[15] That Resolution identified Iran's energy sector as a potential contributor to Iran's "proliferation-sensitive nuclear activities."[16] The sanctions relief in the JCPA includes: [17] (1) energy sanctions, including those that limit Iran's exportation of oil and sanction foreign sales to Iran of gasoline and energy sector equipment, and which limit foreign investment in Iran's energy sector – core provisions of the Iran Sanctions Act (P.L. 104-172 as amended, Section 1245(d)(1) of the National Defense Authorization Act for FY2012 (P.L. 112-81), and provisions of the Iran Threat Reduction and Syria Human Rights Act (P.L. 112-158); (2) sanctions on foreign banks that conduct transactions with Iranian banks – the core of the Comprehensive Iran Sanctions, Accountability, and Divestment Act of 2010 (CISADA); (3) sanctions on Iran's auto sector and trading in the *rial*; (4) the EU ban on purchases of oil and gas from Iran; and (5) the ban on Iran's use of the Society for Worldwide Interbank Financial Telecommunication (SWIFT)

---

[12] Complete references to the laws and Executive Orders discussed in this section can be found in: CRS Report RS20871, *Iran Sanctions*, by Kenneth Katzman; and CRS Report R43311, *Iran: U.S. Economic Sanctions and the Authority to Lift Restrictions*, by Dianne E. Rennack. http://www.politico.com/story/2015/07/full-text-iran-deal-120080.html

[13]   http://www.politico.com/story/2015/07/full-text-iran-deal-120080.html

[14] The U.S. importation of these luxury goods was permitted during 2000-2010, under a modification to the Executive Order 12959 that imposed a ban on U.S. trade with Iran.

[15] The exact U.S. sanctions laws whose provisions might be waived are discussed in: CRS Report RS20871, *Iran Sanctions*, by Kenneth Katzman, and CRS Report R43311. *Iran: U.S. Economic Sanctions and the Authority to Lift Restrictions*, by Dianne Rennack.

[16] The text of the Resolution is at: https://www.iaea.org/sites/default/files/unsc_res1929-2010.pdf

[17]   http://iranmatters.belfercenter.org/blog/translation-iranian-factsheet-nuclear-negotiations;   and author conversations with a wide range of Administration officials, think tank, and other experts, in Washington, D.C. 2015.

electronic payments system that enables Iran to move funds from abroad to its Central Bank or its commercial banks.

- Easing the U.S. sanctions that are required under the JCPA will necessitate also terminating the following Executive Orders: 13574, 13590, 13622, 13645, and sections 5-7 and 15 of Executive Order 13628.[18]

- Under the JCPA, the United States is to revoke the designations made under various Executive Orders of numerous specified Iranian economic entities and personalities, including the National Iranian Oil Company (NIOC), various Iranian banks, and many energy and shipping-related institutions. That step would enable foreign companies to resume transactions with those Iranian entities without risking being penalized by the United States.

- The JCPA requires the Administration, within eight years, to request that Congress lift virtually all of the sanctions that will be suspended under the JCPA. The JCPA requires all U.N. sanctions to terminate after ten years of adoption of the JCPA.

- The JCPA does not commit the United States to suspend U.S. sanctions on Iran for terrorism, human rights abuses, and on proliferation-sensitive technology. As an example, the U.S. Administration has not pledged to revisit, as a direct consequence of a nuclear accord, Iran's designation as a state sponsor of terrorism. That designation triggers numerous U.S. sanctions, including a ban on any U.S. foreign aid to Iran and on U.S. exportation to Iran of controlled goods and services, and a prohibition on U.S. support for international lending to Iran.

- Other U.S. sanctions that are not required to be suspended, according to the JCPA, include: (1) E.O. 13224 sanctioning terrorism entities (not specific to Iran); (2) the Iran-Iraq Arms Non-Proliferation Act that sanctions foreign firms that sell arms and weapons of mass destruction-related technology to Iran; (3) the Iran-North Korea-Syria Non-Proliferation Act (INKSNA);[19] and (4) the Executive Orders and the provisions of CISADA and the Iran Threat Reduction and Syria Human Rights Act that pertain to human rights or democratic change in Iran. Iran also will be remaining on the "terrorism list" and all sanctions triggered by that designation will remain in place, at least for now.

- One issue that arose after the April 2, 2015 framework accord was the suspension of U.N. sanctions on Iran's development of nuclear-capable ballistic

---

[18] For more information on these Executive Orders and their provisions, see CRS Reports RS20871 and R43311, op.cit.

[19] The JCPA does commit the United States to terminate sanctions with respect to some entities designated for sanctions under INKSNA.

missiles and on Iran's importation or exportation of conventional weaponry. The April 2 framework accord indicated that these sanctions would remain in place in the JCPA. However, as subsequently negotiated, according to President Obama, the ban on Iran's development of nuclear-capable ballistic missiles might be lifted within eight years of the JCPA and the ban on conventional arms sales to Iran might be lifted in five years.[20]

Automatic Re-imposition of Sanctions ("Snap-Back")

In the course of negotiating the JCPA, President Obama reportedly directed U.S. negotiators to try to focus on ways to put sanctions back in place ("snap back") if Iran violates the terms of the deal, rather than focus on delaying sanctions relief.[21] According to the April 2 framework agreement, if a dispute over Iran's compliance with the accord cannot be resolved through a specified dispute resolution mechanism, all U.N. sanctions "could" be re-imposed. Treasury Secretary Lew said on April 29, 2015 that this provision for a "snap back" of U.N. Security Council sanctions would not be subject to a veto by any permanent member of the U.N. Security Council.[22]

The JCPA (paragraph 36 and 37) contains a mechanism for the "snap back" of U.N. sanctions if Iran does not satisfactorily resolve a dispute over its compliance. According to the JCPA, the United States (or any veto-wielding member of the U.N. Security Council) would be able to block a U.N. Security Council resolution that would continue the lifting of U.N. sanctions despite Iran's refusal to resolve the dispute. In that case, "the provisions of the old U.N. Security Council resolutions would be re-imposed, unless the U.N. Security Council decides otherwise."

Even if the sanctions are re-imposed through the "snap back" process, a related question is whether the same degree of international compliance with the sanctions would obtain. The effect of the sanctions has depended largely on the substantial degree of international compliance and cooperation with the sanctions regime that has taken place since 2010. A wide range of countries depend on energy and other trade with Iran and might be reluctant to restore cooperation with U.S. sanctions unless Iran commits clear and egregious violations of its commitments.

---

[20] White House. Office of the Press Secretary. Statement by the President on Iran. July 14, 2015.
[21] Peter Baker. "President Favors Way to Give Iran Political Cover." *New York Times*, April 18, 2015.
[22] Department of the Treasury. Remarks of Secretary Jacob J. Lew at the Washington Institute for Near East Policy 30th Anniversary Gala. April 29, 2015.

Verification

According to the JCPA, the IAEA will monitor Iranian compliance with the provisions concerning its enrichment program and the Arak program. The IAEA will increase its number of inspectors in Iran and use modern verification technologies. In addition, Tehran "has agreed to implement" the Additional Protocol to its safeguards agreement. Iran is also to implement the modified code 3.1 of the subsidiary arrangements to its IAEA safeguards agreement. It is worth noting that Iran's IAEA safeguards obligations last for an indefinite duration. Potential nuclear-related exports to Iran would remain subject to the Nuclear Suppliers Group's export guidelines.[24]

The JCPA also describes other monitoring and inspections. For 15 years, the IAEA will monitor the stored Iranian centrifuges and related infrastructure. During this time, Iran will also permit the IAEA "daily access" to "relevant buildings" at the Natanz facilities. For 20 years, Tehran will allow the agency to verify Iran's inventory of certain centrifuge components and the manufacturing facilities for such components. Additionally, Iran is to allow the IAEA to monitor the country's uranium mills for 25 years and to monitor Iran's plant for producing heavy water.[25] IAEA Director General Yukiya Amano told reporters on July 14, 2015, that the agency's "workload will increase" under the JCPA. Amano intends to request additional resources from the agency's Board of Governors.[26]

Access to Other Sites. The JCPA also describes arrangements for the IAEA to gain access to Iranian sites other than those Tehran declares to the agency "if the IAEA has concerns regarding undeclared nuclear materials or activities, or activities inconsistent with" the JCPA. If the IAEA has "concerns regarding undeclared nuclear materials or activities, or activities inconsistent with the JCPOA" at one of these sites, the agency "will provide Iran the basis for such concerns and request clarification." The IAEA could request access to the site if Iran's explanation did not provide such clarification. Tehran may respond to such a request by proposing "alternative means of resolving the IAEA's concerns." If such means did not resolve the IAEA's concerns or the two sides did not "reach satisfactory arrangements... within 14 days of the IAEA's original request for

---

[23] The section entitled "Other Provisions" is derived verbatim from Kenneth Katzman et. al, "Iran Nuclear Agreement," *CRS Report R43333* (July 16, 2015), *available at* http://www.crs.gov/pdfloader/R43333.

[24] For information about the Nuclear Suppliers Group, see CRS Report RL 33865, *Arms Control and Nonproliferation: A Catalog of Treaties and Agreements*, by Amy F. Woolf, Paul K. Kerr, and Mary Beth D. Nikitin.

[25] This plant is currently not under IAEA safeguards.

[26] "IAEA Director General Amano's Remarks to the Press on Agreements with Iran," July 14, 2015.

access," Iran "would resolve the IAEA's concerns through necessary means agreed between Iran and the IAEA." Tehran would make such a decision "in consultation with the members of the Joint Commission" provided for by the JCPA. If the two sides could not reach agreement, the Commission "would advise on the necessary means to resolve the IAEA's concerns" if at least a majority of the Commission's members agreed to do so. The Joint Commission would have 7 days to reach a decision; "Iran would implement the necessary means within 3 additional days."

The JCPA contains several provisions apparently designed to address Iranian concerns that IAEA inspectors may try to obtain information unrelated to the country's nuclear program. For example, the IAEA may only request access to the types of facilities described above "for the sole reason to verify the absence of undeclared nuclear materials and activities or activities inconsistent with the JCPOA." In addition, the agency would provide Iran with written "reasons for access" and "make available relevant information."

Procurement Channel to Be Established. The U.N. Security Council resolution endorsing the JCPA is to establish a "procurement channel" for Iran's nuclear program. The Joint Commission established by the JCPA will monitor and approve transfers made via the channel. IAEA officials will have access to information about, and may participate in meetings regarding, proposed such transfers.

The JCPA also indicates that the IAEA will pursue drawing a "Broader Conclusion that all nuclear material in Iran remains in peaceful activities" According to the IAEA, the agency can draw such a conclusion for states with comprehensive safeguards agreements and additional protocols in force. According to the IAEA,

> The conclusion of the absence of undeclared nuclear material and activities is drawn when the activities performed under an additional protocol have been completed, when relevant questions and inconsistencies have been addressed, and when no indications have been found by the IAEA that, in its judgement [sic], would constitute a safeguards concern.[27]

Formal Congressional Review[28]

Legislation providing for congressional review was enacted as the Iran Nuclear Agreement Review Act of 2015 (P.L. 114-17). Because the agreement was reached after July 10, the congressional review period is 60 days from the date of

---

[27] *2001 IAEA Safeguards Glossary.*
[28] The section entitled "Formal Congressional" and subsequent sections are derived verbatim from Kenneth Katzman et. al, "Iran Nuclear Agreement," *CRS Report R43333* (July 16, 2015), *available at* http://www.crs.gov/pdfloader/R43333.

submission to Congress, which is to be within five days of finalization of the accord. The transmission is to include a report assessing the degree to which the United States will be able to verify Iranian compliance, as well as all annexes. No statutory sanctions can be waived for the review period. If a resolution of disapproval is passed by both chambers, President Obama could not waive sanctions for another 12 days during which he would presumably exercise his threat, stated on July 14, to veto a resolution of disapproval. Congress would have 10 days to try to override the veto, during which sanctions could not be waived. So, the maximum period during which statutory sanctions could not be waived is 82 days after receipt of the agreement. For other provisions of that law, please see CRS Report RS20871, *Iran Sanctions*, by Kenneth Katzman.

Congressional Oversight of an Agreement with Iran[29]

Although Congress may potentially exercise oversight of any agreement reached with Iran, the nature of legislative involvement may depend upon whether the agreement is intended to operate as controlling domestic law and supersede existing statutory requirements.[30] On March 11, 2015, Secretary of State John Kerry indicated that a nuclear agreement with Iran might not be legally binding in nature.[31] If Congress disagrees with any commitments made by the executive branch to Iran that do not modify U.S. law, it would likely need to pass legislation (potentially with sufficient support to override a presidential veto) to limit U.S. adherence to the agreement. However, if the Obama Administration (or a future administration) seeks to conclude a legally binding agreement with Iran intended to have the force of domestic law, such as an agreement intended to modify existing sanctions laws applicable to Iran, congressional action would likely be required.

Congressional Oversight of Arrangements That Do Not Modify U.S. Law

The Obama Administration did not seek legislative approval of the JPA, and the Administration has opined that legislative action would not be constitutionally required to enter any future arrangement with Iran that did not impose legal

---

[29] This section was contributed by Michael John Garcia, Legislative Attorney.

[30] The U.S. sanctions regime against Iran is primarily a creature of statute. In some cases, federal statutes directly require the imposition of sanctions against Iranian entities, but may provide the Executive with authority to waive certain sanction requirements in specified circumstances. In other instances, Congress has delegated broad authority to the Executive to impose sanctions against foreign entities in order to protect U.S. interests, and the Executive has exercised this statutorily delegated authority to impose sanctions against Iranian entities. For further discussion, see CRS Report R43311, *Iran: U.S. Economic Sanctions and the Authority to Lift Restrictions*, by Dianne E. Rennack.

[31] See Felicia Schwartz, "Iran Nuclear Deal, If Reached, Wouldn't Be 'Legally Binding,' Kerry Says," *Wall Street Journal,* March 11, 2015.

obligations upon the United States.[32] The JPA is not crafted as a legally binding agreement, but instead as a political commitment among the participants.[33] The agreement does not modify the participants' existing domestic legal authorities or obligations. Moreover, by its terms, commitments made by JPA participants are understood to be voluntary.[34] Nonetheless, adherence to these commitments may carry significant moral and political weight with the United States, Iran, and other JPA participants. Pursuant to the JPA, the Obama Administration has pledged to exercise its existing statutory authority to waive the application of certain sanctions against Iran, provided that the Iranian government freezes aspects of its nuclear program and allows inspections. The JPA does not purport to confer U.S. agencies with authority to waive sanctions against Iran that cannot be waived under current statute.

The Executive's authority to enter political arrangements like the JPA, without first obtaining the approval of Congress, has been the subject of long-standing dispute between the political branches.[35] Nonetheless, the executive branch has long claimed the authority to make such commitments on behalf of the United States without congressional authorization, asserting that the Executive is not subject to the same constitutional constraints in making political commitments to foreign countries as is the case when entering legally binding international agreements.[36]

If Congress seeks to modify U.S. adherence to an agreement with Iran that did not seek to modify U.S. law, it would likely need to pass legislation to that

---

[32] White House, Letter from Denis McDonough, Asst. to President and Chief of Staff, to Senator Bob Corker, March 14, 2015, available at http://images.politico.com/global/2015/03/15/mcdonoughletter.html (noting several examples when the Executive has entered political commitments concerning nuclear issues without congressional authorization).

[33] For further background on non-legal agreements, see CRS Report RL32528, *International Law and Agreements: Their Effect upon U.S. Law*, by Michael John Garcia.

[34] See Joint Plan of Action, Nov. 24, 2013, at pp. 1-2 (describing the "voluntary measures" agreed upon by the JPA participants), available at http://eeas.europa.eu/statements/docs/2013/131124_03_en.pdf. For discussion of common features distinguishing the wording and format of legal and non-legal international agreements, see State Department Office of the Legal Adviser, *Guidance on Non-Binding Documents*, at http://www.state.gov/s/l/treaty/guidance/.

[35] See S.REPT. 91-129 (1969) (Senate Committee on Foreign Relations report in favor of the National Commitments Resolution, S. Res. 85, criticizing the undertaking of "national commitments" by the Executive, either through international agreements or unilateral pledges to other countries, without congressional involvement).

[36] See generally Robert E. Dalton, Asst. Legal Adviser for Treaty Affairs, *International Documents of a Non-Legally Binding Character*, State Department, Memorandum, March 18, 1994, available at http://www.state.gov/documents/organization/65728.pdf (discussing U.S. and international practice with respect to non-legal, political agreements); Duncan B. Hollis and Joshua J. Newcomer, *"Political" Commitments and the Constitution*, 49 VA. J. INT'L L. 507 (2009) (discussing U.S. political commitments made to foreign States and the constitutional implications of the practice).

effect. For example, Congress could potentially pass legislation to bar the Executive from waiving applicable sanctions against Iran unless the Executive certified to Congress that Iran had complied with the terms of the agreement. Congress might also, if it deemed such action appropriate, enact legislation that statutorily barred certain sanctions against Iran from being lifted, notwithstanding the terms of any agreement reached with Iran. Conversely, Congress could pass legislation to facilitate the implementation of the JPA or future agreements (whether legal or political in nature) negotiated by the Executive with respect to Iran's nuclear program.

Congressional Oversight Concerning a Legal Agreement with Iran

A comprehensive agreement reached with Iran could contemplate a modification of U.S. sanctions laws. Any agreement that seeks to supersede existing U.S. law would likely require legislative action to be given effect. Indeed, in a letter to Senator Bob Corker on March 14, 2015, the White House indicated that

> We agree that Congress will have a role to play—and will have to take a vote—on any comprehensive deal that the United States and our international partners reach with Iran. As we have repeatedly said, only Congress can terminate the existing Iran statutory sanctions.[37]

There are a number of possible methods by which a legally binding agreement may be entered by the United States. As a matter of historical practice, some types of international agreements have traditionally been entered as treaties, while others are typically done as executive agreements, which may take different forms. There is not an extensive body of legally binding international agreements concluded by the United States in which it has pledged to modify its sanctions laws in exchange for another party to the agreement freezing its nuclear program.[38]

A comprehensive, legally binding agreement with Iran could potentially take the form of a treaty, ratified by the President after obtaining the approval of a two-thirds majority of the Senate, or a congressional-executive agreement, which is a particular type of executive agreement that is authorized by legislation passed by both houses of Congress and enacted into law. If a legal agreement with Iran were entered as a treaty, it would need to be approved by a two-thirds majority of the

---

[37] White House Letter to Senator Corker, *supra* footnote 33.

[38] Indeed, perhaps the most relevant precedent for U.S.-Iran negotiations is the 1994 Agreed Framework with North Korea, a multilateral arrangement under which North Korea agreed to freeze its plutonium-based nuclear program, in exchange for the provision of light water reactors and other energy alternatives. The text of the agreement may be viewed at http://www.armscontrol.org/documents/af. The State Department characterized it as a non-legal arrangement which did not pose legal commitments upon its participants. Contemporary State Department correspondence to Congress concerning the non-legal nature of the arrangement is on file with the authors of this report.

Senate and thereafter ratified by the President before it would have the force of law. Moreover, the Senate could potentially condition its consent on certain reservations, understandings, and declarations concerning the treaty's meaning and application. Such conditions may potentially limit and/or clarify U.S. obligations under the agreement.[39] For example, the Senate could condition its approval of a treaty with Iran upon the agreement being deemed "non-self-executing" under U.S. law. Such a condition would mean that the ratified treaty would be understood not to have immediate domestic legal effect, and Congress would need to pass legislation to implement the treaty's requirements.[40]

A legal compact with Iran concerning that country's nuclear program would not necessarily have to take the form of a treaty. The United States has frequently undertaken international legal obligations by means of congressional-executive agreements,[41] and the constitutionality of this practice appears well established. Congressional-executive agreements have been made for a wide variety of topics, such as lessening trade restrictions between parties or allowing the transfer of nuclear materials.[42] Typically, a congressional-executive agreement both

---

[39] Certain conditions to Senate approval of treaty ratification, such as a reservation purporting to limit acceptance of a particular treaty provision, would require the consent of the other parties to the treaty. The Senate may also propose to amend the text of the treaty itself. The other parties to the agreement would have to consent to these changes in order for them to take effect. If such proposed conditions or alterations are not accepted by the other parties to the treaty, then the ratification process cannot be completed and the treaty will not enter into force for the United States. For further discussion of the Senate role in the treaty-making process, see TREATIES AND OTHER INTERNATIONAL AGREEMENTS: THE ROLE OF THE UNITED STATES SENATE, A STUDY PREPARED FOR THE SENATE COMM. ON FOREIGN RELATIONS 6-14
(Comm. Print 2001).
[40] See, e.g., Medellin v. Texas, 552 U.S. 491, at 505 (2008) ("In sum, while treaties may comprise international
commitments ... they are not domestic law unless Congress has either enacted implementing statutes or the treaty itself conveys an intention that it be 'self-executing' and is ratified on these terms.") (internal citations and quotations omitted).
[41] While there is some scholarly debate as to whether a congressional-executive agreement may always serve as an alternative to a treaty, it does not appear that a congressional-executive agreement that had the primary legal effect of modifying an existing federal statutory regime concerning commerce with Iran would raise significant constitutional questions.
[42] Some policymakers have identified the process by which Congress has approved bilateral agreements authorizing the transfer of nuclear materials to a foreign country (commonly referred to as "123 agreements") as a potentially relevant precedent for congressional involvement in approving any agreement concerning Iran's nuclear program. See, e.g., Senate Committee on Foreign Relations, *Hearing on Iranian Nuclear Negotiations: Status of Talks and the Role of Congress*, January 15, 2015 (opening statement of Chairman Bob Corker, suggesting that 123 agreements may serve as a useful model for patterning legislation approving or disapproving of a final agreement concerning Iran's nuclear program). The relevance of this precedent can be subject to debate, in the sense that 123 agreements typically concern the transfer of nuclear materials between parties for peaceful energy-related purposes, while an agreement with Iran could potentially turn on that country halting its nuclear program in exchange for a reduction or elimination in U.S.
trade sanctions.

authorizes a particular agreement (or type of agreement) and also provides any necessary implementing authorities to executive agencies.

It should be noted that executive agreements may sometimes be entered into by the United States that do not take the form of a congressional-executive agreement, but these other categories of agreements do not seem applicable here. For example, the United States does not appear to be a party to any treaty that would give the Executive the authority to enter an agreement with Iran that has the effect of superseding the requirements of existing federal sanctions laws. Additionally, while the Executive is recognized as being able to enter legally binding agreements concerning matters falling under his independent constitutional authority (a category referred to as sole executive agreements), the weight of judicial and scholarly opinion recognizes that the President may not, by way of an executive agreement based solely upon his constitutional authority, supersede or modify a federal statute.[43] Accordingly, it appears that Congress would need to authorize and implement any executive agreement intended to modify or supersede existing U.S. statutes regarding Iran.[44]

---

[43] See, e.g., United States v. Guy W. Capps, Inc., 204 F.2d 655 (4th Cir. 1953) (finding that executive agreement
contravening provisions of import statute was unenforceable), affirmed on other grounds, 348 U.S. 296 (1955); RESTATEMENT (THIRD) OF FOREIGN RELATIONS §115 reporters' n.5 (1987). In limited circumstances, an exception to this rule might exist on matters where Congress has historically acquiesced to the President. See Dames & Moore v. Regan, 453 U.S. 654 (1981) (upholding sole executive agreement concerning the handling of Iranian assets in the United States, despite the existence of a potentially conflicting statute, given Congress's historical acquiescence to sole executive agreements concerning claims settlement). See *Medellin*, 552 U.S. at 531-532 (suggesting that *Dames & Moore* analysis regarding significance of congressional acquiescence might be relevant only to a "narrow set of circumstances," where presidential action is supported by a "particularly longstanding practice" of congressional acquiescence). However, there has not been a consistent or longstanding practice of legislative acquiescence to the Executive entering legal agreements with foreign nations pursuant to his independent constitutional authority which override existing U.S. laws barring or limiting trade with a particular country.

[44] Indeed, even if an arrangement obligated the President to waive a particular sanction that he is already permitted to waive under current U.S. laws, such an arrangement would arguably require congressional approval if it was understood to obligate the United States not to modify its sanctions laws in the future in a manner that would limit applicable waiver authority. On the other hand, an arrangement under which the President pledged to waive application of sanctions against Iran, only *to the extent that such waiver was authorized by U.S. laws in effect at the time the waiver was issued*, arguably would not require congressional approval. On March 9, 2015, forty-seven Senators signed an open letter to Iranian leaders indicating the Senators' position that any agreement with Iran would need to take the form of a treaty or congressional-executive agreement to be considered binding upon the United States. The letter further observed that adherence to an arrangement entered as a sole executive agreement could be modified at any time by
either a legislative enactment or through "the stroke of a pen" of a future President. See Senator Tom Cotton et al., Open Letter to the Leaders of the Islamic Republic of Iran, March 9, 2015, *available at*
http://www.cotton.senate.gov/sites/default/files/150309%20Cotton%20Open%20Letter%20to%20Irani an%20Leaders.pdf.

There might be some question (and possibly debate) over whether a legally binding nuclear agreement with Iran should take the form of a treaty or a congressional-executive agreement. Some observers and policymakers have argued that such an agreement should take the form of a treaty due to the perceived significance of the obligations taken by the parties.[45] Others have suggested that such an agreement could be authorized by an act of Congress, similar to the process used to approve agreements (commonly referred to as "123 agreements")[46] concerning the sharing of nuclear material with other countries for energy purposes.[47] More broadly, the Senate may prefer that significant international commitments be entered as treaties, and fear that reliance on executive agreements will lead to an erosion of the treaty power. The House may want an international compact to take the form of a congressional-executive agreement, so that it may play a greater role in its consideration.

State Department regulations prescribing the process for coordination and approval of international agreements (commonly known as the "Circular 175 procedure")[48] include criteria for determining whether an international agreement should take the form of a treaty or an executive agreement. Congressional preference is one of several factors considered when determining the form that an international agreement should take.[49]

---

[45] See David B. Rivkin Jr. and Lee A. Casey, "How Congress Can Use Its Leverage on Iran," *Wall Street Journal,*
January 20, 2015. It should be noted that arms control and reduction agreements entered by the United States have historically been entered as treaties. However, an agreement in which the United States commits to reduce sanctions in exchange for another country freezing its nuclear program is arguably not analogous to the kind of compacts typically considered arms control agreements.

[46] For further discussion of 123 agreements, including the statutory framework authorizing their adoption, see CRS Report R41910, *Nuclear Energy Cooperation with Foreign Countries: Issues for Congress,* by Paul K. Kerr, Mary Beth D. Nikitin, and Mark Holt.

[47] See, e.g., Senate Committee on Foreign Relations, *Hearing on Iranian Nuclear Negotiations: Status of Talks and the Role of Congress,* January 15, 2015 (opening statement of Chairman Bob Corker, suggesting that 123 agreements may serve as a useful model for patterning legislation approving or disapproving of a final agreement concerning Iran's nuclear program). The relevance of this precedent can be subject to debate, in the sense that 123 agreements typically concern the transfer of nuclear materials between parties for peaceful energy-related purposes, while an agreement with Iran could potentially turn on that country halting its nuclear program in exchange for a reduction or elimination in U.S. trade sanctions.

[48] Circular 175 initially referred to a 1955 Department of State Circular that established a process for the coordination and approval of international agreements. These procedures, as modified, are now found in 22 C.F.R. Part 181 and 11 Foreign Affairs Manual (F.A.M.) chapter 720.

[49] 11 F.A.M. §723.3 (2006).

September 9, 2015, Task Force to Investigate Terrorism Financing hearing titled "Could America Do More? An Examination of U.S. Efforts to Stop the Financing of Terror"

Introduction

Terrorist financing is commonly described as a form of financial crime in which an individual or entity provides, stores, collects, and transports funds by any means, with the knowledge that such funds are intended to be used, in full or in part, to carry out acts of terrorism and sustain a terrorist organization, including the recruitment, retention, and training of terrorist group members.

While terrorist financing is likely only a small subset of financial crimes in terms of volume of transactions in the international financial system, it has long been a national security concern and became a renewed priority following the Al Qaeda attacks against the United States on September 11, 2001. In response to this threat, policymakers have sought to implement measures designed to halt the ability of terrorist groups to raise, move, and use funds.

Threats to the U.S. Financial System

Drawing on 2013 guidance produced by the Financial Action Task Force (FATF), an inter-governmental organization that promotes global anti-money laundering and counter-terrorist financing standards, the U.S. government issued two national risk assessments in June 2015, one on terrorist financing and another on money laundering. These documents update and add to a money laundering threat assessment issued a decade ago by the George W. Bush Administration. A June 2015 Task Force hearing also addressed the issue of U.S. financial sector security.[1] According to the Treasury Department's June 2015 *National Terrorist Financing Risk Assessment*, the United States continues to face a "residual" risk of exposure to terrorist financing threats, due largely to the size and scope of international transactions that flow through the U.S. financial system. Terrorist financiers use various criminal schemes to fundraise in the United States, including through the charitable sector. Social media and other online communication platforms have provided financiers with new methods to solicit funds and recruits. Other emerging fundraising techniques involve the use of cybercrime and identity theft schemes. The *National Terrorist Financing Risk Assessment* further concludes that terrorist groups continue to move funds through and place funds in the U.S. financial system by exploiting correspondent banking relationships with foreign financial institutions, conspiring with complicit money service business employees in the United States, and using unlicensed money transmitters to send funds abroad.

---

[1] Task Force to Investigate Terrorism Financing, hearing on "Evaluating the Security of the U.S. Financial Sector," June 24, 2015.

Bulk cash smuggling continues to be a favored method of moving funds across U.S. borders. New payment systems may also be exploited by terrorists to move and place funds in the international financial system.

The *National Money Laundering Risk Assessment* notes that the underlying vulnerabilities within the U.S. financial system today "remain largely the same as those identified in 2005." Major vulnerabilities include the unreported use and movement of cash and monetary instruments below record-keeping and reporting thresholds, challenges with implementing customer due diligence requirements and other anti-money laundering compliance deficiencies, use of shell companies to obfuscate beneficial ownership, and complicity of merchants and financial institutions to facilitate illicit transactions. Criminal proceeds annually generate an estimated $300 billion that are in turn laundered through the international financial system, according to the Risk Assessment. Most of these proceeds are derived from fraud- and drug trafficking-related crimes.

FATF-Designated High-Risk and Non-Cooperative Jurisdictions and U.S. Guidance

Three times each year, FATF's International Cooperation Review Group (ICRG) evaluates jurisdictions around the world for anti-money laundering and counter-financing of terrorism (AML/CFT) deficiencies. To protect the international financial system from those with the most concerning AML/CFT deficiencies, FATF recommends that all jurisdictions "apply effective counter-measures." The results of the most recent review were released on June 26, 2015, identifying 17 countries of concern.[2]

    Jurisdictions that have strategic AML/CFT deficiencies and to which counter-measures apply: Iran and North Korea

    Jurisdictions with strategic AML/CFT deficiencies that have not made improvements: Algeria and Burma

    Jurisdictions with strategic AML/CFT deficiencies that have made political commitments to improve: Afghanistan, Angola, Bosnia and Herzegovina, Ecuador, Guyana, Laos, Panama, Papua New Guinea, Sudan, Syria, Uganda, Yemen

    Jurisdictions with strategic AML/CFT deficiencies that are not making sufficient progress: Iraq

In response to FATF's ICRG review, the U.S. Department of the Treasury's Financial Crimes Enforcement Network (FinCEN) issued an advisory on July 20, 2015 that reminded financial institutions of the counter-measures in place against Iran and North Korea, including a broad array of U.S. and U.N. sanctions programs.[3] With respect to Algeria and Burma, FinCEN advised financial institutions to apply enhanced due diligence procedures when maintaining correspondent accounts for foreign banks operating under banking licenses issued by those countries. For all other listed countries, FinCEN advised financial institutions to ensure compliance with general due diligence obligations and, if appropriate, enhanced policies, procedures, and controls to detect and report suspected money laundering activity.

Global Terrorist Fundraising Sources

In the Task Force's first congressional hearing in April 2015, witnesses testified to the diversity and scope of today's terrorist financing threat, which has evolved since the Al Qaeda terrorist attacks of September 11, 2001, becoming more varied and

---

[2] Financial Action Task Force, High-Risk and Non-Cooperative Jurisdictions, http://www.fatf-gafi.org/topics/high-riskandnon-cooperativejurisdictions/.

[3] Financial Crimes Enforcement Network, FIN-2015-A002, July 20, 2015.

localized.[4] Common methods for terrorist organizations to raise funds can include a combination of state sponsors, private donors, and licit and illicit revenue streams.

State Sponsors. Although fewer countries are identified today as state sponsors of international terrorism compared to during the Cold War era, overt and covert government sponsors reportedly remain active. Since 1984, for example, the State Department's has identified Iran as providing support to multiple terrorist groups (e.g., Palestinian terrorist groups in Gaza, including Hamas; Lebanese Hezbollah; various groups in Iraq and throughout the Middle East, including Iraqi Shia militias such at Kata'ib Hizballah; as well as through the Islamic Revolutionary Guard Corps-Qods Force). The issue of Iran's role in terrorist financing was featured in a July 2015 Task Force hearing.[5] Other State Department-listed state sponsors of international terrorism include Sudan, designated as such since 1993, and Syria, designated since 1979.[6]

Private Donors. Private donors may include both a core group of wealthy individuals who are sympathetic to certain terrorist group goals as well as a broader network of local and diaspora community members who may or may not be aware that their donations are diverted for use by terrorist groups. According to the Obama Administration's 2011 *National Strategy for Counterterrorism*, Al Qaeda's main sources of financial support were wealthy private donors and charity organizations in the Arabian Peninsula.[7] The June 2015 *National Terrorist Financing Risk Assessment* identified Kuwait and Qatar as particularly permissive environments for donor-driven terrorist financing. Such financial support in turn flows from the region to Al Qaeda's affiliates and adherents around the world.

Self-Generated Profits. Sources of terrorist funds may include the proceeds of legitimate businesses, non-profit organizations, as well as illicit activities, such as drug trafficking, kidnapping for ransom, and extortion. In congressional testimony from February 2015, the Director of National Intelligence (DNI) James Clapper identified terrorism and transnational organized crime as among the top eight global threats to U.S. national security.[8] According to DNI Clapper, both terrorist and transnational criminal groups thrive in highly insecure regions of the world, with terrorist groups contributing to regional instability and internal conflict, while transnational organized crime groups exploit these environments for financial gain and corruptive influence. The February 2015 *National Security Strategy* echoed this concept of terrorism, crime, and corruption representing mutually reinforcing

---

[4] See for example prepared statement of Juan C. Zarate for a hearing held by the Task Force to Investigate Terrorism Financing, April 22, 2015. See also H. Hrg. 112-93.

[5] Task Force to Investigate Terrorism Financing, hearing on "The Iran Nuclear Deal and its Impact on Terrorist Financing," July 22, 2015.

[6] State Department, *2014 Country Reports on Terrorism*, June 2015.

[7] Obama Administration, *National Strategy for Counterterrorism*, June 2011.

[8] James Clapper, Director of the Office of National Intelligence, *Worldwide Threat Assessment of the U.S. Intelligence Community,* statement for the record, U.S. Senate, Committee on Armed Services, February 26, 2015.

and interconnected threats—as did a May 2015 Task Force hearing on the financial implications of this nexus threat.[9]

Methods of Moving Terrorist Proceeds

Multiple methods for hiding and transporting terrorist funds exist. Despite regulatory controls and legal prohibitions, terrorists have exploited the international financial system through the following means: vulnerable non-financial businesses and professions, including charities, lawyers, accountants, and casinos; informal value transfer systems; and international trade systems. Selected examples include the following.

Financial Institutions. Terrorist organizations have used banks and non-bank financial institutions, such as currency exchange houses and other money services businesses, to store and move funds. Terrorists, including the 9/11 hijackers, have reportedly opened personal checking accounts, deposited and withdrawn cash, conducted international wire transfers, used travelers checks, and accumulated transactions on conventional credit cards.[10] According to the June 2015 *National Terrorist Financing Risk Assessment*, foreign correspondent banking presents a particular challenge; in cases where insufficient customer due diligence safeguards were not in place, foreign banks with known links to terrorist organizations or terrorist financing have gained access to the U.S. financial system.

Informal and Unlicensed Value Transfer Mechanisms. Beyond the formal financial sector, unregulated mechanisms exist to anonymously transfer funds internationally. One such mechanism includes unregulated *hawala* transfers, which were reportedly used to facilitate the May 2010 attempted car bombing in New York City's Times Square and other previous terrorist activities.[11] According to the June 2015 *National Money Laundering Risk Assessment*, suspicious activity

---

[9] White House, Administration of President Barack Obama, *National Security Strategy*, February 6, 2015; Task Force to Investigate Terrorism Financing, hearing on "A Dangerous Nexus: Terrorism, Crime, and Corruption," May 21, 2015.

[10] John Roth, Douglas Greenburg, and Serena Wille, *Monograph on Terrorist Financing*, National Commission on Terrorist Attacks Upon the United States (9/11 Commission), Staff Report to the Commission, Washington, DC, 2004.

[11] *Hawala* refers to an informal method for transferring funds that is commonly used in parts of the Middle East and South Asia where the formal banking system has limited presence. A *hawala* transfer typically involves a network of trusted money brokers, or *hawaladars*, who rely on each other to accept and disburse funds to third-party clients on their behalf. Settlement of account balances among *hawaladars* takes place subsequently, but not necessarily through bank and non-bank financial institutions. Such informal value transfer systems are often preferred because of their perceived quickness, reliability, and lower cost. Unregulated *hawala* systems, however, are perceived by government authorities as lacking sufficient transparency and investigations have revealed that they are vulnerable to abuse by terrorist groups. See U.S. Department of Justice, "Pakistani Man Sentenced on Unlicensed Money Transmitting Charges and Immigration Fraud," press release, April 12, 2011 and U.S. Department of the Treasury, Financial Crimes Enforcement Network (FinCEN), "Informal Value Transfer Systems," Advisory, FIN-2010-A011, September 1, 2010.

associated with informal money transmitters involve countries in the Middle East, particularly the United Arab Emirates, Yemen, and Iran, as well as in Latin America, including Venezuela, Argentina, and Mexico.

Charities. Charitable organizations are attractive for terrorist financing because of their presence in distressed parts of the world where terrorists often operate. Such organizations may be exploited as a source of income or as a cover for moving funds internationally in a nontransparent way. Although some donors may be sympathetic to radical causes, others are unaware that their funds may be clandestinely diverted for non-legitimate purposes. One such charity alleged to have been exploited by Al Qaeda and used to funnel funds to Chechen rebels includes the now-defunct, Saudi-based Al Haramain Islamic Foundation.[12] More recently, the June 2015 *National Terrorist Financing Risk Assessment* reported an emerging trend in which financiers solicit funds under the auspices of a charity or charitable cause with no connections to a charitable organization registered and recognized by the U.S. government.

Bulk Cash Movements. Another mechanism used to bypass the formal financial sector involves courier-facilitated transport of bulk cash or substitutes for cash, including gold or precious stones, often undeclared at ports of entry. According to the National Commission on Terrorist Attacks Upon the United States (9/11 Commission), Al Qaeda regularly used couriers, recruited internally within the organization, to physically transport cash. Cross-border movements of Al Qaeda cash, upward of $1 million, have been reported.[13] For the 9/11 plot, Khalid Sheikh Mohammad reportedly couriered $120,000 to a contact in Dubai. The June 2015 *National Terrorist Financing Risk Assessment* concluded that cash smuggling will continue to be used as a means to move funds by a variety of terrorist organizations, including Al Qaeda and its affiliates, the Islamic State (ISIS or ISIL), Al Shabaab, Hezbollah, and the Revolutionary Armed Forces of Colombia (FARC).

Trade-Based Money Laundering (TBML). Trade-based money laundering involves the use of trade transactions to disguise the origin of illicit funds and move value internationally through the import or export of merchandise. TBML schemes vary in sophistication, but a simple example may involve the under- or over-invoicing of the price, quantity, or value of goods in a trade transaction. In 2011, U.S. officials alleged that Hezbollah was involved in a TBML scheme involving the laundering of cocaine proceeds from South America through the sale of used cars

---

[12] Use of charities to raise funds for terrorist groups is not new. In the 1970s, for example, the Irish-American diaspora reportedly provided between $3 million and $5 million for the Irish Republican Army (IRA) through the purported charitable organization Irish Northern Aid Committee (NORAID). Daniel Byman, *Deadly Connections: States that Sponsor Terrorism* (New York: Cambridge University Press, 2005) and Roth, Greenburg, and Wille (2004).

[13] Roth, Greenburg, and Wille (2004).

shipped and resold in West Africa.[14] The June 2015 *National Money Laundering Risk Assessment* notes that TBML is both a particularly difficult form of money laundering to investigate because it involves complicit merchants and also that it "can have a more destructive impact on legitimate commerce than other money laundering schemes." Illicit actors may dump imported goods at below-market prices to expedite the money laundering process, leaving legitimate businesses at a competitive disadvantage. Governments are also affected by lost tax revenue and customs duties on undervalued and fraudulently imported products.

Cyber Threats and Illicit Actors

In February 2015 congressional testimony on the U.S. intelligence community's assessment of worldwide threats, DNI Clapper highlighted cyber threats as a concern for U.S. national and economic security. According to Clapper, cyber threats are "increasing in frequency, scale, sophistication, and severity of impact."[15] A variety of actors, including terrorist organizations, nation states, ideological-driven criminals, and financially motivated entities, have, or are pursuing, cyber-capabilities that would allow them to finance their organization's operations and/or threaten the U.S. financial sector.

With respect to terrorists, Clapper stated in the same February 2015 congressional testimony that such actors would "continue to experiment with hacking" and could ultimately "develop more advanced capabilities." Additionally, he noted that "sympathizers will probably conduct low-level cyber attacks on behalf of terrorist groups and attract attention of the media, which might exaggerate the capabilities and threat posed by these actors." In remarks to the Aspen Security Forum in July 2015, FBI Director James Comey noted that the Bureau considered cyber threats by terrorists a "small but potentially growing problem"—and one that particularly piqued the interest of groups that have otherwise been thwarted in infiltrating or recruiting followers in the United States.[16]

The U.S. financial services business community appears to be a prime target of such cyber threats, variously attracting illicit cyber actors seeking access to funds, personally identifiable information, and client intellectual property.[17] During the 2012-2013 time period, the U.S. financial sector sustained one of the largest distributed denial of service (DDOS) attacks reportedly perpetrated by Iranian actors. Iranian actors were also implicated in the February 2014 cyber attack on the Las Vegas Sands casino company. Russia-based hackers were reportedly behind the 2014 data breaches of JP Morgan Chase & Co. and several other financial companies. North Korea has also been implicated in a 2013 hacking of several South Korean banks and media outlets.

Policy Responses in Historical Perspective

The foundations of contemporary U.S. policy to combat terrorist financing are grounded in anti-money laundering and counterterrorism policies that date back to the 1970s. The cornerstone of contemporary requirements for U.S. financial

---

[14] Financial Crimes Enforcement Network, U.S. Department of the Treasury, "Finding That the Lebanese Canadian Bank SAL Is a Financial Institution of Primary Money Laundering Concern," 76 *Federal Register* 33, February 17, 2011; U.S. Congress, House Committee on the Judiciary, Subcommittee on Crime, Terrorism, and Homeland Security, *Combating Transnational Organized Crime: International Money Laundering As A Threat To Our Financial Systems*, 112th Cong., 2nd sess., February 8, 2012, Serial No. 112-86 (Washington: GPO, 2012).

[15] Prepared statement of Director of National Intelligence James R. Clapper for a Senate Armed Services Committee hearing on the "Worldwide Threat Assessment of the U.S. Intelligence Community," February 26, 2015.

[16] Damian Paletta, "FBI Director Sees Increasing Terrorist Interest in Cyberattacks Against U.S.," *Wall Street Journal*, July 22, 2015.

[17] See for example the House Financial Services Committee Oversight and Investigations Subcommittee hearing on "A Global Perspective on Cyber Threats," June 16, 2015.

institutions to detect and report on suspicious transactions indicative of large-scale money laundering and criminal activities stems from the Bank Secrecy Act of 1970. Designations and prohibitions against state sponsors of terrorism and foreign terrorist organizations (FTOs) emerged in the late 1970s and evolved through the 1990s to include statutes that criminalized "material support" to terrorists and designated terrorist organizations (18 U.S.C. 2339A and 2339B; enacted in 1994 and 1996, respectively) and established targeted financial sanctions against FTOs and terrorist groups that were disrupting the Middle East Peace Process (Antiterrorism and Effective Death Penalty Act of 1996 and Executive Order 12947). The United Nations Security Council also mirrored U.S. policy in 1999, when it adopted Resolution 1267, to require U.N. member states to impose financial sanctions on the Taliban for providing support and sanctuary to Al Qaeda.

9/11 Commission Assessments

In reviewing the status of counterterrorism efforts prior to the Al Qaeda attacks on the United States on September 11, 2001, the 9/11 Commission concluded in a staff monograph devoted specifically to terrorist financing that U.S. and international efforts to target terrorist financiers and transnational funding flows were relatively weak.[18] The 9/11 Commission found efforts to deter financing were not a priority for domestic or international intelligence collection and lacked interagency and strategic planning and coordination. The existing statutes criminalizing material support for terrorists were reportedly rarely used to prosecute terrorist financing cases. Internationally, the 9/11 Commission reported that there was little emphasis on the enforcement and implementation of UNSCR 1267. Moreover, prior to 9/11, the United States had not ratified 1999 International Convention for the Suppression of the Financing of Terrorism.

As Al Qaeda plotted its attacks on the United States in 2001, the group relied on a wide range of methods to raise and transfer funds to its membership worldwide, according to the 9/11 Commission. Major sources of fundraising included wealthy private donors from Gulf countries in the Middle East and the diversion of funds from Islamic charitable organizations. Funds transfers involved a combination of formal financial sector mechanisms, informal value transfer mechanisms (e.g., *hawala*), and bulk cash movements involving trusted couriers. According to the 9/11 Commission, some $300,000 of the overall $400,000-$500,000 cost of the 9/11 attacks passed through U.S. bank accounts. The hijackers directly involved in the 9/11 attacks regularly deposited money into U.S. accounts through overseas wire transfers, cash deposits, and foreign travelers checks. They accessed such funds in the United States through conventional ATM withdrawals and credit card transactions.

Notably, the 9/11 Commission emphasized that the existing financial regulatory framework for anti-money laundering did not fail in 2001, as it was designed to

---

[18] Roth, Greenburg, and Wille (2004).

detect and flag anomalous transactions more often associated with international drug trafficking and large-scale financial fraud rather than the routine-looking transactions conducted by the 9/11 hijackers.

9/11 Aftermath

Terrorist financing emerged as one of the key counterterrorism policy issues addressed during the immediate aftermath of Al Qaeda's September 2001 attacks. As the 9/11 Commission stated: "It is common to say the world has changed since September 11, 2001, and this conclusion is particularly apt in describing U.S. counterterrorist efforts regarding financing...."[19]

Immediately following 9/11, departments, bureaus, and agencies throughout the U.S. government sought to enhance intra- and inter-agency coordination on terrorist financing issues. The FBI established the Terrorism Financing Operations Section (TFOS) with its Counterterrorism Division to coordinate and centralize its efforts to track the financial underpinning of terrorist activity. The National Security Council (NSC) established the interagency Terrorist Financing Working Group (TFWG) in 2001 to coordinate the interagency delivery of training and technical assistance to combat terrorist financing, chaired by the State Department. In subsequent years, in the context of a changing mission brought on by the creation of the Department of Homeland Security (DHS) and an enhanced national security role, the Treasury Department underwent several institutional changes that emphasized counterterrorism finance.[20]

On September 23, 2001, President George W. Bush issued Executive Order 13224, blocking property and prohibiting transactions with persons who commit, threaten to commit, or support terrorism. In his public remarks on issuing EO 13224, President Bush explained: "Today, we have launched a strike on the financial foundation of the global terror network.... We have developed the international financial equivalent of law enforcement's 'Most Wanted' list. And it puts the financial world on notice.... Money is the lifeblood of terrorist operations. Today, we're asking the world to stop payment."[21]

---

[19] Id.

[20] These changes culminated in 2004 with the establishment of the Office of Terrorism and Financial Intelligence (TFI) with a mission to marshal all of the Treasury Department's policy, enforcement, regulatory, and intelligence functions under the leadership of an Under Secretary-level office. Treasury's TFI, the Department of Justice's DEA, and the Department of Defense (DOD) also began establishing foreign-deployed "threat finance cells" as an interagency mechanism to collect, analyze, and act on financial intelligence related to the financial flows and transactions of priority insurgent and terrorist actors. The first such threat finance cell was established in 2005 in Iraq and the second in 2008 in Afghanistan. The Afghan Threat Finance Cell (ATFC), for example, was reportedly instrumental in discovering the illicit hawala-related financial activities of the New Ansari Exchange.

[21] President George W. Bush, *President Freezes Terrorists' Assets*, Remarks in the Rose Garden, Washington, DC, September 24, 2001.

In addition to redoubling efforts to use existing authorities and enforce existing regulations, Congress took additional actions following 9/11 through the enactment of several public laws, including the:

> International Money Laundering Abatement and Anti-Terrorist Financing
>   Act of 2001 (Title III of the USA PATRIOT Act, P.L. 107-56);
> Suppression of the Financing of Terrorism Convention Implementation
>   Act of 2002 (Title II of P.L. 107-197);
> Intelligence Authorization Act for Fiscal Year 2004 (P.L. 108-177);
> Intelligence Reform and Terrorism Prevention Act of 2004 (P.L. 108-458);
> Combating Terrorism Financing Act of 2005 (Title IV of P.L. 109-177); and
> Implementing Recommendations of 9/11 Commission Act of 2007 (P.L.
>   110-53).

In November 2001, the U.S. Senate also approved the 1999 International Convention for the Suppression of the Financing of Terrorism for ratification.[22] This treaty was intended to require the United States and other States Parties to criminalize terrorist financing and commit to international cooperation for the extradition and prosecution of suspects. In order for the United States to fulfill its obligations under this treaty, Congress enacted the Suppression of the Financing of Terrorism Convention Implementation Act of 2002 (Title II of P.L. 107-197).

Office of Terrorism and Financial Intelligence (TFI)
Subsequent congressional efforts to enhance U.S. efforts to combat threat finance included the establishment within the Treasury Department of the Office of Terrorism and Financial Intelligence (TFI) (P.L. 108-447), which leverages a combination of financial policy, enforcement, and intelligence capabilities to fulfill its mission of protecting the financial system "against illicit use and combating rogue nations, terrorist facilitators, weapons of mass destruction (WMD) proliferators, money launderers, drug kingpins, and other national security threats."[23]

Bureaus and offices within TFI include the Office of Terrorist Financing and Financial Crimes (TFFC), the Financial Crimes Enforcement Network (FinCEN), the Office of Foreign Assets Control (OFAC), and the Office of Intelligence and Analysis (OIA)—each of which have contributed to U.S. efforts to combat threats related to crime, terrorism, and corruption.

---

[22] U.S. Congress, Senate, *Anti-Terrorism Conventions*, 107th Cong., 1st sess., November 27, 2001, Exec. Rpt. 107-2 (Washington: GPO, 2001).
[23] U.S. Department of the Treasury, *Terrorism and Financial Intelligence*, http://www.treasury.gov/about/organizational-structure/offices/Pages/Office-of-Terrorism-and-Financial-Intelligence.aspx.

FinCEN, for example, has administered a procedure, authorized pursuant to the USA PATRIOT Act and popularly known as Section 311, to apply enhanced regulatory requirements, called "special measures," against designated jurisdictions, financial institutions, or international transactions deemed to be of "primary money laundering concern." Among the jurisdictional factors that can be considered when applying Section 311 measures, are "evidence that organized criminal groups, international terrorists, or both, have transacted business in that jurisdiction" as well as "the extent to which that jurisdiction is characterized by high levels of official or institutional corruption."

OFAC administers multiple sanctions programs to block transactions and freeze assets within U.S. jurisdiction of specified foreign terrorist, criminal, and political entities, including specially designated individuals and nation states. Authorities for OFAC to designate such entities are derived from executive order and legislative statutes, which include the International Emergency Economic Powers Act (IEEPA), the Antiterrorism and Effective Death Penalty Act of 1996 (AEDPA), and the Foreign Narcotics Kingpin Designation Act.

TFFC is the policy development and outreach office for TFI, which, among other priorities, leads the U.S. delegation to FATF.[24] OIA, which was established by the Intelligence Authorization Act for Fiscal Year 2004 (P.L. 108-177), contributes all-source financial threat assessments and products as a formal member of the U.S. Intelligence Community. Its analysts have been central in interagency efforts such as the Afghanistan Threat Finance Cell (ATFC) as well as its predecessor, the Iraq Threat Finance Cell (ITFC).

Selected Issues

As the House Financial Services Committee Task Force to Investigate Terrorism Financing conducts its fifth hearing in 2015 examining U.S. efforts to combat the financing of terrorism, several ongoing policy issues facing the 114th Congress include:

Information sharing. Some have called for congressional action to improve and expand existing information sharing tools between financial institutions and government authorities and among financial institutions in cases of suspected money laundering and terrorist financing—including changes to the scope of liability safe harbors and the types of information that may be shared. In testimony before the Task Force, Chip Poncy of the Foundation for Defense of Democracies included gaps in information sharing as a "systemic challenge to financial transparency." Similar policy concerns also affect financial institutions with respect to cyber

---

[24] The Intelligence Reform and Terrorism Prevention Act of 2004 (P.L. 108-458) authorized the Secretary of the Treasury, or the Secretary's designee, as the lead U.S. government official to the Financial Action Task Force.

threat-related information sharing. John Carlson of the Financial Services Information Sharing and Analysis Center also testified before the Task Force, noting the private sector's interests in enhanced cyber threat information sharing legislation that would provide a variety of liability and disclosure protections for sharing and receiving cyber threat information.

Beneficial ownership. According to a FATF-conducted mutual evaluation of the U.S. AML/CFT system in 2006, one of the few areas in which the United States was rated "non-compliant" with international AML/CFT standards involved information collection on beneficial ownership and control of legal entities. The risk of terrorist, criminals, and corrupt actors exploiting beneficial ownership information gaps in the United States to create and use shell companies for illicit purposes has long been a concern to Congress as well. Several witnesses at Task Force hearings have raised the issue, including New York County District Attorney Cyrus Vance, Jr.. For its part, the Obama Administration has also sought to address this issue through international commitments and proposed legislative and regulatory changes. The next FATF mutual evaluation of the United States is scheduled for 2016.

Islamic State. As the 114th Congress continues to consider and evaluate U.S. policy responses to address the Islamic State, a focus of concern may center on whether U.S. counterterrorist financing tools are capable of diminishing IS sources of funds. Key questions may include whether current U.S. efforts are effective and sufficiently resourced, or require new legislative authorities, to respond to the Islamic State's ability to accumulate and distribute funds. Although Congress has been active in evaluating U.S. policy responses and options to address the Islamic State, particularly the military response and prospects for congressional authorization for the use of military force, legislative proposals to stem the Islamic State's access to and use of funds have been limited. Many observers recognize that a strategy focused on counter-finance may weaken, but not destroy, the Islamic State. For its part, the Department of the Treasury has cautioned against expectations that efforts to combat the Islamic State's finances will bear fruit quickly.

Iran. Observers have cautioned that the July 2015 negotiated Iran nuclear deal, known as the Joint Comprehensive Plan of Action (JCPOA), could have implications for terrorist financing, a topic that was addressed in a recent Task Force hearing. Although proliferation-related sanctions relief pursuant to the JCPOA would leave in place existing terrorism-related sanctions against Iran, some remain concerned about the possibility that Iran may allocate more resources to terrorist financing as its economic prospects improve. Should the JCPOA be implemented, a potential challenge for the United States and the international financial services community would be how to ensure that the terrorist financing risks emanating from Iran are effectively mitigated.

February 3, 2016, Task Force to Investigate Terrorism Financing titled "Trading with the Enemy: Trade-Based Money Laundering is the Growth Industry in Terror Finance"

Introduction

Trade-based money laundering (TBML) involves the exploitation of the international trade system for the purpose of transferring value and obscuring the true origins of illicit wealth. The Financial Action Task Force (FATF), an intergovernmental standard-setting body on anti-money laundering and combating the financing of terrorism (AML/CFT), has described TBML as the process of disguising proceeds of crime and moving value through trade transactions in order to legitimize their illicit origin—a process that varies in complexity, but typically involves the misrepresentation of the price, quantity, or quality of imports or exports.[1] When used by terrorist groups to finance their activities, move money, or otherwise disguise the source and beneficiaries of their funds, TBML schemes are sometimes referred to as TBML/ Financing of Terrorism (FT). Financial institutions are wittingly or unwittingly implicated in TBML and TBML/FT schemes when they are used to settle, facilitate, or finance international trade transactions (e.g., through the processing of wire transfers, provision of trade finance, and issuance of letters of credit and guarantees).

In June 2015, the U.S. Department of the Treasury issued two reports related to money laundering: a *National Money Laundering Risk Assessment* and a *National Terrorist Financing Risk Assessment*. The *National Money Laundering Risk Assessment* identified TBML as among the most challenging and pernicious forms of money laundering to investigate.[2] Citing information from U.S. Immigration and Customs Enforcement (ICE), Treasury described TBML schemes as capable of laundering billions of dollars annually. An earlier advisory on TBML, issued by the Treasury Department's Financial Crimes Enforcement Network (FinCEN) in February 2010, stated that more than 17,000 Suspicious Activity Reports (SARs) described potential TBML activity between January 2004 and May 2009, which involved transactions totaling in the aggregate more than $276 billion.[3]

---

[1] Financial Action Task Force (FATF), *Trade Based Money Laundering*, June 23, 2006. The basic techniques of trade-based money laundering (TBML) include over- and under-invoicing of goods and services, multiple-invoicing of goods and services; over- and under-shipment (i.e., short shipping) of goods and services; and falsely described goods and services, including phantom shipping.

[2] U.S. Department of the Treasury, *National Money Laundering Risk Assessment*, June 12, 2015.

[3] Financial Crimes Enforcement Network (FinCEN), *Advisory to Financial Institutions on Filing Suspicious Activity Reports Regarding Trade-Based Money Laundering*, advisory, FIN-2010-A001, February 18, 2010.

Although TBML is widely recognized as one of the most common manifestations of international money laundering as well as a known value transfer and reconciliation method used by terrorist organizations, TBML appears to be less understood among academics and policymakers, in contrast with traditional forms of money laundering through the international banking system and through bulk cash smuggling. Considering the volume of global trade and the value of such transactions, however, TBML's effects can result in substantial consequences for international commerce and government revenue. The *National Money Laundering Risk Assessment* concludes that:

> TBML can have a more destructive impact on legitimate commerce than other money laundering schemes. According to ICE HSI [Homeland Security Investigations], transnational criminal organizations may dump imported goods purchased with illicit proceeds at a discount into a market just to expedite the money laundering process. The below-market pricing is a cost of doing business for the money launderer, but it puts legitimate businesses at a competitive disadvantage. This activity can create a barrier to entrepreneurship, crowding out legitimate economic activity. TBML also robs governments of tax revenue due to the sale of underpriced goods, and reduced duties collected on undervalued imports and fraudulent cargo manifests.

Global Hotspots

The U.S. government has historically focused on TBML schemes involving drug proceeds from Latin America, particularly the Black Market Peso Exchange (BMPE). BMPE emerged as a major money laundering method when Colombian drug traffickers used sophisticated trade-based schemes to disguise as much as $4 billion in annual narcotics profits in the 1980s.[4] According to FinCEN, TBML activity is growing in both volume and global reach. In an analysis of SARs between January 2004 and May 2009, TBML activity was most frequently identified in transactions involving Mexico and China. Panama was ranked third, potentially due to TBML activity linked to the Panama Colon Free Trade Zone (FTZ), while the Dominican Republic and Venezuela were identified as "countries with the most rapid growth in potential TBML activity."[5]

---

[4] Broadly, the Black Market Peso Exchange (BMPE) facilitated the "swap" of dollars owned by drug cartels in the United States for pesos already in Colombia by selling the dollars to Colombian businessmen who sought to buy U.S. goods for export. See FinCEN, *Colombian Black Market Peso Exchange*, advisory, issue 9, November, 1997; U.S. government, National Money Laundering Strategy, May 3, 2007; and FATF, *Trade Based Money Laundering*, June 23, 2006.

[5] FinCEN, *Advisory to Financial Institutions on Filing Suspicious Activity Reports Regarding Trade-Based Money Laundering*, advisory, FIN-2010-A001, February 18, 2010.

According to the U.S. Department of State's March 2015 edition of its annual report on money laundering and financial crimes, Volume II of the *International Narcotics Control Strategy Report*, TBML concerns have surfaced in countries or jurisdictions such as Afghanistan, Belize, Brazil, Canada, China, Colombia, Greece, Hong Kong, India, Iran, Iraq (and "the surrounding region"), Kenya, Lebanon, Mexico, Pakistan, Panama, Paraguay, Singapore, St. Maarten, Taiwan, the United Arab Emirates (UAE), Uruguay, Venezuela,[6] and the West Bank and Gaza.[7]

Links to Terrorism

Although a number of anecdotal case studies in recent years have revealed instances in which TBML is used by known terrorist groups and other non-state armed groups, including Hezbollah, the Treasury Department's June 2015 *National Terrorist Financing Risk Assessment* concluded that TBML is not a dominant method for terrorist financing.[8] It stated:

> Broadly speaking, based on an analysis of U.S. law enforcement investigations and prosecutions relating to TF [terrorist financing], two methods of moving money to terrorists and terrorist organizations have been predominate in the convictions and cases pending since 2001: the physical movement of cash and the movement of funds through the banking system…. The physical movement of cash accounted for 28 percent of these cases while movement directly through banks constituted 22 percent, movement through licensed MSBs [money services businesses] 17 percent, and movement by individuals or entities acting as unlicensed money transmitters constituted 18 percent.

The footnote following the last sentence quoted above continued: "The remaining 15 percent were a mix of checks, wire transfers through unspecified financial institutions, and TBML."

In its latest *Country Reports on Terrorism*, issued in June 2015, the State Department identified TBML as a terrorism-related concern in Tunisia and Syria, particularly as a technique used by *hawala* brokers in conjunction with corrupt customs and immigration officials (*hawala* is an informal value transfer system, often used to send remittances, that can operate outside the formal international financial system to move funds internationally and anonymously).[9] The State

---

[6] The 2015 report notes that "Venezuelan government officials—including the president, the executive vice president, an central bank president, a finance minister, and an interior minister—have all admitted publicly over the past 12-18 months that 30-40 percent of the roughly $53 billion the Venezuelan government spent on imports in 2013 were paid out for over-invoiced or completely fictitious transactions…." U.S. Department of State, *International Narcotics Control Strategy Report (INCSR)*, Vol. 2, Money Laundering and Financial Crimes, March 2015.

[7] U.S. Department of State, *INCSR*, Vol. 2, March 2015.

[8] U.S. Department of the Treasury, *National Terrorist Financing Risk Assessment*, June 12, 2015.

[9] U.S. Department of State, *Country Reports on Terrorism 2014*, June 2015.

Department's March 2015 report on money laundering and financial crimes also identified some specific countries that may be vulnerable to TBML/ Financing of Terrorism (FT) schemes. For example, the report notes that TBML in the United Arab Emirates (UAE), particularly linked to *hawala* transactions and counter-valuation through trading companies, "might support sanctions-evasion networks and terrorist groups in Afghanistan, Pakistan, and Somalia."[10]

Vulnerabilities

The potential is vast for criminal organizations and terrorist groups to exploit the international trade system with relatively low risk of detection. According to FATF, key characteristics of the international trade system have made it both attractive and vulnerable to illicit exploitation. Quoting FATF, vulnerabilities include the following:

> The enormous volume of trade flows, which obscures individual transactions and provides abundant opportunity for criminal organizations to transfer value across borders;
> The complexity associated with (often multiple) foreign exchange transactions and recourse to diverse financing arrangements;
> The additional complexity that can arise from the practice of comingling illicit funds with the cash flows of legitimate business;
> The limited recourse to verification procedures or programs to exchange customs data between countries; and
> The limited resources that most customs agencies have available to detect illegal trade transactions.[11]

Selected Case Studies

Hezbollah-Linked TBML

In an elaborate TBML scheme purported to be linked to Hezbollah, a Lebanon-based group that was designated in 1997 by the State Department as a Foreign Terrorist Organization (FTO), U.S. officials claimed that the Lebanese Canadian Bank (LCB) and multiple foreign exchange houses had facilitated the laundering of South American drug proceeds through the Lebanese financial system and through TBML schemes involving used cars and consumer goods.

In one such scheme, LCB facilitated wire transfers to U.S. banks for the purchase of used cars in the United States. Cars would be purchased in the United States and shipped to countries in West Africa and elsewhere while the proceeds from the car sales would reportedly be repatriated back to Lebanon through the use of bulk cash deposits among conspiring exchange houses. In another scheme associated with the same Hezbollah-linked drug trafficking network, Asian-supplied consumer goods

---

[10] U.S. Department of State, *INCSR*, Vol. 2, March 2015.
[11] FATF, *Trade Based Money Laundering*, June 23, 2006.

would be shipped to Latin America while the proceeds would be laundered through a BMPE-styled scheme. The funds sent to pay for the consumer goods were reportedly sent through LCB's U.S. correspondent accounts.

In its February 2011 designation of LCB as a financial institution of primary money laundering concern, FinCEN stated that, according to U.S. government information, Hezbollah "derived financial support" from these drug and money laundering schemes. Ultimately, Lebanon's central bank and monetary authority, the Banque du Liban, revoked LCB's banking license in September 2011 and LCB's former shareholders sold its assets and liabilities to the Lebanese Societé Generale de Banque au Liban SAL (SGBL). Some of the individuals and entities associated with this illicit network have also variously been subject to financial sanctions and law enforcement investigations in the United States.[12]

Toys-for-Drugs BMPE Scheme

In a BMPE scheme involving a Los Angeles-based toy wholesaler, Woody Toys, Inc., its owners received millions of dollars in cash payments generated from Colombian and Mexican narcotics trafficking. The cash payments reportedly were placed directly into the company's bank account from multiple locations in small deposits that were consistently under $10,000 to avoid reporting requirement (i.e., structuring). The toy company used the cash deposits to purchase toys from China, which, in turn, were exported to Colombia. The Colombia pesos generated by the toy sales in Colombia were used to reimburse the Colombian drug traffickers through the BMPE. Some of the employees of Woody Toys had previously worked for Angel Toy Company, whose owners had also been implicated in a similar toys-for-drugs BMPE scheme. The law enforcement investigation into this case benefitted from an information sharing arrangement between the United States and Colombia on trade data through the Trade Transparency Units (TTUs) established in both countries. [13]

Trade Finance and *Hawala* Networks

According to the Asia/Pacific Group on Money Laundering (APG), a FATF-style regional body (FSRB), another scheme to launder funds derived from multiple major international drug traffickers involved cash couriers, money transfer services, alternate value transfer systems (e.g., *hawala*), and formal mechanisms of trade

---

[12] Asia/Pacific Group on Money Laundering (APG), *APG Typology Report on Trade Based Money Laundering*, July 20, 2012; Jo Becker, "Beirut Bank Seen As Hub of Hezbollah's Finances," *New York Times*, December 13, 2011; Sebastian Rotella, "Government Says Hezbollah Profits from U.S. Cocaine Market Via Link to Mexican Cartel," *ProPublica*, December 13, 2011; "Prosecutors Say Hezbollah Laundered Millions of Dollars into U.S.," Associated Press, December 15, 2011, http://www.foxnews.com/us/2011/12/15/prosecutors-say-hezbollah-laundered-millions-dollars-into-us.html; Devlin Barrett, "U.S. Intensifies Bid to Defund Hezbollah," *Wall Street Journal*, December 16, 2015

[13] APG, *APG Typology Report on Trade Based Money Laundering*, July 20, 2012; U.S. Immigration and Customs Enforcement (ICE), "Co-Owner of Los Angeles-Area Toy Company Sentenced in Drug Money Laundering Case," press release, May 6, 2013; https://www.ice.gov/news/releases/co-owner-los-angeles-area-toy-company-sentenced-drug-money-laundering-case.

finance, managed and directed by an Indian national living in Dubai. The individual involved operated numerous businesses in Dubai as well as numerous affiliates in Europe, Asia, Africa, and the United States.

In Dubai, the individual opened letters of credit (LCs) through his various companies for various importers, also located in Dubai. These LCs were opened to benefit various affiliated exporters located in India and in other locations and were in amounts that were substantially higher than the market value of the exports. In opening the LCs, the individual used his businesses connections with certain issuing banks and certain advising banks to transmit the LCs to the affiliated exporters in India. The individual also arranged for trade documents to be prepared that reflected the inflated value of the exports in order to make them acceptable to the issuing and advising banks. Next, the LCs, with inflated export values, along with funds received from drug trafficking, were remitted to the exporters in India, essentially moving money through the financial system in the guise of trade financing. Once in India, the exporters distributed the drug proceeds to the various affiliates and sold the exports at market value.

The same Indian national also used various techniques to move funds offshore through *hawala* operators. In one scheme, the individual facilitated trade in banned goods (in this example, a "pulses," or agricultural crops) by falsifying trade documents through his network of businesses in India to export banned goods from India. In order to circumvent the restrictions, the goods were falsely described and falsely valued in trade documents. *Hawala* operators were used to settle the difference between the true value of the exported goods and the falsely documented value of the goods.[14]

Selected Policy Responses

Role of the Financial Action Task Force (FATF)
FATF was organized to develop and promote AML/CFT guidelines.[15] It currently comprises 34 member countries and territories and two regional organizations.[16]

---

[14] APG, *APG Typology Report on Trade Based Money Laundering*, July 20, 2012.

[15] For additional information, see CRS Report RS21904, *The Financial Action Task Force: An Overview*, by James K. Jackson.

[16] FATF members are Argentina, Australia, Austria, Belgium, Brazil, Canada, Denmark, Finland, France, Germany, Greece, Hong Kong, Iceland, India, Ireland, Italy, Japan, Luxembourg, Mexico, Netherlands, New Zealand, Norway, People's Republic of China, Portugal, Russian Federation, Singapore, South Africa, South Korea, Spain, Sweden, Switzerland, Turkey, United Kingdom, and the United States; the two international organizations are the European Commission, and the Gulf Cooperation Council. The following organizations have observer status: Asia/Pacific Group on Money Laundering; Caribbean Financial Action Task Force; Council of Europe Select Committee of Experts on the Evaluation of Anti-Money Laundering Measures; Eastern and Southern Africa Anti-Money Laundering Group; Financial Action Task Force on Money Laundering in South America; other international organizations including the African Development Bank; Asia Development Bank; European Central Bank; International Monetary Fund; Organization of American States,

Although FATF has no enforcement capabilities, FATF relies on a combination of annual self-assessments and periodic mutual evaluations on the compliance of its members to FATF guidelines. It can suspend member countries that fail to comply on a timely basis with its guidelines. When it was established in 1989, FATF was charged with examining money laundering techniques and trends, reviewing actions already taken, and setting out the measures to be taken to combat money laundering. In 1990, FATF issued a new report containing 40 recommendations,[17] which provided a comprehensive plan of action to fight against money laundering.

In February 2012, FATF members adopted a revised set of the FATF 40 Recommendations (subsequently updated again October 2015), which integrated CFT guidelines into the core set of recommendations and added the proliferation of financing of weapons of mass destruction to FATF's areas of surveillance. The new mandate is intended to:

- deepen global surveillance of evolving criminal and terrorist threats;
- build a stronger, practical and ongoing partnership with the private sector; and
- support global efforts to raise standards, especially in low capacity countries.

In addition, the revised recommendations address new and emerging threats, while clarifying and strengthening many of the existing obligations. The new standards strengthen the requirements for higher risk situations and allow countries to take a more focused approach to areas where high risks remain or where implementation could be enhanced. The standards also address transparency requirements related to the adequate, accurate, and timely information on the beneficial ownership and control of legal persons and arrangements to address tax transparency, corporate governance, and various types of criminal activity.

Recommendations specifically to counter TBML, however, are not included in the current set of FATF's 40 Recommendations, despite recognition that the rapid growth and complexity of the international trade and financing system has multiplied the opportunities for abuse of this system by money launderers and terrorist financiers. FATF, however, has occasionally issued stand-alone reports that address TBML and best practices.[18] Surveys conducted by FATF, for example, indicate that there is no comprehensive data set on the extent and magnitude of TBML. In part, FATF determined that this lack of data reflected the fact that most jurisdictions do not identify TBML as a separately identifiable activity under the

---

Organization for Economic Cooperation and Development; United Nations Office on Drugs and Crime; and the World Bank.

[17] FATF, *International Standards on Combating Money Laundering and the Financing of Terrorism and Proliferation: The FATF Recommendations*, adopted on February 16, 2012 and updated in 2013 and 2015.

[18] FATF, *Best Practices Paper on Trade-Based Money Laundering*, June 20, 2008.

general topic of money laundering and, therefore, did not collect or share data on this specific type of activity. FATF also concluded that most jurisdictions do not offer training to trade and finance specialists specifically related to TBML activities.[19]

U.S. Department of the Treasury

Central to the Treasury Department's efforts to combat TBML is FinCEN, which issues advisories and geographic targeting orders, and applies special measures to jurisdictions determined to be of primary money laundering concern.

What is FinCEN?

FinCEN's mission is to safeguard the financial system through the collection, analysis and dissemination of financial intelligence to law enforcement. FinCEN's Director is appointed by the Secretary of the Treasury and reports to the Under Secretary of the Treasury for Terrorism and Financial Intelligence. FinCEN also acts as the U.S. financial intelligence unit (FIU), one of the over 100 FIUs that comprise the Egmont Group, an international body focused on information sharing and cooperation among FIUs.[20] FinCEN receives data, such as suspicious transaction reports (SARs) from banks and other financial firms, analyzes the data, and disseminates it to law enforcement. It also cooperates with foreign FIUs in exchanging information, largely through its membership and participation in the Egmont Group.

FinCEN exercises regulatory functions primarily under the Currency and Financial Transactions Reporting Act of 1970,[21] as amended by Title III of the USA PATRIOT Act of 2001[22] and other legislation, together commonly referred to as the Bank Secrecy Act (BSA). The BSA is the United States' first and most comprehensive Federal AML/CFT statute. It authorizes the Secretary of the Treasury to issue regulations requiring banks and other financial institutions to establish AML programs and to file reports on financial activity that may have relevance for criminal, tax, and regulatory investigations or for intelligence or counter-terrorism.

Advisories

The purpose of a FinCEN advisory, in general, is to red flag for financial institutions activities that may be indicative of certain types of money laundering,

---

[19] Ibid.

[20] An FIU is a national agency responsible for receiving (and, as permitted, requesting), analyzing, and disseminating to the competent authorities disclosures of financial information concerning suspected proceeds of crime and potential financing of terrorism or as otherwise required by national legislation or regulation, in order to combat money laundering and terrorism financing. See https://www.fincen.gov/about_fincen/wwd/.

[21] 31 U.S.C. 5311 *et seq.*

[22] P.L. 107-56.

in line with recent investigations, to assist financial institutions in filing suspicious activity reports (SARs). FinCEN first highlighted TBML in November 1997 and then again in June 1999 with advisories on the Black Market Peso Exchange (BMPE).[23]

In February 2010, FinCEN issued an advisory on TBML, based on law enforcement experience involving U.S. trade with Central and South America.[24] The purpose of the advisory was to aid financial institutions in reporting suspicious activity related to TBML. The advisory noted the basic schemes behind TBML and offered more specific red flags. The 2010 advisory further noted that reporting on suspected TBML had been inconsistent and requested that financial institutions include the abbreviation TBML or BMPE on SARs.[25] FinCEN also described substantial delays in the reporting of suspected TBML activity.[26]

FinCEN issued an additional TBML advisory in May 2014 related to Mexican TBML activity involving funnel accounts.[27] A funnel account is an individual or business account in one geographic area receiving multiple cash deposits, often below the jurisdiction's cash reporting threshold, and from which the funds are withdrawn in a different geographic area with little time elapsing between the deposits and withdrawals.[28] The advisory also provides several specific red flags associated with such activity conducted by Mexican criminal and drug trafficking organizations.

Geographic Targeting Orders

FinCEN appears to have also begun to rely more heavily on Geographic Targeting Orders (GTOs) in recent years, a tool that was first authorized in 1988. A GTO imposes additional, but time-limited, recordkeeping and reporting requirements on domestic financial institutions or nonfinancial businesses in a particular geographic area in order to assist regulators and law enforcement agencies in identifying

---

[23] The two early FinCEN advisories on TBML were also followed in 2005 by additional sections in the Federal Financial Institutions Examination Council (FFIEC) BSA/AML Examination Manual, issued in collaboration with FinCEN, aimed at providing more guidance to bank examiners on assessing the adequacy of bank systems on risks associated with trade finance activities. See http://www.ffiec.gov/bsa_aml_infobase/pages_manual/manual_online.htm.

[24] FinCEN, *Advisory to Financial Institutions on Filing Suspicious Activity Reports Regarding Trade-Based Money Laundering*, advisory, FIN-2010-A001, February 18, 2010.

[25] Ibid. Of the approximately 17,000 SARs between January 2004 and May 2009 that FinCEN determined may have indicated TBML activity, only 24% of them clearly identified the suspected activity as TBML. The remaining 76% were identified by FinCEN based on complex queries including "trade" and other terms derived from various red flags.

[26] Ibid. For example, 14% of suspected TBML activity reported in SARs in 2004 occurred in 2004. However, 30% of such activity was not reported by financial institutions until 2009, five years after the activity occurred.

[27] FinCEN, *Update on U.S. Currency Restrictions in Mexico: Funnel Accounts and TBML*, advisory, FIN-2014-A005, May 28, 2014.

[28] Ibid.

criminal activity. In the absence of extensions, GTOs may only remain in effect for a maximum of 180 days. Violators may face substantial civil or criminal liability. Several recent GTOs have been used to enhance U.S. efforts to combat TBML.

In April 2015, FinCEN issued a GTO that lowered cash reporting thresholds and triggered additional recordkeeping requirements for certain financial transactions for about 700 Miami-based electronics exporters.[29] The GTO required targeted businesses to file forms with FinCEN reporting any single transaction or related transactions in which they receive more than $3,000 in cash—a stricter standard than the ordinary $10,000 filing threshold for cash transactions imposed pursuant to BSA. FinCEN stated that the new reporting requirements are aimed at combating complex TBML-related schemes employed by the Sinaloa and Los Zetas drug and transnational crime organizations. In October 2015, FinCEN renewed the GTO for an additional 180 days.[30]

In October 2015, FinCEN issued a similar GTO that also lowered cash reporting to $3,000 and triggered additional recordkeeping requirements. This GTO targeted businesses in the Los Angeles Fashion District in an effort to frustrate suspected Mexican and Colombian drug traffickers who had been exploiting fashion industry businesses to engage in BMPE schemes.[31]

Special Measures

Pursuant to BSA, as amended by the USA PATRIOT Act, FinCEN may require financial institutions and agencies within U.S. jurisdiction to take certain regulatory special measures against a foreign jurisdiction, foreign financial institution, class of transaction, or type of account determined to be of "primary money laundering concern."[32] The enumerated five special measures, which may be imposed individually, in any combination, and in any sequence, range from requiring enhanced due diligence to prohibiting the opening or maintaining of correspondent or payable-through accounts. In some cases, such action corresponds with other administrative actions taken by the Treasury Department, including by the Office of Foreign Asset Control (OFAC), which is responsible for administering financial sanctions that target specially designated foreign nationals and entities.

---

[29] FinCEN, *Geographic Targeting Order*, April 15, 2015; see also FinCEN, "FinCEN Targets Money Laundering Infrastructure with Geographic Targeting Order in Miami: 'GTO' Addresses Trade-Based Money Laundering Activity Involving Drug Cartels," press release, April 21, 2015.
[30] FinCEN, *Geographic Targeting Order*, October 20, 2015; see also FinCEN, "FinCEN Renews Geographic Targeting Order (GTO) Requiring Enhanced Reporting and Recordkeeping for Electronics Exporters Near Miami, Florida," press release, October 23, 2015.
[31] FinCEN, *Geographic Targeting Order*, September 26, 2014; see also FinCEN, "FinCEN Issues Geographic Targeting Order Covering the Los Angeles Fashion District as Part of Crackdown on Money Laundering for Drug Cartels," press release, October 2, 2014.
[32] 31 U.S.C. 5318A, as added by Sec. 311 of Title III of the USA PATRIOT Act (P.L. 107-56), and subsequently amended.

Among the 10 active cases, several were designated for their involvement in TBML, including the following:

Halawi Exchange and Rmeiti Exchange. In April 2013, FinCEN separately designated two Lebanese exchange houses, Halawi Exchange and Rmeiti Exchange, as financial institutions of primary money laundering concern. According to U.S. government information, both exchange houses facilitated transactions associated with a large-scale TBML scheme, involving the purchase of used cars in the United States for export to West Africa. Moreover, U.S. authorities claim that both exchange houses had been providing money laundering services for an international narcotics trafficking and money laundering network linked to Hezbollah.[33]

Banca Privada d'Andorra (BPA). In March 2015, FinCEN designated BPA as a financial institution of primary money laundering concern. FinCEN found high-level managers to have facilitated transactions on behalf of Third-Party Money Launderers (TPMLs) linked to individuals and organizations associated with organized crime, corruption, human trafficking, TBML, and fraud. One of these TPMLs laundered the proceeds of Venezuelan public corruption through TBML schemes, among others.[34]

U.S. Department of Homeland Security

Within the U.S. Department of Homeland Security (DHS), Immigration and Customs Enforcement's Homeland Security Investigations (ICE/HSI) established the first Trade Transparency Unit (TTU) in Washington, D.C., in 2004. Using a specialized computer system called the "Data Analysis and Research for Trade Transparency System" (DARTTS), TTUs examine trade anomalies and financial irregularities in domestic and foreign trade data to identify instances of TBML, customs fraud, contraband smuggling, and tax evasion that warrant further law enforcement investigation. With funding support from the Department of State's Bureau for International Narcotics and Law Enforcement Affairs (INL), HSI has stood up TTUs in Argentina, Brazil, Colombia, Ecuador, Guatemala, Mexico, Panama, and Paraguay. According to the State Department, these eight international TTUs form the basis of broader plans to develop an international network of TTUs, similar to the Egmont Group of FIUs.[35] The 2007 *National Money Laundering Strategy* established attacking TBML at home and abroad as a national goal and specifically called on the deployment of ICE-led TTUs to facilitate the exchange and analysis of trade data among trading partners. According to one

---

[33] FinCEN, *Notice of Finding that Halawi Exchange Co. is a Financial Institution of Primary Money Laundering Concern*, April 23, 2013; FinCEN, *Notice of Finding that Kassem Rmeiti & Co. For Exchange is a Financial Institution of Primary Money Laundering Concern*, April 23, 2013.
[34] FinCEN, *Notice of Finding that Banca Privada d'Andorra is a Financial Institution of Primary Money Laundering Concern*, March 10, 2015.
[35] U.S. Department of State, *INCSR*, Vol. 2, March 2015.

estimate, more than $1 billion has been seized since the creation of the U.S.- and foreign-based TTU effort.[36]

---

[36] John Cassara, *Trade-Based Money Laundering: The Next Frontier in International Money Laundering Enforcement* (Hoboken, NJ: John Wiley & Sons, 2016).

March 1, 2016, Task Force to Investigate Terrorism Financing hearing titled "Helping the Developing World Fight Terror Finance"

Introduction

U.S. and international efforts to combat terrorist financing abroad include a number of interdependent activities. These include targeted sanctions, intelligence and law enforcement, global guidance and regulatory standard-setting, as well as training and technical assistance to build the capabilities of national government anti-money laundering and combating the financing of terrorism (AML/CFT) efforts. Despite the existence of international conventions, standards, initiatives, regulations, and oversight bodies that commit participating countries and institutions to AML/CFT goals, there is no central coordination body mandated to facilitate AML/CFT capacity building efforts on a global level through training and technical assistance. While there has been substantial convergence on the specific requirements of the various conventions and initiatives, coherence among the various national and international agencies involved has been identified as an area of concern.

In remarks delivered in April 2015, Yury Fedetov, Executive Director of the United Nations Office on Drugs and Crime, commented that:

> [The] most frequently identified technical assistance needs in countering terrorist financing are one, strengthening the effective cooperation between national agencies which are involved directly or indirectly in fighting terrorist financing, and two, enhancing cooperation between regional and international networks.[1]

As terrorist financing and other illicit financial activity continues to pose risks to the international financial system, some have called for greater AML/CFT cooperation between, and among, national and international agencies.[2] The international community has yet to clarify the varying roles that state, regional bodies, and international and intergovernmental entities may play in the coordination and implementation of AML/CFT capacity building assistance. Instead, a wide range of donor entities are actively engaged in providing a broad array of AML/CFT technical assistance and training offerings, which are not consistently catalogued or coordinated. It is believed that "improved coordination among donor governments... could make global development assistance more efficient and effective."[3] Donor coordination, which is called "harmonization," has

---

[1] Yury Fedetov, Remarks at the UNODC High-Level Special Event on Strengthening National and International Cooperation in Preventing and Countering Terrorist Financing, April 14, 2015.

[2] Financial Action Task Force, Emerging Terrorist Financing Risks, October 2015.

[3] *See*, for example, Congressional Research Service Memo, Foreign Aid: International Donor Coordination of Development Assistance, February 2013.

been a major theme of international development cooperation agreements in the last decade, including the 2005 Paris Declaration on Aid Effectiveness, to which the U.S. and other major donors have committed themselves.[4] As described in international guidance on AML/CFT capacity building, however, there are inherent tensions between international interests to coordinate technical assistance and national prerogatives that seek to avoid perceptions of outside influence to control or constrain the mandates and activities of donor and recipient countries.[5]

Key issues for policymakers include whether and how to prioritize AML/CFT technical assistance at the international level and what role the United States can or should play to coordinate, fund, and implement such efforts. Some observers have questioned the effectiveness of recent AML/CFT capacity building efforts. A 2015 report by the Organization for Economic Cooperation and Development (OECD), for example, found that while countries' compliance with key AML/CFT standards has improved, particularly following international responses after the Al Qaeda terrorist attacks of September 11, 2001, compliance with the key OECD recommendations and obligations remains low.[6] Compliance is an even greater concern in developing countries, since larger Gross Domestic Product (GDP) levels and a higher quality of domestic economic and legal institutions are associated with greater compliance with AML/CFT standards.[7] The Financial Action Task Force (FATF) has cautioned that the aggressive implementation of AML/CFT standards and procedures can have the unintended consequence of preventing low-income households from accessing the formal financial sector.

International Framework

Although there are international standard-setting bodies, such as FATF and the OECD, in addition to global and regional forums to address AML/CFT policy issues, there is no central coordination body to set a global direction or policy agenda on AML/CFT capacity building efforts. This has been mitigated, to an extent, through the involvement of informal groups such as the G-20, which has taken leadership on various financial sector issues.

International legal obligations to combat terrorist financing have been negotiated within the framework of the United Nations (UN). The UN Security Council has issued specific mandates to target individuals and funding streams associated with Al Qaeda and the Islamic State (also known as ISIL, ISIS, and Da'esh). Nevertheless, most international AML/CFT activity has been voluntary and policy

---

[4] Id.

[5] See, for example, Financial Action Task Force, Guidance on Capacity Building for Mutual Evaluations and Implementation of the FATF Standards Within Low Capacity Countries, February 29, 2008.

[6] Organization for Economic Cooperation and Development, Illicit Financial Flows from Developing Countries: Measuring OECD Responses, 2014.

[7] Concepcion Verdugo Yepes, Compliance with the AML/CFT International Standard: Lessons from a Cross-Country Analysis, International Monetary Fund, Working Paper 11/177, 2011.

concerns are raised in informal decision-making forums like the G-20. National authorities are the primary actors, responsible for devising regulatory requirements for and guidance to the financial industry and other economic sectors vulnerable to money laundering and terrorist financing abuse, as well as providing oversight and supervision of financial institutions operating under their jurisdiction. National authorities also voluntarily participate in the international standard-setting bodies. International financial institutions, primarily the International Monetary Fund (IMF), provide overall surveillance of national compliance with the agreed upon international financial standards, among its other functions. The IMF, as well as the World Bank and numerous other international, regional, and national entities, provide a wide range of technical assistance and training to various countries each year.

Support for Bilateral and International Technical Assistance

Several U.S. federal departments, agencies, and offices provide bilateral technical assistance and training on AML/CFT topics. The U.S. government also supports multilateral organizations that provide AML/CFT assistance, whether in the form of direct U.S. participation or funding. According to the U.S. Department of State, in a 2015 report to Congress on Money Laundering and Financial Crimes, the U.S. government provided AML/CFT support to more than 100 countries in 2014, both bilaterally and with other donor nations and international organizations, in the form of training, mentoring, and other support for the full range of AML/CFT stakeholders.[8] Such stakeholders included supervisory, law enforcement, prosecutorial, customs, and financial intelligence unit government personnel, as well as private sector entities. U.S. agencies involved in implementing such international AML/CFT support include the:

- Board of Governors of the Federal Reserve System (FRB);
- U.S. Department of Homeland Security (DHS), including Customs and Border Protection (CBP) and the Immigration and Customs Enforcement's Homeland Security Investigations (ICE-HSI);
- U.S. Department of Justice (DOJ), including the Drug Enforcement Administration (DEA), Offices within the Criminal Division (including the Office of Overseas Prosecutorial Development, Assistance, and Training (OPDAT), and the Asset Forfeiture and Money Laundering Section (AFMLS), and the National Security Division (NSD));
- U.S. Department of State, including the International Narcotics and Law Enforcement Affairs Bureau (INL) and Counterterrorism Bureau (CT);
- U.S. Department of the Treasury, including the Financial Crimes Enforcement Network (FinCEN), International Revenue Service-Criminal Investigations (IRS-CI), Office of the Comptroller of the Currency (OCC), and Office of Technical Assistance (OTA); and

---

[8] U.S. Department of State, International Narcotics Control Strategy Report, Vol. II, Money Laundering and Financial Crimes, March 2015.

- Federal Deposit Insurance Corporation (FDIC).

These U.S. federal entities provide an array of international programming that spans several AML/CFT topics. Illustrative programming includes DHS-CBP training workshops in bulk cash smuggling, ICE-HSI cross-border financial investigation training (CBFIT), DOJ-OPDAT and DOJ-AFMLS training on financial investigations and asset recovery, State Department-managed trainings through its five International Law Enforcement Academies (ILEAs), and Treasury-OTA's comprehensive support to develop internationally-compliant AML/CFT regimes through its Economic Crimes Team (ECT).

DHS special agents have also been placed on temporary assignment overseas as cross-border financial investigations advisors (CBFIAs) and federal prosecutors have been placed overseas on long-term assignments funded by the State Department and managed by OPDAT, as resident legal advisors (RLAs). In 2014, RLAs were located in Algeria, Bangladesh, Iraq, Kenya, Panama, Senegal, Turkey, and UAE; they focused on supporting host nations with the development and implementation of AML/CFT legal regimes.

Additionally, the State Department provides multilateral AML/CFT support to the UN through its Global Programme Against Money Laundering (GPML); FATF, including selected FATF-Style Regional Bodies (FSRBs); the Egmont Group; and the Organization of American States Inter-American Drug Abuse Control Commission (OAS-CICAD), particularly to its Experts Group to Control Money Laundering and the OAS Counter-Terrorism Committee. AML/CFT technical assistance projects have primarily been funded with foreign assistance accounts administered by the State Department's INL and CT bureaus and Treasury's OTA, but have also received funding from the U.S. Agency for International Development (USAID), U.S. Embassies, and the Millennium Challenge Corporation, among others. Prior to 2015, earlier annual volumes of the State Department's Money Laundering and Financial Crimes report described the coordination of U.S. AML/CFT technical assistance through an interagency entity called the Terrorist Finance Working Group (TFWG), which was co-chaired by INL and CT bureaus. Although the TFWG was not mentioned in the 2015 edition of the Money Laundering and Financial Crimes report and has apparently not met recently, working-level discussions of AML/CFT assistance coordination reportedly continue.[9]

U.S. funding for AML/CFT technical assistance across all government stakeholders is not comprehensively presented in an interagency format to Congress as part of the President's annual budget plans, but some illustrative trends in funding are available for specific accounts, including technical assistance funded by Treasury's OTA (see **Table 1**) and State Department funding specifically for combating terrorist financing, which is appropriated out of the Non-Proliferation, Anti-

---

[9] State Department response to CRS, February 17, 2016.

Terrorism, Demining, and Related Programs (NADR) foreign aid account (see **Table 2)**.

Table 1. Treasury's OTA: Technical Assistance Funding, FY2010-present
(in US$ current millions)

FY2010	FY2011	FY2012	FY2013	FY2014	FY2015	FY2016	FY2017 Request
25	25.4	27	23.6	23.5	23.5	23.5	33.5

Source: U.S. Department of the Treasury, International Programs, Congressional Justification for Appropriations, FY2012-FY2017.
Notes: Unless otherwise noted, funding represents enacted levels.

Table 2. State Department's Foreign Assistance to Combat Terrorist Financing, FY2010-present
(in US$ current millions)

FY2010	FY2011	FY2012	FY2013	FY2014	FY2015	FY2016 Request	FY2017 Request
21	20.7	17	16.1	7.1	15	16	not available

Source: U.S. Department of State, response to CRS.
Notes: This programming category specifically includes only State Department foreign assistance for combating terrorist financing under Sub-Element 1.1.1.3 "Deny Terrorist Access to Finance," as defined by the *Standardized Program Structure and Definitions*. Other State Department funding for technical assistance for anti-money laundering and capacity building for financial institutions, more broadly defined, is not included here. Sub-Element 1.1.1.3 is exclusively budgeted out of the Nonproliferation, Anti-Terrorism, Demining and Related Programs (NADR) foreign assistance account. According to the State Department's *Standardized Program Structure and Definitions* document, this Sub-Element includes programming to "[i]dentify, disrupt, and deny access to sources, means, and mechanisms of terrorist finance including technical assistance to strengthen foreign government legislative, regulatory, law enforcement, and prosecutorial capabilities and the establishment of multilateral organizations to ensure legal/enforcement standards for formal financial systems."

Figures reported by the United States and other donors to the OECD, however, help illustrate how donors spend official development assistance (ODA) funds on programs related to AML/CFT.

For example, at the global level, OECD categorizes a subset of ODA under the "Government and Civil Society" category, which reportedly captures foreign aid related to governance capacity building, including CFT (**Figure 1**). Within the "Governance and Civil Society" sector, several sub-categories of funding would capture some CFT-related support including:

- Anti-corruption organizations and institutions, which totaled $229 million (or 1.6% of total spending in the governance category) in 2014;
- Public financial management, which totaled $1.9 billion (10.6%) in 2014, and includes support for bank supervision, AML-related issues, customs and border controls, and strengthened tax systems;
- Legal and judicial development, which totaled $3.1 billion (21.3%) in 2014 and which helped to build the capacity of judicial authorities to investigate and prosecute economic and financial crimes;
- Democratic participation and civil society, which totaled $2.5 billion (17.3%) in 2014; and
- Media and free flow of information, which totaled $481 million (3.3%) in 2014, can help non-governmental actors investigate illegal activities and advocate for reforms.

Figure 2. Total Development Assistance to the Sector "Government and Civil Society" in the OECD's DAC Sector Classification, 2014

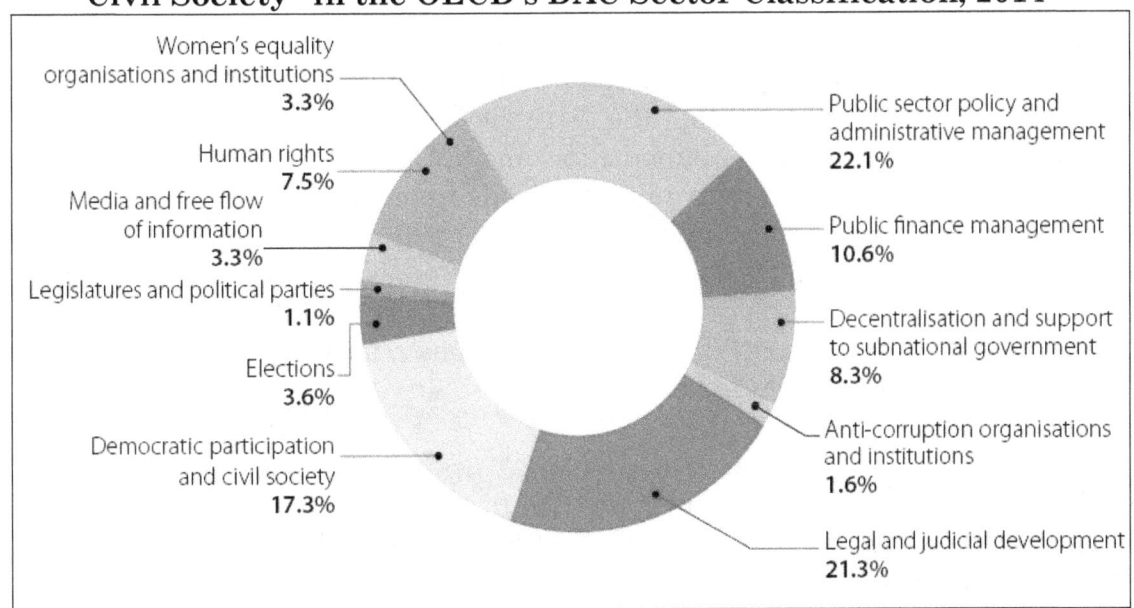

Source: OECD.

Table 3. Selected U.S. Development Assistance to the Sector "Government and Civil Society" in the OECD's DAC Sector Classification
(in US$ current millions)

	2009	2010	2011	2012	2013	2014
Anti-corruption organizations and institutions	84.16	75.05	68.32	155.62	41.67	42.59
Public finance management	266.10	104.72	59.13	55.70	37.68	58.47
Legal and judicial development	1,588.84	1,621.31	1,863.28	1,905.51	1,757.04	1,975.21
Democratic participation and civil society	241.04	343.09	331.41	323.46	295.36	282.15
Media and free flow of information	57.53	63.79	82.19	82.67	79.59	66.45

Source: OECD

International Fora for AML/CFT Technical Assistance

Technical assistance for AML/CFT is coordinated and supported by multiple international organizations, including the FATF and its FATF-Style Regional Bodies (FSRBs), the Egmont Group, the IMF, the World Bank, and the UN. The U.S. government provides donor support to some but not all of these organizations. Although there may be awareness among officials from donor nations that AML/CFT technical assistance may be provided on a bilateral, regional, or multilateral basis, such efforts do not appear to be consistently coordinated for possible redundancy. While there is broad recognition that AML/CFT capacity in many developing countries remains limited, decisions regarding where to prioritize international support appears to be diffuse.

United Nations Office on Drugs and Crime (UNODC)

Established in 1997, the UNODC is mandated to provide technical assistance to Member States in their struggle to combat drugs, crime, and terrorism consistent with their obligations pursuant to relevant UN treaties, including the 1999 UN International Convention for the Suppression of the Financing of Terrorism. Central to the UNODC's effort to address AML/CFT is the Global Programme Against Money Laundering, Proceeds of Crime and the Financing of Terrorism (GPML). According to the State Department, which provides financial support to GPML, GPML is "the focal point for AML policy and activities within the UN system and a key player in strengthening CFT."[10] Through GPML, UNODC supports Member States with AML/CFT technical assistance in the form of advisory services, workshops, seminars, other training platforms, as well as in-country mentoring. Various national and international organizations, including the World Bank, IMF, Egmont Group, EU, OSCE, and the United States, partner with UNODC on AML/CFT technical assistance. GPML also maintains observer status

---

[10] U.S. Department of State, International Narcotics Control Strategy Report, Vol. II, Money Laundering and Financial Crimes, March 2015.

with FATF and its FSRBs. According to the State Department, GPML deployed three in-country AML/CFT mentors overseas in 2014, including one who was shared with the World Bank. In addition, GPML hosts an international information sharing platform, which includes contacts for inter-country assistance on AML/CFT capacity building.

In April 2015, on the sidelines of the 13th UN Congress on Crime Prevention and Criminal Justice, the UNODC organized a *High-Level Special Event on Strengthening National and International Cooperation in Preventing and Countering Terrorist Financing*. This event explored ongoing CFT work carried out by Member States and key organizations, highlighting areas where gaps still exist and exploring potential for capacity building programs. Several participants, including the Nigerian and Brazilian representatives called for greater coordination among donor agencies on their technical assistance efforts and increased use of unconditional contributions to the UNODC's efforts.[11]

Financial Action Task Force (FATF) and FATF-Style Regional Bodies (FSRBs)

FATF is an intergovernmental body established in 1989, whose current mandate (2012-2020) focuses on setting global standards for the implementation of legal, regulatory, and operational measures for AML/CFT and other threats to the integrity of the international financial system.[12] FATF has issued a set of 40 recommendations on international AML/CFT standards that have been endorsed by over 180 countries. It collaborates with other international stakeholders to identify and follow up on national-level AML/CFT vulnerabilities, particularly through periodic mutual evaluations that review participating country AML/CFT legal, financial, and regulatory systems. Currently, FATF identifies 13 "high risk and non-cooperative jurisdictions."[13] FATF's mandate document also clarifies that the IMF and the World Bank are responsible for providing technical assistance and capacity building on combating money laundering, terrorist financing, and other related threats.

In February 2008, FATF issued special guidance on AML/CFT capacity building consistent with the FATF standards in low-capacity countries.[14] It noted that while implementation of FATF standards in all countries can be challenging, their

---

[11] UNODC, Thirteenth United Nations Congress on Crime Prevention and Criminal Justice, Draft Report: High Level Segment of the Conference, April 14, 2015.

[12] Financial Action Task Force, Mandate (2012-2020), April 20, 2012.

[13] Against two of these, Iran and North Korea, FAFT calls on its participating membership to "apply counter-measures to protect the international financial system" from AML/CFT risks arising from these two countries. FATF also identifies the following countries as jurisdictions to monitor: Afghanistan, Bosnia and Herzegovina, Guyana, Iran, Iraq, Laos, Myanmar (Burma), Papua New Guinea, Syria, Uganda, Vanuatu, and Yemen.

[14] Financial Action Task Force, Guidance on Capacity Building for Mutual Evaluations and Implementation of the FATF Standards Within Low Capacity Countries, February 29, 2008.

implementation in low-capacity countries is particularly difficult due to several structural characteristics that are "severely" constraining, including:

- competing priorities for scarce government resources;
- a severe lack of resources and skilled workforce to implement government programs;
- overall weakness in legal institutions;
- a dominant informal sector and cash-based economy;
- poor documentation and data retention systems; and
- a very small financial sector.

The FATF guidance further notes that care should be taken in defining a proper sequence for implementation of AML/CFT reforms and that FSRBs, regional entities whose primary purpose is to promote the implementation of FATF standards, can play an important role in facilitating requests for technical assistance and training. The guidance notes that several FSRBs have established coordination mechanisms to facilitate AML/CFT technical assistance and training (e.g., the Asia/Pacific Group on Money Laundering (APG), to which the United States is a member). Although FSRBs can be relevant in the coordination of efficient and effective technical assistance between donor and recipient nations, the FATF guidance cautions that they are not to "control or constrain the mandates and activities of the donors, nor act as a 'buffer zone' between the countries requesting assistance and the donor/provider."

In February 2016, FATF held its most recent plenary session in Paris and focused in particular on terrorist financing, identifying the issue as "the top priority" for FATF.[15] At the plenary session, FATF members adopted a consolidated FATF Strategy on Combating Terrorist Financing. Included among the FATF Strategy's goals is to "identify and take measures in relation to any country with strategic deficiencies for terrorist financing."[16] To this end, FATF updated members on the status of jurisdictions with fundamental shortcomings in the implementation of FATF recommendations 5 and 6 (on criminalizing terrorist financing and applying targeted financial sanctions). As of February, FATF reported that 36 jurisdictions, including 40% that had lacked in 2015 legal powers to prosecute terrorist financiers or apply targeted financial sanctions, have already taken remedial actions.[17] There reportedly remain, however, 15 jurisdictions that FATF identifies as requiring "urgent action to address their shortcomings, including requesting technical assistance from relevant bodies if necessary."[18]

---

[15] Financial Action Task Force, Outcomes of the Plenary Meeting of the FATF, Paris, 17-19 February 2016.

[16] Financial Action Task Force, Consolidated FATF Strategy on Combatting Terrorist Financing, February 2016.

[17] Id.

[18] Financial Action Task Force, Outcomes of the Plenary Meeting of the FATF, Paris, 17-19 February 2016.

Egmont Group of Financial Intelligence Units

The Egmont Group began in 1995 as a small group of 14 national financial intelligence units (FIUs) seeking international cooperation on financial intelligence matters. The State Department describes the Egmont Group as the "international standard setter" for FIUs, whose guidance documents are interlinked with the FATF standards.[19] Since its inception, it has grown to a recognized membership of 151 FIUs as of 2015. According to its revised 2013 charter, the Egmont Group aims, among other purposes, to support member capacity development through the offering of training and technical assistance, personnel exchanges, operational and strategic collaboration, and access to secure information exchanges between Egmont FIUs.[20] The Egmont Group's annual report for the 2013-2014 time period describes its Secretariat's role in coordinating the delivery of technical assistance and training and support for such activities by regional representatives.[21]

International Monetary Fund and the World Bank

In November 2001, IMF and World Bank member countries agreed to expand their work to cover the problems of terrorist financing through the provision of technical assistance and the conduct of the IMF's annual surveillance. In 2002, IMF member countries approved the Fund's involvement in the conduct of assessments of country's compliance with the FATF AML/CFT standard. Specifically, the Board agreed to adopt, subject to certain conditions, the FATF standard for the purposes of the Reports on the Observance of Standards and Codes (ROSC) program and to launch a twelve-month pilot program of AML/CFT assessments. During the pilot, the IMF and the World Bank evaluated 33 countries and assessed their compliance with the FATF AML/CFT recommendations. This program was made permanent in 2004 and since then, AML/CFT issues have been an integral component of many IMF surveillance products. In a limited number of cases, AML/CFT measures have been incorporated into conditionality under Fund-supported programs.[22]

One of the benefits of IMF and World Bank membership is technical assistance and training. The IMF and the World Bank are the only global institutions that have a permanent staff of assessors and a global reach that facilitates conducting assessments and providing technical assistance/capacity building. Since 2007, the World Bank has led the development of an analytical risk assessment tool to guide countries in conducting their AML/CFT risk assessment at the national level.[23]

---

[19] U.S. Department of State, International Narcotics Control Strategy Report, Vol. II, Money Laundering and Financial Crimes, March 2015.

[20] Egmont Group of Financial Intelligence Units, Charter, approved by the Egmont Group Heads of Financial Intelligence Unit, July 2013, published October 30, 2013.

[21] Egmont Group of Financial Intelligence Units, Annual Report 2013-2014, 2014.

[22] For example, Afghanistan, Cyprus, Greece, Kyrgyzstan, Sao Tome and Principe, and Uganda.

[23] More information is available at: http://www.worldbank.org/en/topic/financialmarketintegrity/brief/antimoney-laundering-and-combating-the-financing-of-terrorism-risk-assessment-support.

This AML/CFT technical assistance is provided on a voluntary, cooperative basis, i.e., at the request and with the assistance of the authorities of that country. Prior to the 2009, the IMF's AML/CFT capacity development programs were financed primarily through internal resources. Since 2009, most of the AML/CFT technical assistance is externally financed through a multi-donor trust fund. The United States is not a contributing member.

The IMF's AML/CFT trust fund was renewed for a five-year term in May 2014. Donors (France, Japan, Luxembourg, the Netherlands, Norway, Qatar, Saudi Arabia, Switzerland and the United Kingdom) have pledged more than $20 million through 2019. As of September 2015, 17 projects have already started under the second phase. The trust fund complements existing accounts that finance the IMF's AML/CFT capacity development activities in member countries, bringing the number of countries assisted each year to over 30 and totaling over $6.5 million annually in direct technical assistance and training.[24] In addition to their own technical assistance efforts, the World Bank has become involved in providing detailed AML/CFT risk assessments.

Selected Issues
U.S. Government Interagency Coordination

According to a U.S. Government Accountability Office (GAO) report from July 2015, the formal interagency Terrorist Financing Working Group (TFWG), which had previously been the primary mechanism "to discuss and reach consensus on CTF programming outcome and goals," is on hiatus.[25] Part of the reason for its recent inactivity is the result of organizational restructuring within the State Department's CT Bureau, whose CFT unit, which was disbanded, had been a co-chair of the TFWG. A Treasury official reported to GAO that, despite ongoing informal coordination, the current status quo could have deleterious consequences for stakeholder awareness. The TFWG was also the subject of a 2005 GAO study, which identified gaps in coordination, including interagency disagreement over the roles, procedures, delivery, and evaluation of CFT training and technical assistance.[26] In light of the TFWG's current status, some may question whether the U.S. government's ability to coordinate on CFT assistance among international donors has been affected by recent gaps in interagency coordination—and how to avoid returning TFWG to the interagency malfunctions described in the 2005 GAO report.

---

[24] International Monetary Fund, "Fact Sheet: The IMF and the Fight Against Money Laundering and the Financing of Terrorism," September 14, 2015.

[25] U.S. Government Accountability Office (GAO), "Combating Terrorism: State Should Evaluate Its Countering Violent Extremism Program and Set Time Frames for Addressing Evaluation Recommendations," GAO-15-684, July 2015.

[26] GAO, "Terrorist Financing: Better Strategic Planning Needed to Coordinate U.S. Efforts to Deliver Counter-Terrorism Financing Training and Technical Assistance Abroad," GAO-06-19, October 2005.

FATF Role and Counter-ISIL Financing Coordination

As part of the U.S.-led global coalition to combat the Islamic State, the United States, Italy, and Saudi Arabia are co-chairing a Counter-ISIL Finance Group (CIFG) focused on disrupting the Islamic State's sources of revenue and its ability to move and use funds. In February 2016, the CIFG jointly met with FATF to discuss the ISIL threat, exchange information, and identify opportunities for future action. One of these, according to the FATF-CIFG Communique following the joint meeting, is to facilitate "efforts to improve multilateral information sharing and capacity building."[27] As the international community, including the United States, proceeds to translate such statements into action, a key question for policymakers will be how to coordinate, prioritize, and implement multilateral efforts to build CFT capacity broadly and counter-ISIL financing capacity specifically.

Building Policy Coherence

The OECD has identified tensions between national and international systems for combatting terrorist financing. A 2014 OECD study found that countries face a range of challenges implementing standards related to combatting money laundering, tax evasion, international bribery, and freezing, recovering, and repatriating stolen assets.[28] While many of the policies required of national governments by the FATF standards do not leave countries any discretion, there are others such as FATF's risk-based approach, in which countries are required to ensure their risks apply proportionate measures. These include enhanced or simplified measures and exemptions from the FATF requirements depending on their unique risk assessment.

A further challenge is that any country's efforts to combat terrorist financing are embedded in a deep and wide national framework of polices and institutions with diverse priorities (e.g., criminal justice, financial regulation and supervision, tax, government and public administration, etc.). Policymakers may also choose to consider how best to help governments create holistic/whole-of-government AML/CFT strategies.

---

[27] FATF-CIFG Communique, February 2016.
[28] Organization for Economic Cooperation and Development, "Illicit Financial Flows from Developing Countries: Measuring OECD Responses," 2014.

April 19, 2016, Task Force to Investigate Terrorism Financing hearing titled "Preventing Cultural Genocide: Countering the Plunder and Sale of Priceless Cultural Antiquities by ISIS"

Introduction

The theft, fraud, looting, and trafficking of artifacts and cultural materials, including antiquities, is a longstanding transnational phenomenon that can enrich criminal actors and destroy the cultural heritage of nations. Despite international efforts to address the problem, trafficking in art and cultural property continues unabated.[1] Current concern has focused in particular on the situation in Iraq and Syria, where multiple armed actors in the region are believed to profit from looting.[2] One of these groups is the terrorist organization known as the Islamic State (IS or ISIS or ISIL or Daesh[3]), which controls or contests territory that includes some of the most archaeologically treasured sites of ancient civilization. Reports indicate that the Islamic State has institutionalized antiquities looting as a source of revenue, although estimates on how much the antiquities sector contributes to its total revenue remain imprecise. The Islamic State also publicly destroys symbols of cultural heritage that are inconsistent with its ideology.[4]

Observers describe a large scale and systematic process of cultural heritage destruction in Iraq and Syria, which has, over the course of the Syrian civil war and the ensuing regional instability, expanded. There are some 4,500 archaeological sites located in IS territory that are at risk—vulnerable to looting, destruction, or both. France Desmarais of the International Council of Museums describes the situation as the "largest-scale mass destruction of cultural heritage since the Second World War."[5] United Nations Educational, Scientific, and Cultural Organization

---

[1] Steven Lee Myers and Nicholas Kulish, "'Broken System' Allows ISIS to Profit From Looted Antiquities," *New York Times*, January 9, 2016; Rachel Shabi, "Looted in Syria and Sold in London: The British Antiquities Shops Dealing in Artefacts Smuggled by ISIS," *The Guardian (UK)*, July 3, 2015; Graham Bowley, "Antiquities Lost, Casualties of War: In Syria and Iraq, Trying to Protect a Heritage at Risk," *New York Times*, October 3, 2014.

[2] For examples of comparative satellite imagery of archaeological site looting in Syria, see http://eca.state.gov/cultural-heritage-center/syria-cultural-heritage-initiative/imagery-archaeological-site-looting.

[3] The term "Daesh" is an Arabic acronym formed from the group's previous name in Arabic- "al-Dawla al-Islamiya fil Iraq wa al-Sham". The term has negative connotations and has therefore gained currency as a way of challenging the legitimacy of the group. See, http://www.bbc.com/news/world-middle-east-27994277

[4] Illustrative of the brutality that the Islamic State exhibits against those with opposing views regarding cultural heritage preservation was the kidnapping and subsequent murder in 2015 of Syrian archaeologist Khaled al-Asaad, known as "Mr. Palmyra." Others involved in the protection of Syrian cultural heritage have reportedly been targeted by the Islamic State. "Syrian Archaeologist 'Killed in Palmyra' by IS Militants," *BBC*, August 19, 2015; Bowley (New York Times), October 3, 2014.

[5] Myers and Kulish (New York Times), January 9, 2016.

(UNESCO) Director-General Irina Bokova considers the Islamic State's destruction of cultural heritage sites to be an international war crime.[6]

Global Context

Concrete data on the global value of the illicit art and cultural property trade are not available, but the U.S. Federal Bureau of Investigation (FBI) estimates that such crimes result in annual financial losses "in the billions of dollars."[7] In 2011, the non-governmental group Global Financial Integrity (GFI) conservatively averaged and aggregated existing figures to estimate that the value of the illicit trade of cultural property may range between $3.4 and $6.3 billion annually.[8] Drawing on GFI's estimates, the United Nations Office on Drugs and Crime (UNODC) estimated in 2011 that art and cultural property crime represented 0.8% of global proceeds of transnational crime.[9] Some substantially smaller portion of this total likely represents the illicit trade in antiquities, which is a narrow subset of the global art trade.[10]

According to a survey of archaeologists published in 2013, antiquities looting is neither isolated nor confined to certain regions or countries. Respondents to the survey reported archaeological looting activity in 103 of the 118 countries (87%) where they were conducting fieldwork.[11] In addition to the economic harm such illicit activity can produce, the theft, fraud, looting, and trafficking of cultural heritage can jeopardize the preservation of a nation's identity, culture, and history.[12] Also contributing to cultural heritage loss, particularly during periods of armed conflict, is the damage to or destruction of artifacts, heritage sites, and cultural materials of national and international importance.

In 2011, the RAND Corporation described the illegal trade in cultural property as typically involving six stages in the supply chain (see **Figure 1** below).[13] The

---

[6] United Nations Educational, Scientific, and Cultural Organization (UNESCO), "UNESCO Mobilizes the International Community to End Cultural Cleansing in Iraq," press release, March 11, 2015.

[7] Federal Bureau of Investigation (FBI), *Art Theft*, https://www.fbi.gov/about-us/investigate/vc_majorthefts/arttheft.

[8] Jeremy Haken, *Transnational Crime in the Developing World*, Global Financial Integrity, February 2011.

[9] United Nations Office on Drugs and Crime (UNODC), *Estimating Illicit Financial Flows Resulting from Drug Trafficking and Other Transnational Organized Crimes*, research report, October 2011.

[10] According to the International Association of Dealers in Ancient Art, the global licit trade in antiquities roughly amounts to less than $200 million per year. See Angela M.H. Schuster, "The Power 100 of 2015: The Pillaging of the Middle East," *Blouin ArtInfo*, December 28, 2105.

[11] Blythe Bowman Proulx, "Archaeological Site Looting in 'Glocal' Perspective: Nature, Scope, and Frequency," *American Journal of Archaeology*, Vol. 117 (2013), pp. 111-125.

[12] INTERPOL, Office of Legal Affairs, *Countering Illicit Trade in Goods: A Guide for Policy-Makers*, 2014.

[13] Siobhán Ní Chonaill, Anaïs Reding, and Lorenzo Valeri, *Assessing the Illegal Trade in Cultural Property from a Public Policy Perspective*, RAND Europe, 2011.

process begins with the supplier who loots or otherwise steals the cultural object or artifact. The typical looter receives less than 1% of the retail value of the stolen object (other estimates range up to 2%), while the dealers and traders receive the largest share of the profits.[14] Along the supply chain, the illicit antiquities trade may intersect with networks of organized criminals, corrupt officials and arts brokers, and, at times, terrorist or insurgent groups. In recent years, the growing use of the Internet, through peer-to-peer sales websites, online auctions, and social media platforms, has complicated law enforcement efforts to thwart the smuggling and sale of cultural artifacts.[15]

Figure 1. The Six Stages of the Illegal Trade in Cultural Property
(an illustrative typology)

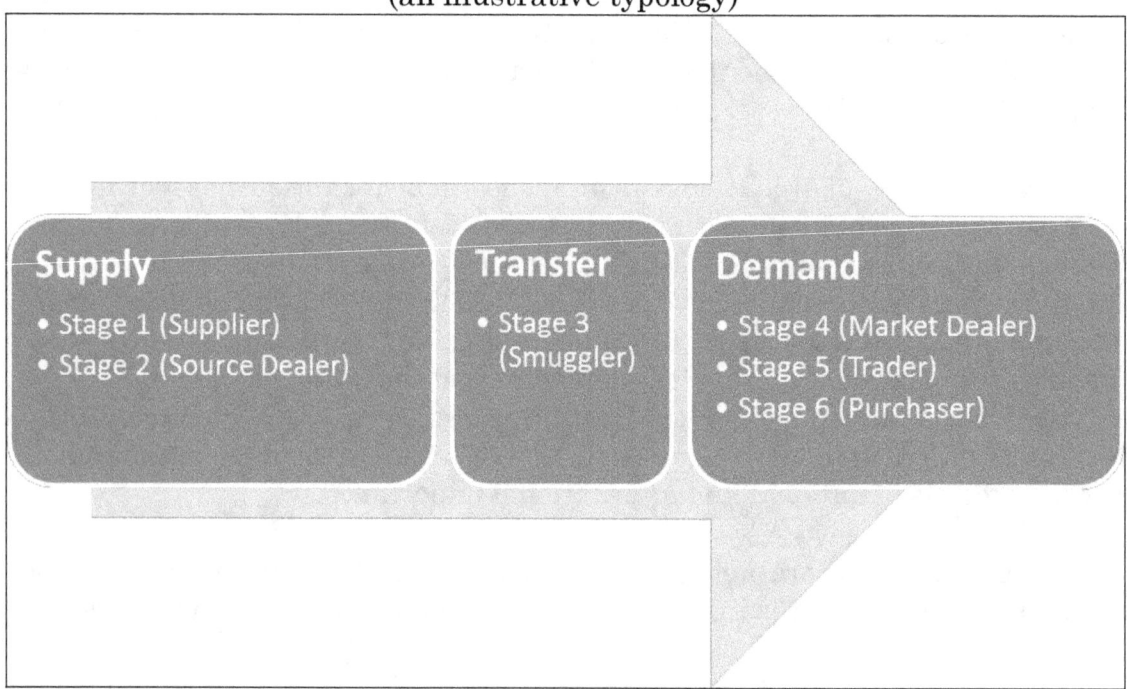

Supply
- Stage 1 (Supplier)
- Stage 2 (Source Dealer)

Transfer
- Stage 3 (Smuggler)

Demand
- Stage 4 (Market Dealer)
- Stage 5 (Trader)
- Stage 6 (Purchaser)

Source: CRS adaptation of the RAND Corporation's study (2011).
Notes: The RAND study indicates that the illegal trade in cultural property begins with the supplier who loots or steals a desirable cultural artifact. Next in the supply chain is the source dealer who arranges transport, via a smuggler, to a market dealer, usually a professional art or antiquities dealer. The source dealer often has advanced knowledge of art history or archaeology in order to create false documents certifying authenticity and provenance. Smugglers, in turn, receive a fee for providing the logistics of physically transporting the looted good from the supplying source location to locations where market demand for the item exists. Market dealers often have close connections to the source zones and supply retail outlets with artifacts and cultural objects currently in demand.

The final retail purchaser obtains the product from a cultural property salesperson or retail outlet (e.g., antique shops, auction houses, or underground art and

---

[14] See also Neil Brodie, Jenny Doole, and Peter Watson, *Stealing History: The Illicit Trade in Cultural Material*, The McDonald Institute for Archaeological Research, 2000.
[15] INTERPOL, *Countering Illicit Trade in Goods*, 2014.

antiquities traders). The final retail purchasers may include criminal groups seeking a non-cash form of stored value to launder proceeds of crime; or private collectors, museums, and other cultural institutions, some of whom may be unaware of the illicit origins of the product due to falsified provenance and import/export paperwork.

Terrorism Links to Looting and Destruction

Reports indicate that illicit armed groups, including terrorists, have sought to benefit opportunistically from the trade in cultural property. In general, terrorist, insurgent, or paramilitary groups may raise funds through the trafficking of antiquities or other cultural property by (1) controlling the illicit network, (2) directly facilitating the movement of contraband items for a fee, or (3) levying "taxes" that authorize criminal smugglers to loot or transit through their controlled territory unharmed.

According to a 2005 article in the German periodical *Der Spiegel*, Mohammed Atta, one of the Al Qaeda hijackers on September 11, 2001, sought advice from a German university professor in 1999 on how to sell potentially valuable cultural artifacts from Afghanistan.[16] German authorities surmised that Atta was exploring terrorist fundraising options. In 2010, a report published by the Counter Terrorism Center (CTC) at West Point found that illicit antiquities traders based in the United Arab Emirates (UAE) would provide the Haqqani Network and the Taliban with protection payments, though often described as donations, in order to "avoid trouble on the road."[17] In 1974, the Irish Republican Army (IRA) stole 19 paintings by artists such as Johannas Vermeer, Francisco Goya, and Diego Velázquez from a Dublin estate and attempted to negotiate their return in exchange for a ransom payment and the release of several political prisoners.[18]

Antiquities smuggling also occurred throughout the 1980s and 1990s under the Iraqi Ba'athist regime of Saddam Hussein, particularly as a means to generate income amid international sanctions.[19] Following Hussein's fall in 2003, antiquities smuggling across the thousands of unguarded archaeological sites in Iraq became a source of financing for both Sunni and Shia militias and insurgents, including Al Qaeda in Iraq (AQI) and the Islamic State of Iraq (ISI), the predecessors to today's Islamic State. In June 2005, for example, the U.S. military discovered both antiquities and weapons caches during a series of raids on insurgent underground

---

[16] "Kunst als Terrorfinancierung?" *Der Spiegel*, July 18, 2005.

[17] Gretchen Peters, *Crime and Insurgency in the Tribal Areas of Afghanistan and Pakistan*, Combating Terrorism Center (CTC) at West Point, October 14, 2010.

[18] See for example Damian Corless, "No Regrets for Renegade IRA Art Robber Rose Dugdale," *Independent (Ireland)*, April 5, 2014.

[19] Phil Williams, *Criminals, Militias, and Insurgents: Organized Crime in Iraq*, Strategic Studies Institute, June 2009; Yaya J. Fanusie and Alexander Joffe, *Monumental Fight: Countering the Islamic State's Antiquities Trafficking*, Foundation for the Defense of Democracies (FDD), Center on Sanctions and Illicit Finance, November 2015.

bunkers.[20] Al-Nusrah Front for the People of the Levant (ANF), an Al Qaeda affiliate in Syria, also reportedly profits, although less pervasively than the Islamic State, from antiquities looting—as have most non-state actors involved in the Syrian conflict and the Bashar al-Assad regime.[21]

In addition to smuggling art and antiquities, armed groups including the Islamic State have also destroyed cultural heritage for ideological reasons. In 2012, the Al Qaeda-affiliated Ansar Dine in Mali destroyed monuments and other cultural heritage in Timbuktu. In 2001, the Taliban destroyed the giant Buddha statues in Bamiyan. More recently, the Al Qaeda-affiliated Ansar Al-Sharia in Yemen also destroyed tombs, shrines, and other archaeological sites. Islamist militants in Libya are also implicated or suspected in cultural heritage destruction. In other instances, conflict, political instability, corruption, and post-conflict insecurity contribute to a surge in antiquities looting and trafficking.[22] Unsanctioned looters may inadvertently destroy some cultural artifacts when using indiscriminate techniques to excavate and bulldozer archaeological sites. It is also possible that public displays of cultural heritage destruction could have the two-fold effect of perpetuating radical ideology while also raising international demand for rare artifacts.

Antiquities and Islamic State Financing

Numerous reports indicate that the Islamic State encourages and profits from antiquities looting in the territory it controls. Experts indicate that antiquities looting in the region predated the Islamic State. As the group seized control of territory, it also began to regulate and tax the pre-existing looting economy. Within the past year, amid greater pressure on its financial resources, the Islamic State ratcheted up its regulatory control and enforcement of antiquities extraction activities.

In November 2014, the United Nation Security Council's (UNSC) Al Qaeda Analytical Support and Sanctions Monitoring Team reported that, although the risk of looting and trafficking of antiquities was known, the Islamic State's involvement

---

[20] Matthew Bogdanos, "The Terrorist in the Art Gallery," *New York Times*, opinion, December 10, 2005.

[21] United Nations Security Council (UNSC), *Assessment by the Analytical Support and Sanctions Monitoring Team of the Impact of the Measures Imposed in Security Council Resolution 2199 (2015), Pursuant to Paragraph 30 of the Resolution: Chair's Summary*, S/2015/739, September 25, 2015; Brigadier General (Ret.) Russell Howard, Jonathan Prohov, and Marc Elliott, "Digging in and Trafficking Out: How the Destruction of Cultural Heritage Funds Terrorism," *CTC Sentinel*, CTC at West Point, February 27, 2015.

[22] Heather Pringle, "New Evidence Ties Illegal Antiquities Trade to Terrorism, Violent Crime: In Cambodia and Beyond, Archaeologists and Criminologists are Fighting the Underground Trade in Cultural Treasures," *National Geographic*, June 13, 2014; Deborah M. Lehr and Katie A. Paul, "Rocking the Cradle of Civilization: Antiquities Theft Funding Terrorists," *Huffington Post*, blog, July 2, 2014; Simon Mackenzie and Tess Davis, "Temple Looting in Cambodia: Anatomy of a Statue Trafficking Network," *British Journal of Criminology*, Vol. 54 (2014), pp. 722-740.

in such activity "has become more systematic and organized."[23] In February 2015, the Financial Action Task Force (FATF), an intergovernmental body that promotes best practices and global guidance to combat money laundering and terrorist financing (AML/CFT), reported that one of several sources of IS revenue stems from the smuggling of cultural artifacts, whether through direct involvement or through the taxation of goods, including antiquities, that move through IS territory.[24]

Iraqi officials claimed in 2015 that the Islamic State could be generating as much as $100 million annually from antiquities.[25] Russian officials in March 2016 stated in a letter to the UNSC President that "[t]he profit derived by the Islamists from the illicit trade in antiquities and archaeological treasures is estimated at US$ 150-200 million per year."[26] In September 2015, the U.S. Department of State's Deputy Assistant Secretary for Counter Threat Finance and Sanctions Andrew Keller stated that: "The U.S. government assesses that ISIL has probably earned several million dollars from antiquities sales since mid-2014, but the precise amount is unknown."[27] Despite the lack of specific estimates, Brigadier General (Ret.) Russell Howard and others in an analysis published by the CTC at West Point nevertheless summarized the Islamic State's likely role in antiquities trafficking as follows:

> From our perspective, ISIL's involvement in antiquities looting and trafficking is clear, based on satellite imagery, anecdotal evidence, documentation by concerned citizens, and the similar involvement of ISIL predecessors al-Qa'ida in Iraq and the Islamic State of Iraq. Terrorists and looters are opportunists; given that ISIL derives much of its income from various illicit activities, it would be surprising if the group were not involved in what is believed to be the world's third

---

[23] UNSC, *The Islamic State in Iraq and the Levant and the Al-Nusrah Front for the People of the Levant: Report and Recommendations Submitted Pursuant to Resolution 2170 (2014)*, S/2014/815, November 14, 2014.

[24] Financial Action Task Force (FATF), *Financing of the Terrorist Organisation Islamic State in Iraq and the Levant (ISIL)*, February 2015.

[25] In June 2014, *The Guardian (UK)* reported that the Iraqi forces raided the home of an IS military leader near Mosul and collected "more than 160 computer flash sticks" with details on the organization's finances. The article quoted an Iraqi intelligence office as stating that the Islamic State had generated "$36m from al-Nabuk alone" and that "the antiquities there are up to 8,000 years old." This quote has generated debate among observers, who question whether the $36 million figure represents only antiquities looting or includes other sources of revenue. See Martin Chulov, "How an Arrest in Iraq Revealed ISIS's $2bn Jihadist Network," *The Guardian (UK)*, June 15, 2014.

[26] UNSC, *Smuggling of Antiquities by the International Terrorist Organization Islamic State in Iraq and the Levant*, letter and annex from the Permanent Representative of the Russian Federation to the United Nations addressed to the President of the Security Council, S/2016/298, March 31, 2016.

[27] U.S. Department of State (DOS), Bureau of Economic and Business Affairs, Deputy Assistant Secretary for Counter Threat Finance and Sanctions, Andrew Keller, "Documenting ISIL's Antiquities Trafficking: The Looting and Destruction of Iraqi and Syrian Cultural Heritage: What We Know and What Can Be Done," remarks at the Metropolitan Museum of Art, New York, September 29, 2015.

largest illicit market, particularly in a region that is home to some of the world's oldest and most valuable antiquities.[28]

Abu Sayyaf Raid

Since 2014, the U.S. Department of the Treasury, in congressional testimony and public remarks, has recognized that the Islamic State profits from a range of criminal activities, including looting and selling antiquities.[29] The U.S. government, however, did not publicly document evidence of the Islamic State's financial role in antiquities looting and trafficking until after the May 2015 U.S. Special Forces raid on the Syrian compound of Abu Sayyaf, the Islamic State's reputed finance chief and head of its administrative department for natural resources, the *Diwan al-Rikaz*. In addition to paperwork describing the bureaucratic processes used by the Islamic State to regulate their illicit antiquities trade (see **Figure 2** below), the U.S. military recovered a variety of archaeological and historical objects and fragments, including a mix of fakes and looted museum artifacts.

Figure 2. Organizational Structure of the Islamic State's Antiquities Division
(English translation of a document discovered during the Abu Sayyaf raid)

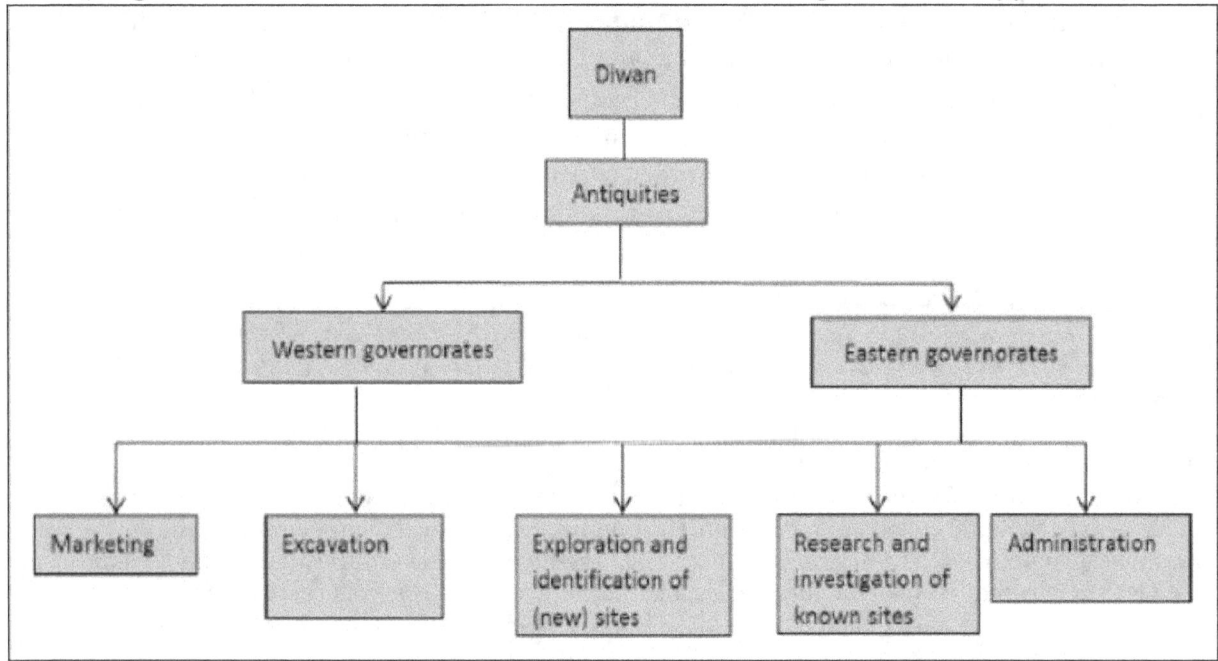

Source: U.S. Department of State (2015), http://www.state.gov/e/eb/rls/rm/2015/247739.htm.

---

[28] Howard, Prohov, and Elliott, "Digging in and Trafficking Out," *CTC Sentinel*, February 27, 2015.
[29] U.S. Department of the Treasury (Treasury), "Remarks of Under Secretary for Terrorism and Financial Intelligence David S. Cohen at the Carnegie Endowment for International Peace, 'Attacking ISIL's Financial Foundation,'" as prepared for delivery, October 23, 2014; Treasury, "Testimony of Under Secretary Cohen before the House Financial Services Committee on 'The Islamic State and Terrorist Financing,'" as prepared for delivery, November 13, 2014.

Based on declassified information collected during the raid, U.S. officials described the organizational infrastructure that the Islamic State has established to regulate the extraction of and profiteering from antiquities. According to the State Department, the *Diwan al-Rikaz* housed an antiquities division with "units dedicated to research of known sites, exploration of new sites, and marketing of antiquities."[30] Included in the cache were official Islamic State memoranda signed by Abu Sayyaf that authorized specific individuals to excavate and supervise excavation of artifacts. Receipts documented the levy of a 20 percent *khums* tax on the proceeds of looting.[31] In one book of receipts discovered during the raid, the Islamic State generated more than $265,000 in *khums* taxes between December 6, 2014 and March 26, 2015. Other documents described prohibitions on looting without an official permit.

Additional documents posted online by the blogger Aymenn Jawad Al-Tamimi appeared to emphasize the Islamic State's focus on regulating the antiquities trade and the revenue generated, including the enforcement of its administrative rules.[32] In congressional testimony from November 2015, the archaeologist Michael Danti acknowledged that the Islamic State has also confiscated and destroyed antiquities from unauthorized smugglers.[33] Archaeologist Amr Al-Azm has further claimed that the Islamic State supports the excavation of antiquities by supplying trucks and bulldozers, as well as hiring work crews; in these circumstances, looters would be required to obtain additional permits from IS authorities and pay enhanced taxes or fees upon sale of the looted artifacts.[34] Leftover artifacts that are not sold directly by the looters are eventually offered for sale in periodic auctions in Raqqa, Syria.[35]

Trafficking Pathways

In August 2015, the FBI issued a public alert about trading in antiquities from the Near East. The alert stated that the FBI has "credible reports that U.S. persons

---

[30] DOS (Keller), remarks at the Metropolitan Museum of Art, New York, September 29, 2015.

[31] Other sources have suggested that the antiquities looting-related fees collected by the Islamic State may be substantially higher in some cases. For example, if the Islamic States provides authorized looters with equipment to unearth the artifacts, the looters may be required to pay an enhanced percentage of the revenue derived from their sale. See Fanusie and Joffe (FDD), November 2015; "Following the Trail of Syria's Looted History," *CBS News*, September 9, 2015.

[32] Aymenn Jawad Al-Tamimi, "The Archivist: Unseen Islamic State Financial Accounts for Deir az-Zor Province," *Jihadology*, blog, October 5, 2015; Al-Tamimi, "The Archivist: Unseen Documents from the Islamic State's Diwan al-Rikaz," *Jihadology*, blog, October 12, 2015. Al-Tamimi's articles are available at http://www.aymennjawad.org/articles/.

[33] Prepared statement of Michael D. Danti, Director of Cultural Heritage Initiatives at the American Schools of Oriental Research, "Terrorist Financing: Kidnapping, Antiquities Trafficking, and Private Donations," hearing before the House Foreign Relations Subcommittee on Terrorism, Nonproliferation, and Trade, Serial No. 114-120, November 17, 2015.

[34] Sangwon Yoon, "Islamic State is Selling Looted Art Online for Needed Cash," *Bloomberg*, June 28, 2015.

[35] Ben Taub, "The Real Value of the ISIS Antiquities Trade," *New Yorker*, December 4, 2015.

have been offered cultural property that appears to have been removed from Syria and Iraq recently."[36] Media reports indicate that some looted antiquities from the region are being offered for retail sale while artifacts of questionable provenance have reportedly been seized by authorities in Turkey, Lebanon, Jordan, Europe, and the United States. Proving that such artifacts were excavated or authorized to be excavated by the Islamic State and that the Islamic State would financially benefit from such sales is difficult.

Observers describe the typical routes for smuggled antiquities flowing mainly through southern Turkey and the Bekaa Valley in Lebanon, potentially comingled among flows of refugees and other contraband items, including drugs.[37] Wholesale dealers will work with smugglers to fabricate provenance and other necessary claims of authenticity. Journalists and independent investigators have described the marketing of looted antiquities through online websites and social networks. Retail buyers may include individuals in the region, who purchase small items at local markets, as well as high-value investors and collectors in Europe, the United States, China, and the Persian Gulf. The archaeologist Markus Hilgert has described a geographic divide in demand for antiquities, with pre-Islamic objects marketed in Europe and North America and Islamic art smuggled to countries in the Gulf.[38]

Some observers have identified gaps between supply and demand of looted antiquities from Syria and Iraq. Although there is a conventional assumption that the black market in antiquities remains lucrative because demand exceeds supply, others note that few Syrian antiquities in recent years have been publicly sold at auction.[39] Experts point to dealer stockpiling as the reason for the seeming disconnect between satellite imagery of apparently looted archaeological sites and the dearth of recent sales of antiquities sourced from Iraq and Syria. Some of the more valuable items may be stored for years or even decades before resurfacing for

---

[36] FBI, "ISIL Antiquities Trafficking," August 25, 2015.

[37] Some have further indicated that smugglers may use trafficking routes through the desert in Jordan as well as potentially through Iran. Shabi (The Guardian), July 3, 2015; Joe Parkinson and Duncan Mavin, "West Seeks Tighter Curbs on Trade in Antiquities Looted by Islamic State: Images of Militants Destroying Artifacts Spurred News Push," *Wall Street Journal*, March 30, 2015; Fanusie and Joffe (FDD), November 2015.

[38] Myers and Kulish (New York Times), January 9, 2016.

[39] In the last eight years, only 50 Syrian objects were reportedly sold by Christie's in the United States and a similar amount was reportedly sold by Sotheby's. See Kate Fitz Gibbon, "Heritage Protection Depends on Stable Governments," *New York Times*, opinion, October 9, 2014. To the extent that black market trends in antiquities trafficking correspond to trends in the import and export licit art, antiques, and artifacts, some analysts have noted upticks in U.S. imports from Iraq, Syria, and other countries in the region of potentially related categories of trade, such as antiques. See Loveday Morris, "Islamic State Isn't Just Destroying Ancient Artifacts – It's Selling Them," *Washington Post*, June 8, 2015; Mark V. Vlasic and Helga Turku, "Countering IS's Theft and Destruction of Mesopotamia," *World Policy Journal*, blog, July 7, 2015; and Fanusie and Joffe (FDD), November 2015.

public sale, providing dealers with time to establish more convincingly false provenance. A U.S. Department of Homeland Security official speculated that some looted antiquities may be located in so-called "free ports," where goods in transit are exempt from customs duty and which are reportedly used by wealthy art collectors to store valuables.[40]

Smaller, potentially more generic artifacts such as statuettes, pottery, carved cylinder seals, and coins, have been reportedly marketed. Photos documenting such items appear to be circulating among prospective buyers. Although such items are typically worth less than rare museum-quality artifacts, their provenance is more easily obscured and thus more marketable in the short term.[41] Coins, for example, are not always easily traceable to specific archaeological sites, particularly to sites under IS control. According to Yaya Fanusi and Alexander Joffe, researchers at the Foundation for Defense of Democracies (FDD):

> Certain categories of artifacts found in Syria during the Classical (roughly the fourth century BCE to the sixth century CE) and early Islamic periods (seventh to 11th centuries CE) are easily mistaken to originate from elsewhere. They share stylistic or artistic features with other regions of the Middle East and the Mediterranean away from the conflict. Misidentifying artifacts or attributing to them a generic origin lessens the scrutiny on the part of middlemen and buyers who want to avoid purchasing looted wartime artifacts.[42]

Selected Policy Considerations

The U.S. government actively investigates cases of art and antiquities trafficking, repatriates looted artifacts, and supports academic, non-governmental, and international efforts to raise awareness as well as to conserve and protect cultural heritage. Efforts to disrupt IS finances, one of nine strategies outlined by President Barack Obama to counter the Islamic State, includes diminishing IS profits from antiquities smuggling. In August 2015, the FBI notified the public that buyers of IS-looted antiquities could face criminal charges of violating U.S. material support for terrorism laws.[43] In September 2015, the State Department announced the offering of a reward—up to $5 million—for "information leading to the significant

---

[40] Freeports were traditionally used to store traded goods and commodities in transit duty free, pending further duty-paid import or re-export to another jurisdiction. Yoon (Bloomberg), June 28, 2015. See also "Freeports: über-warehouses for the Ultra-Rich," *The Economist*, November 23, 2013.
[41] Provenance refers to a cultural item's history of ownership from the time of its recovery until the present. For a possible example of the difficulty of selling on the black market a rare artifact looted in Iraq whose provenance would be difficult to disguise, see Isabel Hunter, "Syria Conflict: The Illicit Art Trade that is a Major Source of Income for Today's Terror Groups is Nothing New," *Independent on Sunday (UK)*, April 25, 2015.
[42] Fanusie and Joffe (FDD), November 2015.
[43] FBI, "ISIL Antiquities Trafficking," August 25, 2015.

disruption" of IS-related antiquities or oil smuggling.[44] As discussed above, antiquities-related information collected during the U.S. military's raid on Abu Sayyaf's compound in May 2015 also significantly contributed to the international community's understanding of how the Islamic State regulates and financially profits from looting.

At the international level, FATF recommended in February 2015 that financial institutions and the private sector improve efforts to prevent suspicious transactions that involve looted antiquities:

> Those who buy the artifacts or their proxies at some point intersect with the regulated financial system in order to send or receive payments.... The financing for the buying and selling of tainted antiquities can be disrupted by auction houses, financial institutions, and other legitimate businesses involved in the antiquities trade, by urging these institutions to adopt or implement policies that require clear, certified documentation that identifies the origin of the artefacts. Banks should refrain from processing transactions for antiquities that originate in Iraq or Syria. Steps could be taken to ensure that private sector actors have a better understanding of the sites in Iraq and Syria that are being plundered and of the routes that are being used. In addition, dealers in the antiquities realm could be urged to report suspicious behavior, fraudulent paperwork or knowledge of stolen artifact circulation.[45]

In February 2015, the United Nations Security Council (UNSC) passed resolution 2199, which requires all Member States to

> take appropriate steps to prevent the trade in Iraqi and Syrian cultural property and other items of archaeological, historical, cultural, rare scientific, and religious importance illegally removed from Iraq since 6 August 1990 and from Syria since 15 March 2011, including by prohibiting cross-border trade in such items, thereby allowing for their eventual safe return to the Iraqi and Syrian people.[46]

In December 2015, the UNSC passed resolution 2253, which has been newly strengthens the existing Al-Qaeda sanctions regime and further UNSC's Al-Qaeda sanctions committee, which has been newly renamed to include the Islamic State in its title, to

---

[44] DOS, Office of the Spokesperson, "Rewards for Justice: Reward Offers for Information that Leads to Disruption of Financing of Islamic State of Iraq and the Levant (ISIL)," media note, September 29, 2015.

[45] FATF, February 2015.

[46] UNSC, S/RES/2199 (2015), February 12, 2015.

immediately consider, in accordance with its resolution 2199 (2015), designations of individuals and entities engaged in financing, supporting, facilitating acts or activities, including in oil and antiquities trade-related activities with ISIL, Al-Qaida, and associated individuals, groups, undertakings and entities.[47]

To date, no IS-affiliated individuals have been designated for such UNSC sanctions. Groups such as the Antiquities Coalition have advocated for further U.S. implementation of UNSCRs 2199 and 2253, including the application of U.S. import restrictions on Syrian antiquities, similar to those already in place for Iraqi antiquities.[48]

In addition, the Treasury Department maintains unilateral sanctions to combat global terrorism, including the Islamic State. To date, one designated individual has been publicly described by the Treasury Department as linked to IS-related antiquities activities: Sami Jasim Muhammad al-Jaburi, designated under Executive Order 13224 in September 2015 and reportedly involved in the supervision of the Islamic State's oil and gas, antiquities, and mineral resources operations.[49] In March 2015, several Members of Congress called on the Treasury Department to "impose sanctions on importers of cultural property unlawfully removed from Syria" that would mirror regulations already established for Iraq.[50] The 114th Congress has also addressed antiquities trafficking through hearings. In June 2015, the House passed H.R. 1493, the Protect and Preserve International Cultural Property Act. In July 2015, the Senate introduced S. 1887 with the same title as the House version. On April 13, 2016, the Senate passed H.R. 1493 with an amendment. Groups such as the Antiquities Coalition have endorsed the proposed legislation, arguing that it would help the United States fulfill its obligations under UNSCRs 1299 and 2253.[51] Others, including advocates of the rare coin trade, have expressed concern that new import restrictions on Syrian antiquities trade would be applied by U.S. border and customs authorities too broadly and that such policy actions would do little to change the current behavior of the Islamic State, as it reaps the financial benefits of antiquities looting well before artifacts reach Western buyers.[52]

---

[47] UNSC, S/RES/2253 (2015), December 17, 2015.

[48] Antiquities Coalition, *#CultureUnderThreat: Recommendations for the U.S. Government*, April 2016.

[49] Treasury, "Treasury Sanctions Major Islamic State of Iraq and the Levant Leaders, Financial Figures, Facilitators, and Supporters," press release, September 29, 2015.

[50] House Foreign Affairs Committee, "Engel, Royce, Keating, And Smith Urge Treasury To Block Import Of Antiquities Looted From Syria," press release, March 30, 2015.

[51] Antiquities Coalition, April 2016.

[52] See for example Peter Tompa, "2015's Questionable Claims on ISIS and Syrian Antiquities: To Hopes for More Accuracy and Less Hype in 2016," *Cultural Property Observer*, blog, January 6, 2016.

May 24, 2016 Task Force to Investigate Terrorism Financing hearing titled "Stopping Terror Finance: A Coordinated Government Effort"

Terrorist Financing Threats

According to the Financial Action Task Force (FATF)—an intergovernmental technical entity long focused on international standards-setting for anti-money laundering (AML) and combating the financing of terrorism (CFT)—terrorist methods for raising and managing funds have evolved since its original 2008 typologies report on terrorist financing.[1] In addition to the traditional means of raising, moving, and using terrorist funds (i.e., fundraising through charities, private donors, state sponsors, etc., and the use of formal financial institutions, informal value transfer methods, and bulk cash smuggling for moving funds internationally), FATF identified in October 2015 four "emerging terrorist financing threats and vulnerabilities," including financial considerations associated with Foreign Terrorist Fighters (FTFs), fundraising through social media, the exploitation of new payment products and services (e.g., virtual currencies), and the appropriation of natural resources for profit.[2]

The U.S. Intelligence Community has identified similar themes in an evolving terrorist financing environment. Director of National Intelligence (DNI) James Clapper identified the Internet as a critical platform made use of by modern terrorist groups, especially the Islamic State, "to organize, recruit, spread propaganda, collect intelligence, raise funds, and coordinate operations."[3] The terrorist financial support provided by FTFs is also an issue of concern, given the sheer number of FTFs known to have traveled to Syria since 2012 and their diverse origins, including from the United States. According to DNI Clapper, the number of U.S.-based IS-supporters arrested by the Federal Bureau of Investigation (FBI), mainly for attempting to provide material support to the Islamic State, grew from "approximately one dozen" in 2014 to "approximately five dozen" in 2015.[4]

According to the U.S. Department of the Treasury (Treasury), these threats collectively represent a source of risk to the U.S. financial system, as some terrorist organizations continue to seek access to the U.S. financial system to facilitate their

---

[1] Financial Action Task Force (FATF), Emerging Terrorist Financing Risks, October 2015.
[2] Ibid.
[3] James Clapper, Director of National Intelligence, prepared statement for a hearing on the "Worldwide Threat Assessment of the U.S. Intelligence Community," Senate Armed Services Committee, February 9, 2016. With respect to the Islamic State, Clapper stated in earlier testimony that "the group has been executing a highly strategic social media campaign using a diverse array of platforms and thousands of online supporters around the globe. The group quickly builds expertise in the platforms it uses and often leverages multiple tools within each platform. ISIL and its adherents' adept use of social media allows the group to maximize the spread of its propaganda and reach out to potential recruits." See Clapper prepared statement for a hearing on "Worldwide Cyber Threats," House Permanent Select Committee on Intelligence, September 10, 2015.
[4] Clapper prepared statement on Worldwide Threats (February 9, 2016).

activities. Treasury's June 2015 National Terrorist Financing Risk Assessment, the first of its kind, concluded that "[t]he central role of the U.S. financial system within the international financial system and the sheer volume and diversity of international financial transactions that in some way pass through U.S. financial institutions expose the U.S. financial system to TF [terrorist financing] risks that other financial systems may not face."[5]

Recent Financing Developments

Islamic State

Recent assessments indicate that the Islamic State's financial assets have declined, but remain significant. According to Daniel Glaser, Treasury's Assistant Secretary for Terrorist Financing, oil revenue generated by the Islamic State has dropped from approximately $500 million per year to "probably... about half of what they previously have been making."[6] Additionally, Glaser estimates that the Islamic State generates approximately $360 million per year broadly in "taxation."[7] Based on open source analysis, the non-governmental organization IHS Conflict Monitor estimated in April 2016 that the Islamic State's overall monthly revenue has fallen since the previous summer.[8] IHS estimates that oil and gas revenue dropped from $31 million to $23 million per month. Despite declines in production, due in part to an intensified military air campaign through Operation Tidal Wave II, the Islamic State has reportedly not increased the price of oil. IHS further estimates that the Islamic State's revenue for taxation and confiscation has also declined in the past year from $39 million to $30 million per month due to declines in territory and population. The Islamic State's financial strains have manifested in reported cuts in FTF salaries and amplified tax collection practices levied against local populations.

Hezbollah

Although Hezbollah has been designated as a Foreign Terrorist Organization by the U.S. Department of State since 1997, U.S. officials describe a reinvigorated U.S. focus on targeting the group's finances in the past five years, which some observers say is paying off.[9] Hezbollah's global reach became more visible during this time period, as plots were uncovered in countries that spanned Bulgaria, Cyprus, Peru, and Thailand. Its role as a regional destabilizer also concerned policymakers, particularly its role in the Syrian conflict as a proxy for Iranian interests and

---

[5] U.S. Department of the Treasury, National Terrorist Financing Risk Assessment, June 12, 2015.

[6] Foundation for Defense of Democracies, transcript of event on "State of Play: Combating Today's Illicit Financial Networks," May 11, 2016.

[7] Ibid.

[8] IHS Conflict Monitor, An Assessment of the Islamic State in Iraq and Syria, monthly report, April 2016.

[9] Foundation for Defense of Democracies, transcript (May 11, 2016). See also Matthew Levitt (Washington Institute for Near East Policy), "The Crackdown on Hezbollah's Financing Network," Wall Street Journal, opinion, January 27, 2016; Devlin Barrett, "U.S. Intensifies Bid to Defund

Hezbollah," Wall Street Journal, December 16, 2015.

supporter of the Bashar al-Assad regime.[10] With Treasury's designation of Lebanese Canadian Bank SAL in February 2011 as a financial institution of primary money laundering concern, pursuant to Section 311 of the USA PATRIOT Act, Hezbollah's role in Latin American cocaine trafficking, West African trade-based money laundering schemes, and exploitation of Lebanese exchange houses were also publicly revealed. Hezbollah spokespeople denied links to such activities.[11] Since 2011, pressure on the group has persisted through targeted financial sanctions, law enforcement investigations, and judicial prosecutions, as well as mounting costs associated with its involvement in Syria and reductions in Iranian financial support.[12] Notably, on December 18, 2015, President Barack Obama signed into law the Hizballah International Financing Prevention Act of 2015 (P.L. 114-102), which requires enhanced restrictions on foreign financial institutions that facilitate financial transactions and services for Hezbollah. Adding pressure, the European Union (in 2013) and more recently the Gulf Cooperation Council and the Arab League (in March 2016) have designated Hezbollah a terrorist organization.[13]

Iran Sanctions

Despite the lifting of U.S. and EU sanctions on Iran's civilian economic sectors on January 16, 2016, known as Implementation Day of the Joint Comprehensive Plan of Action (JCPOA), reports indicate that many major European banks remain hesitant to re-enter the Iran market by providing trade financing and other financial services, causing Iranian officials to complain about the lack of anticipated benefits associated with JCPOA sanctions relief. Iran has increased its oil exports to about 2.35 million barrels per day, close to 2011 levels, and it is able to access approximately $55 billion in foreign exchange assets (this is a Treasury estimate net of funds already obligated or locked in illiquid projects).[14] Still, European banks reportedly remain reluctant to conduct Iran-linked business due in part to the continuation of unilateral U.S. financial sanctions against Iran for purposes other than proliferation, including terrorism, regional destabilization, missile and human rights violations, as well as a lack of transparency in Iran's financial sector. Senior U.S. officials, including Secretary of State John Kerry, have met with various government and financial sector representatives to clarify that most forms of

[10] For further discussion see Matthew Levitt, "Hezbollah's Transnational Organized Crime," Washington Institute for Near East Policy, April 21, 2016.
[11] U.S. Department of the Treasury, "Treasury Identifies Lebanese Canadian Bank SAL as a 'Primary Money Laundering Concern,'" press release, February 10, 2011; Jo Becker, "Beirut Bank Seen as a Hub of Hezbollah's Financing," New York Times, December 13, 2011.
[12] See for example, U.S. Drug Enforcement Administration (DEA), "DEA and European Authorities Uncover Massive Hizballah Drug and Money Laundering Scheme," press release, February 1, 2016.
[13] Justyna Pawlak and Adrian Croft, "EU Adds Hezbollah's Military Wing to Terrorism List," Reuters, July 22, 2013; Hugh Naylor, "In Jab at Iran, Gulf Arab States Declare Hezbollah a Terrorist Group," Washington Post, March 2, 2106; BBC, "Arab League Brands Hezbollah a Terrorist Organization," March 11, 2016.
[14] Glenn Kessler, "Kerry's Claim that Iran Has Only Received '$3 billion' from the Nuclear Deal," Washington Post, fact checker, May 11, 2016.

foreign financial activity with Iran are now permissible and that major
international banks should resume transactions with Iran. Still, the Financial
Action Task Force (FATF) continues to identify Iran as one of two countries in the
world (the other is North Korea) with strategic deficiencies in anti-money
laundering and combating the financing of terrorism (AML/CFT). European banks
such as Standard Chartered and HSBC, which have in the past been targeted for
sanctions violations and lax AML/CFT regimes, have reportedly continued more
conservative policies regarding business with Iranian clients than U.S. and other
laws may require.[15]

Strategic CFT Guidance

The U.S. government does not maintain a single strategic document or interagency
implementation plan for combating the financing of terrorism (CFT). Instead,
policy guidance can be found pertaining to CFT in the 2015 National Security
Strategy and the 2011 Counterterrorism Strategy. CFT policy objectives are also
summarized in Treasury's 2015 National Terrorist Financing Risk Assessment. In
August 2010, the U.S. Department of Defense also issued Directive Number 5205.14
(updated in October 2015) on Counter Threat Finance Policy. At the international
level, the FATF has also recently issued a consolidated CFT strategy (see text box,
below).

2015 National Security Strategy. The most recent National Security Strategy is
organized into four thematic chapters: "security," "prosperity," "values," and
"international order." The security chapter addresses, among other topics,
counterterrorism priorities, particularly with respect to Al Qaeda, the Islamic State,
and their affiliates. CFT is addressed in the prosperity chapter, within the context
of international efforts "to promote financial transparency and prevent the global
financial system from being abused by transnational criminal and terrorist
organizations...."[16]

2011 Counterterrorism Strategy. The most recent Counterterrorism Strategy
identifies eight overarching counterterrorism goals, including the goal to "deprive
terrorists of their enabling means."[17] In a subsection on "terrorist financing," the
strategy notes that "[t]he United States will continue to emphasize disrupting the

[15] Financial Action Task Force (FATF), "FATF Public Statement," February 19, 2016; Martin Arnold,
Geoff Dyer, and Najmeh Bozorgmehr, "European Banks Resist Calls to Increase Ties with Iran,"
Financial Times, May 11, 2016; Stuart Levy, "Kerry's Peculiar Message About Iran for European
Banks," Wall Street Journal, opinion, May 13, 2016. See also: Rep. Ed Royce, "The United States
Must Not Aid and Abet Iranian Money Laundering," Washington Post, opinion, April 5, 2016; Rep.
Peter Roskam, "Don't Be So Quick to Do Business with Iran," Wall Street Journal, opinion, March
31, 2016; Mark Dubowitz and Jonathan Schanzer, "Dollarizing the Ayatollahs," Wall Street Journal,
opinion, March 27, 2016.

[16] White House (Obama Administration), National Security Strategy, February 6, 2015.

[17] White House (Obama Administration), National Strategy for Counterterrorism, June 28, 2011.

access of terrorists—especially al-Qa'ida, its affiliates, and its adherents—to sources of financial support." Specified approaches to address terrorist financing include to:

- "expand and enhance efforts aimed at blocking the flow of financial assets to and among terrorist groups" through sanctions and prosecutions against sanctions violators;
- "push for enhanced unilateral action" against financiers and facilitators located in the Arabian Peninsula and for closer cooperation among Gulf states with the United States, "while retaining our ability to take unilateral action as well;" and
- "encourage countries—especially those in Europe—to adopt a policy against making concessions to kidnappers while using tailored messages unilaterally and with our partners to delegitimize the taking of hostages."

2015 National Terrorist Financing Risk Assessment. Although Treasury's National Terrorist Financing Risk Assessment analyzes risks to the U.S. financial system more than it provides strategic guidance, the executive summary outlines the U.S. government's rationale for CFT activity:

> After the September 11, 2001 terrorist attacks, the United States adopted a preventive approach to combating all forms of terrorist activity. Efforts to combat the financing of terrorism (CFT) are a central pillar of this approach. Cutting off financial support to terrorists and terrorist organizations is essential to disrupting their operations and preventing attacks. To that end, the U.S. government has sought to identify and disrupt ongoing terrorist financing (TF) and to prevent future TF.[18]

FATF's Consolidated CFT Strategy

In February 2016 the intergovernmental Financial Action Task Force (FATF) issued a new "Consolidated FATF Strategy on Combatting Terrorist Financing."[19] According to FATF, "the scope and nature of terrorist threats globally intensified" in 2015, resulting in calls for "further concerted action" to be "urgently" taken "to strengthen global counter-terrorist financing regimes to combat the financing of these serious terrorist threats, and contribute to strengthening the financial and economy system, and security." The new FATF CFT strategy document identified five key policy objectives and specified the priority actions required to achieve these objectives. The key policy objectives are to:

- "Improve and update the understanding of terrorist financing risks, and in particular the financing of ISIL/Da'esh."
- "Ensure that the FATF Standards provide up-to-date and effective tools to

---

[18] U.S. Department of the Treasury, National Terrorist Financing Risk Assessment, June 12, 2015.
[19] Financial Action Task Force (FATF), Consolidated FATF Strategy on Combatting Terrorist Financing, February 19, 2016.

> identify and disrupt terrorist financing activity."
> - "Ensure countries are appropriately and effectively applying the tools, including U.N. Targeted Financial Sanctions, to identify and disrupt terrorist financing activity."
> - "Identify and take measures in relation to any countries with strategic deficiencies for terrorist financing."
> - "Promote more effective domestic coordination and international cooperation to combat the financing of terrorism."

Legislative Reporting Requirements

As required by Congress, the State Department submits two annual reports on matters related to terrorist financing. Until 2007, Congress had also required Treasury to prepare a national money laundering strategy.

Country Reports on Terrorism

One of the current annual reports is the Country Reports on Terrorism, submitted pursuant to Section 140 of the Foreign Relations Authorization Act, Fiscal Years 1988 and 1989 (P.L. 100-204), as amended and codified at 22 U.S.C. 2656f. The most recent report was published by the Bureau of Counterterrorism in April 2015, covering developments in the previous calendar year.[20] It included a chapter on "countering terrorism on the economic front," which listed sanctions designations made by the State Department, including changes to the Foreign Terrorist Organization list and Executive Order 13224. For each country described in the report, there is a section on "countering the financing of terrorism." Also, in the chapter on Foreign Terrorist Organizations, the report includes a brief section on "funding and external aid."

International Narcotics Strategy Report

The second congressionally mandated reporting requirement is the International Narcotics Control Strategy Report (INCSR), submitted pursuant to Section 489 of the Foreign Assistance Act of 1961 (P.L. 87-195), as added by Section 5(a) of the International Narcotics Control Act of 1992 and subsequently amended. The provision is also codified at 22 U.S.C. 2291h. The report is required, among other provisions, to identify "major money laundering countries" defined as "a country whose financial institutions engage in currency transactions involving significant amounts of proceeds from international narcotics trafficking" and to include:

> Information on multilateral and bilateral strategies with respect to money laundering pursued by the Department of State, the Department of Justice, the Department of the Treasury, and other relevant United States Government agencies, either collectively or individually, to ensure the cooperation of foreign governments with

---

[20] Available at http://www.state.gov/j/ct/rls/crt/2014/index.htm.

respect to narcotics-related money laundering and to demonstrate that all United States Government agencies are pursuing a common strategy with respect to major money laundering countries. The report shall include specific detail to demonstrate that all United States Government agencies are pursuing a common strategy with respect to achieving international cooperation against money laundering and are pursuing a common strategy with respect to major money laundering countries, including a summary of United States objectives on a country-by-country basis.

The most recent report was published by the Bureau of International Narcotics and Law Enforcement Affairs in March 2016 and released in two volumes, the first on drug and counternarcotics matters and the second on "money laundering and financial crimes."[21] In practice, Volume II of the INCSR applies to a broader scope of financial crimes than the statutorily defined scope of "major money laundering countries." For example, the INCSR includes a cross-country comparative table of government tools to address not only money laundering but also terrorist financing, including whether the government or jurisdiction has criminalized the financing of terrorism, reports suspected terrorist financing, can free terrorist assets without delay, or is a States Party to the International Convention for the Suppression of Terrorism Financing. As the INCSR explains:

> The complex nature of money laundering transactions today makes it difficult in many cases to distinguish the proceeds of narcotics trafficking from the proceeds of other serious crime. Moreover, financial institutions engaged in transactions that involve significant amounts of proceeds from other serious crimes are vulnerable to narcotics-related money laundering. The... [INCSR] recognizes this relationship by including all countries and other jurisdictions whose financial institutions engage in transactions involving significant amounts of proceeds from all serious crimes or are particularly vulnerable to such activity because of weak or nonexistent supervisory or enforcement regimes or weak political will.... Therefore, the focus in considering whether a country or jurisdiction should be included in this category is on the significance of the amount of proceeds laundered in the entire financial sector, not only banking transactions or on the AML [anti-money laundering] measures taken.[22]

National Money Laundering Strategy and Report

Previously, the President, acting through the Treasury Secretary, in consultation with the Attorney General, had been required by Congress to "develop a national strategy for combating money laundering and related financial crimes" as well as,

---

[21] Available at http://www.state.gov/j/inl/rls/nrcrpt/2016/.
[22] Ibid.

separately, "a report containing an evaluation of the effectiveness of policies to combat money laundering and related financial crimes. Section 2(a) of the Money Laundering and Financial Crimes Strategy Act of 1998 (P.L. 105-310), as amended and codified at 31 U.S.C. 5341, specified that the national strategies were to be submitted in 1999, 2000, 2001, 2002, 2003, 2005, and 2007.[23]

Although there was a statutory requirement that the money laundering strategies include "[d]ata concerning money laundering efforts related to the funding of acts of international terrorism, and efforts directed at the prevention, detections, and prosecution of such funding," the last strategy issued in May 2007 focused "exclusively on deterring money laundering, independent of our efforts to combat the financing of terror" (previous iterations had presented a combined program against both money laundering and terrorist financing) because, as the strategy explained: "Money laundering, in its own right, is a serious threat to our national and economic security."

U.S. CFT Responses

The 2015 National Terrorist Financing Risk Assessment describes the scope of ongoing U.S. government efforts to combat terrorist financing as encompassing three broad categories: law enforcement efforts, financial and regulatory measures, and international engagement.[24]

Law Enforcement. With respect to law enforcement efforts, the 2015 National Terrorist Financing Risk Assessment states that the September 11, 2001, terrorist attacks drove federal law enforcement agencies to undertake "a fundamental reorientation of their institutions, processes, resources, and apparatuses to enhance their ability to disrupt and prevent acts of terrorism before they occur."[25] The U.S. Department of Justice is the principal federal entity responsible for overseeing the investigation and prosecution of terrorist financing-related offenses. Other agencies with CFT-related enforcement responsibilities include including the U.S. Department of Homeland Security and the Internal Revenue Service.

Financial and Regulatory Measures. Ever since September 11, 2001, the U.S. government has stepped up its systemic and targeted regulatory tools aimed at disrupting the finances and funding networks fueling terrorist organizations, and on collecting and disseminating financial intelligence provided by domestic financial institutions.[26] Treasury's Office of Terrorism and Financial Intelligence (TFI) was established in 2004 to lead the U.S. government's CFT efforts. TFI seeks to mitigate terrorist financing risk through both

---

[23] The strategies for 1999-2003 and 2007 are available at https://www.fincen.gov/news_room/rp/nmls.html. In 2006, the Treasury Department released a U.S. Money Laundering Threat Assessment for 2005, which is available at https://www.treasury.gov/resource-center/terrorist-illicit-finance/Pages/Money-Laundering.aspx.
[24] U.S. Department of the Treasury, National Terrorist Financing Risk Assessment, June 12, 2015.
[25] Ibid.
[26] Ibid.

systemic and targeted actions. Targeted actions, usually in the form of targeted financial sanctions administered and enforced by Treasury's Office of Foreign Assets Control (OFAC), are used to identify, disrupt, and prevent terrorists from accessing the U.S. financial system. TFI is composed of: The Office of Terrorist Financing and Financial Crimes (TFFC), which is TFI's policy development and outreach office; OFAC, is charged with administering and enforcing all U.S. economic sanctions programs, including those targeting terrorist financing; the Office of Intelligence Analysis (OIA) is TFI's in-house intelligence office; and the Financial Crimes Enforcement Network (FinCEN) is the financial intelligence unit (FIU) for the United States charged with administering and enforcing the Bank Secrecy Act (BSA).[27]

International Engagement. Recognizing the interconnectedness of the international financial system and the prominent role of the U.S. financial system, international engagement efforts support the implementation of strong international AML/CFT standards through bilateral and multilateral tools. International and technical assistance for AML/CFT is funded primarily by the State Department, but often implemented by a mix of experts and practitioners in the Departments of Justice, Treasury (including through OTA), and Homeland Security. Treasury also represents the U.S. government in international AML/CFT technical bodies, such as FATF.

Financial Crimes Enforcement Network

The mission of the Financial Crimes Enforcement Network (FinCEN) is to safeguard the financial system from illicit activities, combat money laundering and promote national security through the collection, analysis, and dissemination of financial intelligence and strategic use of financial authorities.[28] FinCEN is housed as an independent bureau within TFI, and the director of FinCEN is appointed by the Secretary of the Treasury and reports to the Treasury Under Secretary for Terrorism and Financial Intelligence. FinCEN is also the U.S. government's FIU and as such represents the U.S. at the Egmont Group, the international body of FIUs that facilitates international information exchange on AML/CFT.[29] FinCEN plays an important bridging role across all three dimensions of U.S. AML/CFT efforts. Law enforcement efforts are supported by FinCEN through its unique tools to collect, analyze, and disseminate financial intelligence for law enforcement authorities. As the administrator of the Bank Secrecy Act for the financial sector, FinCEN issues regulations, guidance, advisories, and other orders that require banks and other financial institutions to take precautions against money laundering, terrorism financing and financial crime, such as through filing reports on suspicious financial transactions. Internationally, FinCEN also plays a role in building bilateral and multilateral cooperation and exchanging financial

---

[27] The Bank Secrecy Act of 1970 and its major component, the Currency and Foreign Transactions Reporting Act, are codified at 12 U.S.C. 1829b and 1951-1959; and 31 U.S.C. 5311-5322.
[28] See Financial Crimes Enforcement Network (FinCEN), *FinCEN: What We Do*, at https://www.fincen.gov/about_fincen/wwd/.
[29] The list of jurisdictions and countries which are members of the Egmont Group can be found at: http://www.egmontgroup.org/about/list-of-members.

information on AML/CFT matters, including through the FATF, an international standard-setting body that issues standardized best practice guidelines for AML/CFT internationally. It also participates in the Egmont Group, which facilitates the direct exchange of financial information by allowing Egmont member FIUs to request that another member's FIU search its own databases for financial information that may be relevant for an investigation.

One of FinCEN's recent initiatives related to its financial intelligence and CFT role relates to its IT systems and data collection. The majority of the BSA data FinCEN collects comes from two reporting streams: one on large cash transactions exceeding $10,000, and the other on suspicious transactions identified by financial institutions.[30] FinCEN's data collection spans the following entities, which it considers "financial institutions:"

- Banks and credit unions;
- Money remitters, check cashers, and virtual currency exchangers;
- Dealers in foreign exchange;
- Casinos and card clubs;
- Insurance companies;
- Securities and futures brokers;
- Mutual funds;
- Operators of credit card systems;
- Dealers in precious metals, stones, or jewels; and
- Certain individuals and trades or businesses, transporting or accepting large amounts of cash.

FinCEN's financial intelligence also includes information on cash crossing the U.S. border. The data FinCEN has collected—known in sum as "BSA data"—totals roughly 190 million records.[31] The agency recently concluded a five-year IT modernization project, in which it (1) assumed responsibility for maintaining its own data in a FinCEN system of records; (2) supported a significant shift from the paper filing of BSA reports to the electronic filing of BSA data; (3) developed a new IT system for its many law enforcement and regulatory partners to search, slice, and dice BSA data; and (4) provided advanced analytics tools to FinCEN's analysts to enhance their capabilities to make sense of the data.[32]

Another recent initiative for FinCEN has also been the greater use of coordinated multilateral collaboration, such as through the Egmont Group, to address global criminal and national security threats.[33] Most recently, these initiatives have focused on the threat of foreign terrorist fighters associated with the Islamic State.

---

[30] FinCEN, speech of Director Jennifer Shasky Calvery at Predictive Analytics World for Government Conference, Washington, D.C. (October 13, 2015), p. 2.
[31] Ibid.
[32] Ibid.
[33] FinCEN, speech of Director Jennifer Shasky Calvery at Royal United Services Institute, (May 27, 2015).

The Egmont Group of FIUs has supported an expedited multilateral collaborative effort of 24 FIUs since the project's inception in February 2015. In the project, participating FIUs have shared financial intelligence, strategic reports, and other Islamic State intelligence-related information while identifying important related characteristics of the financial transactions and activity of foreign terrorist fighters as they travel to and from the conflict zone.[34]

Office of Technical Assistance

The mission of the Department of the Treasury's Office of Technical Assistance (OTA) is "to help [the] finance ministries and central banks of developing and transition countries strengthen their ability to manage public finances effectively and safeguard their financial sectors."[35] OTA is an international assistance program within Treasury's Office of International Affairs. OTA offers its technical assistance and capacity building support to countries through five major disciplines:

- **Revenue Policy and Administration Team**: Creates more effective tax administrations that simplify procedures to encourage voluntary compliance on the part of taxpayers, effectively uncover tax evasion, and maintain high standards of fairness and transparency;
- **Budget and Financial Accountability Team**: Strengthens the effectiveness of ministries of finance, the readability and transparency of budget documents, and the management and expenditure of government resources;
- **Government Debt and Infrastructure Finance Team**: Provides strategic and technical assistance to develop market-based means of public finance through the issuance of domestic government securities; increases the efficiency of government debt management; and implements comprehensive debt strategies that diversify sources of finance, reduce liability risk and lower debt service burdens. The team also provides technical assistance to accelerate the development of financially sound infrastructure projects;
- **Banking and Financial Services Team**: Supports the development of strong financial sectors in which institutions are well-regulated, stable and accessible, serve as efficient intermediaries between savers and investors, and are resistant to criminal activity;
- **Economics Crimes Team**: Assists the development and implementation of anti-money laundering and counter terrorist financing regimes that are compliant with international standards.

While the specific number of projects and countries fluctuates from year to year, OTA currently has 100 projects in nearly 50 countries.[36] OTA provides financial sector assistance in five core disciplines: "revenue policy and administration, budget and financial accountability, government debt and infrastructure finance, banking

---

[34] Ibid.

[35] *See* International Affairs, Technical Assistance, U.S. Dep't of Treasury, https://www.treasury.gov/about/organizational-structure/offices/Pages/Technical-Assistance-.aspx. [36]

U.S. Treasury Office of Technical Assistance, OTA Projects (as of Mar. 31, 2016).

and financial services, and economic crimes."[37] With a budget of approximately $23.5 million,[38] OTA has helped developing and transition countries build their capacity to manage government finances more effectively; deliver essential public services; and grow their economies.[39] OTA is also the "first responder" in emerging economic and national security crises, such as recently in Ukraine.[40] Demand for OTA assistance from developing and transitional countries is relatively strong and continues to increase.[41]

---

[37] U.S. Dep't of Treasury, Office of Technical Assistance booklet, (2015).

[38] OTA received $23.5 million for FY 2015 and FY 2016, and the FY2017 request was $33.5 million.; U.S. Dep't of the Treasury, International Programs, Congressional Justification for Appropriations.

[39] Ibid.

[40] Ibid.

[41] Ibid.

June 6, 2016, Task Force to Investigate Terrorism Financing titled "The Enemy in our Backyard: Examining Terror Funding Streams from South America"

Introduction

Illicit financial flows in the Western Hemisphere are characterized by their links to transnational crime, trade-based money laundering, bulk cash smuggling, and corruption. Some international terrorist groups, including a few that operate in South America, also profit from significant criminal activity in the region. In a recent roundtable with the media, Admiral Kurt Tidd, U.S. Commander of Southern Command (SOUTHCOM), even raised concerns regarding the growth of Islamist extremism in the region, noting that the Islamic State has attracted between 100 and 150 recruits from Latin America.[1] Notwithstanding the presence of terrorism in the region, the terrorist threat in Latin America, including concerns regarding terrorist financing, is often downplayed when compared to terrorism issues in other parts of the world. As described in the U.S. Department of State's June 2016 *Country Reports on Terrorism*:

> [t]ransnational criminal organizations continued to pose a more significant threat to the region than terrorism, and most countries made efforts to investigate possible connections with terrorist organizations....[2]

The primary U.S. Department of State-designated Foreign Terrorist Organizations (FTOs) operating in South America are the Revolutionary Armed Forces of Colombia (Fuerzas Armadas Revolucionarias de Colombia, or FARC), the National Liberation Army (Ejército de Liberación Nacional, or ELN), also of Colombia, and the Shining Path (Sendero Luminoso, or SL) of Peru. All three terrorist groups have been officially designated as FTOs by the State Department since October 1997.[3]

Members of other terrorist groups, including the Basque separatist group in Spain (Euskadi Ta Askatasuna, or ETA), have also reportedly been sighted in recent years in South America.[4] According to the State Department, sympathizers and facilitators of other terrorist groups may also reside in the region:

---

[1] Kristina Wong, "U.S. Military Eyes 'Extremist Islamic Movement' in Latin America," *The Hill*, June 1, 2016.

[2] U.S. Department of State, *Country Reports on Terrorism 2015*, June 2016.

[3] For further information see also CRS Report RS21049, *Latin America: Terrorism Issues*, by Mark P. Sullivan and June S. Beittel.

[4] e.g., Jose Ignacio De Juana Chaos, an ETA terrorist reportedly surfaced in Venezuela, according to media reports. See for example "España pide a Venezuela la extradición del etarra De Juana Chaos," *El Universal*, July 3, 2015.

South America and the Caribbean also served as areas of financial and ideological support for ISIL and other terrorist groups in the Middle East and South Asia. In addition, Hizballah continued to maintain a presence in the region, with members, facilitators, and supporters engaging in activity in support of the organization. This included efforts to build Hizballah's infrastructure in South America and fundraising, both through licit and illicit means.[5]

The State Department further noted that the Argentine Federal Prosecutor in charge of Economic Crimes in Argentina had identified at the end of 2015 "a new potential terrorism-financing case" involving a Syrian national carrying out suspicious transactions in the tri-border area (TBA) between Argentina, Brazil, and Paraguay.[6]

Also of note is that in May 2015, the Obama Administration announced the removal of Cuba from the U.S. list of state sponsors of international terrorism —Cuba was the only Western Hemisphere country that has ever been listed.[7]

Much U.S. concern about terrorist financing in South America has focused on the extent of Iranian influence in the region–Iran is one of three countries identified by the United States as state sponsors of international terrorism–but most observers agree that Iran's activities in the region have waned in recent years. One incident that highlights the potential nexus of criminal and Iranian-backed terrorist activity in Latin America is the alleged plot uncovered by the U.S. Department of Justice in October 2011 to assassinate Saudi Arabia's Ambassador in Washington D.C. That plot reportedly involved Iran's Islamic Revolutionary Guards Corps-Quds Force (IRGC-QF) attempting to recruit an agent who it thought was a member of a Mexican drug trafficking organization (Los Zetas), but who was actually a Drug Enforcement Administration confidential source.[8]

Sources of Financing

The State Department's *Country Reports on Terrorism* includes a section on "funding and external aid" for each designated FTO described in the report. According to the most recent report, FTOs operating in or deriving financial support from Latin America, often by means of criminal activity, include FARC, ELN, SL, and Hezbollah.[9]

---

[5] U.S. Department of State, *Country Reports on Terrorism 2015*, June 2016.
[6] Ibid.
[7] For background on Cuba's removal from the list, see CRS Report R43926, *Cuba: Issues for the 114th Congress*, by Mark P. Sullivan.
[8] U.S. Department of Justice, "Two Men Charged in Alleged Plot to Assassinate Saudi Arabian Ambassador to the United States," press release, October 11, 2011; and Charlie Savage and Scott Shane, "Iranians Accused of a Plot to Kill Saudis' U.S. Envoy," *New York Times*, October 11, 2011.
[9] *See* note 3, *supra*: U.S. Department of State, *Country Reports on Terrorism 2015*, June 2016.

- **FARC** obtains funds from extortion, kidnapping for ransom, and drug trafficking. According to recent testimony, drug proceeds benefitting FARC may range from $200 million to $3 billion per year.[10] In recent years, FARC diversified into illegal mining, especially gold mining as gold prices rose.[11] In April 2016, the *Economist* reported that an unpublished Colombian study estimated that FARC had stockpiled some $11 billion in assets by 2012.[12] The Colombian government entered into peace negotiations with FARC in late 2012 and has negotiated with the group for more than 50 rounds of peace talks.

- **ELN** is primarily financed by drug trafficking, extortion of oil and gas companies, and, to a lesser extent, kidnapping for ransom. ELN's efforts to negotiate and communicate with authorities are considerably behind FARC peace talks. The Colombian government has criticized ELN for continuing kidnappings to raise funds and bolster its negotiating position, as it did in late-May 2016 when ELN detained three journalists and prevented the opening of formal talks with the Juan Manuel Santos government.

- **SL** generates most of its funds through drug trafficking. Specifically, according to recent congressional testimony, SL may generate some $50,000 to $100,000 in drug income each month.[13] SL operates in the remote central-southern Valley of the Apurimac, Ene, and Mantaro Rivers (VRAEM), where approximately half of Peru's pure cocaine is produced. SL's strength has been greatly reduced from the late 1980s and early 1990s, when it posed a significant threat to national security. According to *Jane's Sentinel Security Assessment*, SL no longer poses a major security threat outside the VRAEM.[14] Foreign and domestic gas and mining operating in the VRAEM continue to face threats of extortion, sabotage, and kidnapping by the group.[15]

---

[10] Michael Shifter, President of the Inter-American Dialogue, prepared statement for a hearing held by the House Foreign Affairs Subcommittee on Terrorism, Nonproliferation, and Trade, "Terrorist Groups in Latin America: The Changing Landscape," Serial No. 113-121, February 4, 2014.

[11] See Juan Carlos Garzón and Julian Wilches, "The Reasons for the Surge in Coca Cultivation in Colombia," Wilson Center for International Studies, August 25, 2015. The authors examine the idea that coca cultivation and gold price are correlated. Their examination of the data finds that these activities may be complementary.

[12] "Unfunny Money," *Economist*, April 16, 2016. Colombian officials have not corroborated this estimate since the *Economist* article was published. The FARC has also reportedly denied the accuracy of the figure as well.

[13] Michael Shifter, President of the Inter-American Dialogue, prepared statement for a hearing held by the House Foreign Affairs Subcommittee on Terrorism, Nonproliferation, and Trade, "Terrorist Groups in Latin America: The Changing Landscape," Serial No. 113-121, February 4, 2014.

[14] IHS, "Peru: Security," *Jane's Sentinel Security Assessment*, November 23, 2015.

[15] Ibid.

- **Hezbollah** reportedly receives financial support from Lebanese Shia communities worldwide, including in South America. For further discussion of Hezbollah's alleged links to drug trafficking and related money laundering in South America, see section below on "Selected Case Studies."

Criminal Nexus

Transnational crime is a key concern for the region, as are potential links between criminal and terrorist activity. Among the FTOs operating in South America, all are known to exploit porous and permissive borders to engage in drug trafficking, extortion, kidnapping, and other illicit criminal activity.

FARC, for example, has been known to exploit Colombia's porous borders for safe haven, weapons sourcing, and logistical planning in neighboring countries (i.e., Ecuador, Venezuela, Panama, and Brazil). Other illegal armed groups in Colombia, particularly the *"bandas criminales"* (criminal bands, or BACRIM), also reportedly exploit these porous borders to cultivate and transport drugs, operate illegal mines, and extort the local populace.

The TBA of Argentina, Brazil, and Paraguay, for example, has long been a regional nexus for the smuggling of weapons, drugs, people, and counterfeit and pirated goods, as well as money laundering. According to the State Department, "[i]llicit activities within the TBA remained potential funding sources for terrorist organizations, most notably Hizballah."[16]

Panama is also known as a key node for a variety of smuggling and money laundering activity and a potential conduit for terrorist travel. According to the State Department's 2014 *Country Reports on Terrorism*:

> Panama's strategic location as a gateway between Central and South America [as well as its] expansion in the banking and finance sectors, the establishment of a new diamond exchange, offshore banking facilities, tax shelters, and free trade zones leave [it] vulnerable to illicit arms and narcotics trade along with other associated forms of money laundering. Panama's Darien region remained a significant and growing pathway for human smuggling with counterterrorism implications.[17]

Drug Trafficking Proceeds Accrued to Mexican Criminal Groups

Beyond terrorist financing in Latin America, Mexican dominance of the region's drug supply, trafficking, and wholesale distribution of most illicit drugs to the United States represents the most significant source of illicit cash to be laundered. Illicit profits accrued by Mexican criminal organizations—ranging from complex

---

[16]U.S. Department of State, *Country Reports on Terrorism 2014*, June 2015.
[17] Ibid.

transnational criminal organizations (TCOs) to smaller Mexican mafias—remain hard to estimate. Various estimates from 2010 and 2011 characterized the range of Mexican drug-related proceeds as spanning between $4 billion and $29 billion.[18] A more recent study by the Financial Action Task Force (FATF) in 2015 suggests that an annual estimate of bulk cash smuggled over the U.S.-Mexico border is between $6 billion to $36 billion annually ($25 billion is the generally accepted figure).[19] FATF's estimate, however, does not define how much of that total benefits TCOs directly.[20]

According to many observers, the largest portion of TCO criminal proceeds in Mexico continues to be from the drug trade. The major Mexican TCOs—such as the Sinaloa crime group—are producing and trafficking multiple drugs, such as heroin, methamphetamine, and cannabis, or supplying cocaine produced in South America to the large U.S. market. Other TCOs may specialize in a particular drug. Some analysts contend that, in addition to the larger TCOs, there has been a sharp increase in newer criminal organizations splintered from larger groups, often operating inside Mexico or regionalized in their native country. Some observers maintain that these smaller *cartelitos* have continued an overall pattern of fragmentation that has generated 60 to 200 groups. New organizations that have emerged or become prominent in 2015 and 2016 include: the Jalisco Cartel New Generation (JCNG), Los Viagras, Guerreros Unidos, and Los Cuinis, among several others. In addition to fragmentation, there has been a major shift into other types of predatory crime including natural resource theft (e.g., oil smuggling, illegal logging, and illegal mining) and the extortion of legal businesses, particularly in agriculture and construction.

---

[18] According to a 2010 study prepared by the U.S. Department of Homeland Security, Mexican bulk cash criminal proceeds were estimated to range between $19 billion and $29 billion annually. According to the State Department in 2010, the amount of drug proceeds that have been annually repatriated from the United States to Mexico may range between $8 billion and $25 billion. Other estimates have given lower ranges; for example, a RAND Corporation study released in 2010 characterized a total of $6.6 billion annually as the "best estimate." In 2011, the Mexican government estimated that organized crime groups laundered some $10 billion, with drug trafficking making up roughly 40% of that or $4 billion. U.S. Department of Homeland Security, *United States of America- Mexico Bi-National Criminal Proceeds Study*, June 2010; U.S. Department of State, *International Narcotics Control Strategy Report* (INCSR), Vol. 2: Money Laundering and Financial Crimes, March 2010; Beau Kilmer, Jonathan P. Caulkins, and Brittany M. Bond et al., *Drug Trafficking Revenues and Violence in Mexico: Would Legalizing Marijuana in California Help?*, RAND Corporation, Los Angeles, CA, 2010; Mollie Laffin-Rose, "Organized Crime Laundered $10 Bn in Mexico in FY2011,'" *In Sight Crime*, April 20, 2012.
[19] Financial Action Task Force (FATF), "Money Laundering Through the Physical Transportation of Cash," October 2015, available at http://www.fatf-gafi.org/media/fatf/documents/reports/money-laundering-through-transportation-cash.pdf .
[20] Given the wide range of estimates, some analysts maintain that money laundering volume estimates are so imprecise that it undermines anti-money laundering approaches as an effective basis for dismantling the drug trafficking organizations or shutting down their operations. See, for example, Alejandro Hope, "Money Laundering and the Myth of the Ninja Accountant," *InSight Crime*, October 11, 2011.

Mexico's Anti-Money Laundering Efforts

In August 2010, the Mexican government approved limits on U.S. dollars that individuals can deposit or exchange each month to $7,000, and this level was later raised to $14,000. In September 2014, however, the restrictions were eased for border and tourist area businesses due to concerns that the restrictions were harming legitimate commerce.[21] According to the State Department, "[v]ery few Mexican financial institutions have taken advantage of these new regulations."[22] Under the Mérida Initiative, the United States has provided more than $1.6 billion in security assistance to Mexico and provided technology, equipment and training, including $20 million to support the development of a financial intelligence unit (FIU) within the Mexican Attorney General's office.[23] The State Department's International Narcotics and Law Enforcement Affairs office, located at the U.S. Embassy in Mexico, has supported the work of Mexico's FIU, helping the office to bring cases, although few have reportedly resulted in successful asset seizures or prosecutions.

Selected Case Studies

Drug Trafficking and Hezbollah Money Laundering. Several U.S. law enforcement cases in recent years have highlighted Hezbollah's role in drug trafficking, including links to FARC, and related money laundering. A two-year U.S.-Colombian investigation alleged in 2008 that Lebanese kingpin Chekry Harb laundered hundreds of millions of dollars in drug proceeds for the Medellin drug trafficking organization known as La Oficina de Envigado.[24] Harb reportedly laundered drug proceeds through key nodes in Latin America and Asia, while also paying some 12% of his profits to Hezbollah. In 2011, Lebanese-Colombian national Ayman Joumaa was indicted in the United States for cocaine trafficking with links to the Mexican Los Zetas group and laundering millions of dollars in drug proceeds across Latin America, West Africa, and Europe—some portion of which he reportedly reserved as profit to Hezbollah.[25]

---

[21] "Mexico Scraps Dollar Cash Deposit Limits to Spur Trade," *Reuters*, September 12, 2014; "War Against Drug Money Entering U.S. from Mexico Takes a Turn, Banks Back in Picture," *Fox News Latino*, October 11, 2014.

[22] U.S. Department of State, *International Narcotics Control Strategy Report* (INCSR), Vol. 2: Money Laundering and Financial Crimes, March 2016.

[23] For more information on the Mérida Initiative, see CRS Report R41349, *U.S.-Mexican Security Cooperation: The Mérida Initiative and Beyond*, by Clare Seelke and Kristin Finklea.

[24] Celina Realuyo, National Defense University Professor of Practice of National Security Affairs, prepared statement for a hearing held by the House Foreign Affairs Subcommittee on Terrorism, Nonproliferation, and Trade, "Terrorist Groups in Latin America: The Changing Landscape," Serial No. 113-121, February 4, 2014.

[25] U.S. Department of the Treasury, "Treasury Targets Major Lebanese-Based Drug Trafficking and Money Laundering Network," press release, January 26, 2011; Sebastian Rotella, "Government Says Hezbollah Profits from U.S. Cocaine Market Via Link to Mexican Cartel," *ProPublica*, December 13, 2011.

Also in 2011, U.S. authorities took action against the now-defunct Lebanese Canadian Bank, which was used, in combination with several Lebanese exchange houses, as part of a transnational illicit trade and money laundering scheme.[26] The scheme facilitated the laundering of South American drug proceeds through the Lebanese financial system and through trade-based money laundering (TBML) schemes involving used cars and consumer goods.

Most recently, in February 2016, U.S. and European authorities revealed that Hezbollah maintained a specific branch within its organization focused on drug trafficking and money laundering, called the Business Affairs Component (BAC).[27] Authorities also revealed Hezbollah schemes involving the movement of large quantities of South American cocaine, via links with various South American drug cartels, and the laundering of such drug proceeds through informal value transfer mechanisms.

Trade-Based Money Laundering. Anecdotally, in some instances TBML techniques are used by known terrorist groups, including Hezbollah, as well as *hawala* brokers operating beyond the realm of international banking regulatory standards. In comparison to other means, however, the U.S. Department of the Treasury Department's June 2015 *National Terrorist Financing Risk Assessment* concluded that TBML is not a dominant method for terrorist financing.[28] The U.S. government has historically focused on TBML schemes involving drug proceeds from Latin America, particularly the Black Market Peso Exchange (BMPE). BMPE emerged as a major money laundering method when Colombian drug traffickers used sophisticated trade-based schemes to disguise as much as $4 billion in annual narcotics profits in the 1980s.[29] According to the Treasury Department, TBML activity is growing in both volume and global reach. In an analysis of suspicious activity reports (SARs) between January 2004 and May 2009, the Treasury Department's Financial Crimes Enforcement Network (FinCEN) found that TBML activity was most frequently identified in transactions involving Mexico and China. Panama was ranked third, potentially due to TBML activity linked to the Panama

---

[26] Jo Becker, "Beirut Bank Seen as a Hub of Hezbollah's Financing," *New York Times*, December 13, 2011. See also, Renee Novakoff, "Transnational Organized Crime: An Insidious Threat to US National Security Interests, *PRISM*, vol. 5, no. 4 (2015). Novakoff points out that Joumaa was an example of "super fixers" or middlemen who are increasingly serving as providers of intermediary services to criminal clients and terrorist groups alike.

[27] U.S. Drug Enforcement Administration, "DEA and European Authorities Uncover Massive Hizballah Drug and Money Laundering Scheme," press release, February 1, 2016.

[28] U.S. Department of the Treasury, *National Terrorist Financing Risk Assessment*, June 12, 2015.

[29] Broadly, the Black Market Peso Exchange (BMPE) facilitated the "swap" of dollars owned by drug cartels in the United States for pesos already in Colombia by selling the dollars to Colombian businessmen who sought to buy U.S. goods for export. See FinCEN, *Colombian Black Market Peso Exchange*, advisory, issue 9, November, 1997; U.S. government, National Money Laundering Strategy, May 3, 2007; and FATF, *Trade Based Money Laundering*, June 23, 2006.

Colon Free Trade Zone (FTZ), while the Dominican Republic and Venezuela were identified as "countries with the most rapid growth in potential TBML activity."[30]

Panama Papers and Latin American Links. In April 2016, the International Consortium of Investigative Journalists (ICIJ) disclosed the existence of 11.5 million files of leaked financial documents and attorney-client communications related to more than 214,000 offshore companies listed by the Panamanian law firm Mossack Fonseca. While the mere existence of offshore accounts is not necessarily indicative of illicit activity, unscrupulous actors may seek to exploit the anonymity provided by such accounts. These leaked documents, known as the Panama Papers, reveal the use of shell companies by a number of individuals, including alleged drug traffickers from Latin America.[31]

Status of AML/CFT Compliance

The Unites States reviews foreign jurisdictions, including those located in Latin America, for their adherence to international standards on anti-money laundering (AML) and combating the financing of terrorism (CFT) in reports to Congress such as the State Department's *International Narcotics Control Strategy Report* and *Country Reports on Terrorism*, as well as through regular participation in FATF and FATF-style regional bodies such as the Caribbean Financial Action Task Force (CFATF) and the Financial Action Task Force of Latin America (GAFILAT). Multiple federal agencies participate in ongoing law enforcement investigations and operations related to criminal and national security financial matters, including narco-terrorism concerns. Several federal agencies also provide training and technical assistance, as well as advisory and mentoring support to countries in Latin America for AML/CFT purposes.[32] Treasury's Office of Foreign Assets

---

[30] FinCEN, *Advisory to Financial Institutions on Filing Suspicious Activity Reports Regarding Trade-Based Money Laundering*, advisory, FIN-2010-A001, February 18, 2010.

[31] See "Giant Leak of Offshore Financial Records Exposes Global Array of Crime and Corruption," *International Consortium of Investigative Journalists*, April 3, 2016; and Elyssa Pachico, "Panama Papers Highlight How LatAm's Elites Hide Wealth," *InSight Crime*, April 4, 2016.

[32] Such efforts have recently included: initiatives by the Board of Governors of the Federal Reserve System in several Caribbean jurisdictions; cross-border financial investigations trainings and advisors by the Department of Homeland Security in several South American countries; support to trade transparency units (TTUs) in Argentina, Colombia, the Dominican Republic, Ecuador, Guatemala, Mexico, Panama, Paraguay, and Peru; trainings by the Drug Enforcement Administration (DEA) on money laundering, TBML, undercover financial operations, financial investigations, and financial intelligence; Federal Bureau of Investigations (FBI) courses, seminars, and workshops on illicit finance and terrorist financing in countries such as Brazil, Colombia, and Paraguay; a train-the-trainer program on financial investigations and money laundering to Panama by the Justice Department's Office of Overseas Prosecutorial Development, Assistance and Training (OPDAT); technical assistance by the Justice Department's Asset Forfeiture and Money Laundering Section (AFMLS); resident or intermittent legal advisors funded by the State Department to support CFT efforts in countries such Panama, Colombia, and Paraguay; State Department funding for UN support and assistance for South American asset recovery efforts and for regional capacity building efforts on money laundering and terrorist financing through the Organization of American States (OAS); Strategic analysis training by FinCEN for Egmont members in Latin America; technical

Control (OFAC) also administers several financial sanctions programs on counterterrorism, counternarcotics, and transnational organized crime that target individuals and entities in Latin America.

State Department Report

According to the State Department's March 2016 *International Narcotics Control Strategy Report* (INCSR), 20 Latin American countries or jurisdictions were identified as "major money laundering countries" in 2015.[33] They include: Antigua and Barbuda, Argentina, the Bahamas, Belize, Bolivia, Brazil, the British Virgin Islands, the Cayman Islands, Colombia, Costa Rica, Curacao, Dominican Republic, Guatemala, Haiti, Mexico, Panama, Paraguay, Sint Maarten, Uruguay, and Venezuela. Latin America accounts for approximately 30% of the State Department's global list of 67 major money laundering countries, which includes the United States. The State Department reports terrorist financing-related concerns for these major money laundering countries in Latin America:

- **Argentina** suffers from "[i]nstitutionalized corruption, drug trafficking, high levels of informal and contraband trade, and an active informal exchange market" whose "general vulnerabilities in the financial system also expose Argentina to a risk of terrorism financing." In the past, FinCEN, a Treasury Department bureau that serves as a national financial intelligence unit (FIU), has suspended information sharing privileges with Argentina's FIU. The first time was in July 2009, and the suspension lasted three and a half years. The second time was in June 2015, after an unauthorized disclosure of information received from FinCEN. On March 21, 2016, FinCEN and Argentina's FIU re-established information sharing.[34]

- **Belize** has a substantial and reportedly "loosely monitored" offshore financial sector that is vulnerable to money laundering and terrorist financing.

- **Brazil**, as the second-largest economy in the Americas, a major drug-transit country, and a regional financial center for Latin America, is also attractive as a location to launder proceeds of drug trafficking, corruption, organized crime, and other contraband and counterfeit goods. Although a new law signed in October 2015 provides procedures for freezing assets

assistance by the Internal Revenue Service-Criminal Investigations (IRS-CI) and the Economic Crimes Team of the Treasury Department's Office of Technical Assistance (OTA); and training of foreign banking supervisors by the Office of the Comptroller of the Currency.

[33] U.S. Department of State, *International Narcotics Control Strategy Report* (INCSR), Vol. 2: Money Laundering and Financial Crimes, March 2016.

[34] U.S. Department of the Treasury, Financial Crimes Enforcement Network (FinCEN), "U.S. and Argentine Financial Intelligence Unis Restore Cooperation to Fight Terrorism and Organized Crime," press release, March 21, 2016.

related to United Nations terrorist sanctions and bilateral information sharing, "[t]errorism and terrorist financing are still not criminalized in a manner consistent with international standards."

- In **Colombia**, money laundering is "a significant avenue for terrorist financing" and involves nearly all conceivable methods of laundering, including bulk cash smuggling and TBML. Although the State Department's *Country Reports on Terrorism* describes Colombia as "a regional leader in the fight against terrorist financing," the INCSR is far more critical of Colombia, stating that:

  > Key impediments to developing an effective AML/CFT regime are underdeveloped institutional capacity, limited interagency cooperation, lack of experience, and an inadequate level of expertise in investigating and prosecuting complex financial crimes. Colombian laws are limited in their respective authorities to allow different agencies to collaborate and pursue financial crimes, and there is a lack of clear roles and responsibilities among agencies. Despite improvements, regulatory institutions have limited analytical capacity and tools, and lack the technology to effectively utilize the vast amount of available data.

- **Costa Rica** has not prosecuted anyone for terrorist financing, but authorities have detected in recent years drugs- and weapons-trafficking linked to FARC, as well as "bulk cash smuggling by nationals from countries at higher risk for terrorist financing." In 2015, Costa Rica issued a National Strategy to Counter Money Laundering and Terrorist Financing, but the country reportedly "remains deficient... with respect to [countering] the financing of terrorism."

- **Panama** has a dollarized economy and has long been an attractive haven for laundering proceeds of drug trafficking. In 2015, it passed new legislation to criminalize money laundering, address terrorist financing, and regulate designated non-financial businesses and professions. Panama is in the early stages of implementing these new laws and establishing the framework for freezing terrorist assets pursuant to international standards.

- **Venezuela's** vulnerability to money laundering and terrorist financing is a function of several factors, including weak regulatory enforcement, lack of political will, and endemic corruption. Recent U.S. legal activity relating to Venezuelan citizens has "exposed questionable financial activities related to money laundering and terrorism finance." In September 2015, the Southern District of Florida unsealed an indictment against Pedro Luis Martin, former head of financial intelligence for Venezuela's secret police and allegedly "a primary financial manager responsible for laundering drug trafficking proceeds for top Venezuelan officials." In 2006, FinCEN suspended information sharing with Venezuela's FIU for an unauthorized disclosure of information and the suspension remains in effect.

Financial Action Task Force List

Several times each year, FATF publicly identifies "jurisdictions with strategic AML/CFT deficiencies" with whom FATF works to develop an action plan to implement political commitments to address relevant AML/CFT deficiencies. Among the 11 identified by FATF in February 2016, one is located in Latin America: **Guyana** (not a State Department-listed major money laundering country).[35] With respect to Guyana, FATF states:

> In October 2014, Guyana made a high-level political commitment to work with the FATF and CFATF to address its strategic AML/CFT deficiencies. Since October 2015, Guyana has taken steps towards improving its AML/CFT regime, including by enacting further amendments to the AML/CFT Act and AML/CFT Regulations, and issuing FIU guidelines on targeted financial sanctions. However, the FATF has determined that certain strategic deficiencies remain. Guyana should continue to implement its action plan, including by ensuring and implementing an adequate legal framework for identifying, tracing and freezing terrorist assets. The FATF encourages Guyana to address its remaining deficiencies and continue the process of implementing its action plan.[36]

In its February 2016 report, FATF also announced that **Panama** would be removed from the list of jurisdictions with strategic deficiencies, noting that "FATF welcomes Panama's significant progress in improving its AML/CFT regime and notes that Panama has established the legal and regulatory framework to meet its commitments in its action plan regarding the strategic deficiencies FATF had identified in June 2014."

---

[35] Financial Action Task Force (FATF), "Improving Global AML/CFT Compliance: On-going Process," February 19, 2016.
[36] Ibid.

Appendix B: Hearing Summaries

This Appendix provides summaries of ten hearings, in reverse chronological order, held by the House Financial Services Committee's Task Force to Investigate Terrorism Financing over a two-year period. It was originally intended to support a final summation hearing of the Task Force, which was held on June 23, 2016.[1]

June 8, 2016: "The Enemy in Our Backyard: Examining Terror Funding Streams from South America"

Overview. At this hearing, the Task Force reviewed how terrorist organizations fund their operations in Latin and South America, and the impact of anonymous offshore companies on anti-money laundering/countering the financing of terrorism (AML/CFT) efforts. The Task Force heard from three witnesses: (1) Mariano Federici, President of Argentina's Financial Intelligence Unit; (2) Michael Braun, Managing Partner of SGI Global LLC; and (3) Emanuele Ottolenghi, Fellow at the Center on Sanctions and Illicit Finance at the Foundation for Defense of Democracies.

Witness Testimony. Federici described how low morale, scarce funding, and lack of strategic vision have plagued Argentina's law enforcement, judiciary, and regulatory bodies, resulting in a system of generalized corruption. He lamented his country's historic lack of political will to advance financial integrity issues, based on a mistakenly low estimate of the threat posed by terrorism financing to the country, but he noted that a new President and administration of which he is a part have set a new course and are determined to reshape anti-terror finance efforts. In conclusion, Federici launched an appeal to the United States to continue providing diplomatic, technical and material support to Argentina's new government to help set them firmly on a path of continued improvement in AML/CFT.

Braun stressed the unique nature of Hezbollah's AML efforts. He described in detail the organization's role in the trafficking of cocaine out of the area connecting Argentina, Brazil and Paraguay (also known as the Tri-Border Area, or TBA) directed towards Europe, as well as Hezbollah's unparalleled capacity to move currency around the world. He offered his opinion that the United States has been focusing too much on the dictum "follow the money" and too little on the supply side of the terrorist organization's business model – i.e. addressing how terrorist organizations are generating revenue in the first place. In conclusion, Braun suggested refocusing U.S. AML/CFT efforts toward disrupting Hezbollah's supply chain: the virtually unopposed drug trafficking operation it is conducting in South America. To that end, Braun proposed a massive employment of intelligence and

---

[1] This memorandum was prepared by the Congressional Research Service (CRS) at the Task Force's request, and has been reviewed and approved by staff of the Financial Services Committee.

surveillance assets provided by the U.S. Department of Defense as well as joint kinetic operations by U.S. military forces and the Drug Enforcement Agency.

Ottolenghi testified that his research indicates the presence of a high degree of cooperation in Latin America between drug traffickers and terrorist groups. He further stressed that Hezbollah has been devoting considerable resources to establish a solid, reliable and permanent network of contacts, charitable organizations and cells exploiting the Lebanese diaspora communities in the southern western hemisphere with the aim of ensuring a continuous stream of funding and a springboard for asymmetric conflict against the U.S. and its interests in the region. He offered the example of the trade-based money laundering (TBML) case recently uncovered in Ciudad del Este, Paraguay and highlighted that the AML scheme involved shipments of goods to Miami and, via Dakar, to Dubai. According to Ottolenghi, this case highlights the shortcomings plaguing the ability of U.S. authorities to tackle trade-based ploys. He strongly advocated for the enforcement of stricter border controls over merchandise originating from, transiting through or destined to at-risk jurisdictions. In his opinion, if those stricter regulations cannot be enforced in the U.S., the government should exert its influence to strengthen controls over weak access points to the global financial system.

Questions and Discussion. Task Force Members raised questions regarding the perceived low priority attributed to fighting domestic terrorism financing issues in Latin American countries, and options available to counter that perception. Other members solicited the witnesses' opinions on the United State's performance to date in keeping pace with the evolution of terrorist and criminal organizations, on the efficiency of continuing to operate principally via the network of Financial Investigative Units (FIUs) and the Financial Action Task Force (FATF), and on Argentina's progress in reforming its own FIU. Additional questions focused on the issue of beneficial ownership, on the policies implemented to date to improve law enforcement and judiciary presence in ungoverned areas such as the TBA, and whether Iran's influence in Latin America has been growing.

May 24, 2016: "Stopping Terror Finance: A Coordinated Government Effort"

Overview. This hearing reviewed the actions and policies carried out by two entities within the U.S. Department of the Treasury (Treasury) to combat terrorism financing: the Financial Crimes Enforcement Network (FinCEN) and the Office of Technical Assistance (OTA). The hearing provided a snapshot into the current state of, and the emerging challenges associated with, AML/CFT. It also highlighted coordination efforts among various federal agencies involved in AML/CFT efforts. The Task Force heard from two witnesses: FinCEN Director Jennifer Shasky Calvery; and Deputy Assistant Secretary Larry McDonald.

Witness Testimony. Shasky Calvery, whose resignation as FinCEN Director became effective three days after the hearing, stressed the necessity of a proper legal and regulatory framework, the increased need of funding for FinCEN, and the importance of information sharing with domestic and foreign counterparts, as well as enlisting the support and active participation of the industry and private sector. She also highlighted the difficulty of balancing the transparency required to acquire and share data with the protection of sensitive corporate and individual data. Shasky Calvery mentioned the major proposals recently put forward by FinCEN regarding increased Customer Due Diligence (CDD) regulations, transparency in beneficial ownership provisions, and extended authority for Geographical Targeting Orders (GTOs). She stressed that the focus of FinCEN has been on the intermediaries that help launder the money (the "gatekeepers" or professional enablers). Shasky Calvery concluded by mentioning the potential risks posed in the cyber realm and new technologies that continue to be exploited by bad actors in the absence of a prompt regulatory response from government.

McDonald described the work that OTA performs in AML/CFT technical assistance. Specifically, he noted that OTA assists foreign FIUs in strengthening their AML/CFT efforts to reach FATF standards. He stressed the importance of providing assistance only to those countries that show serious interest in making reforms, which he defined as "demand driven assistance," not duplicating assistance efforts offered by other parties, and focusing on areas of proven excellence of the agency. McDonald highlighted the difficulties faced by foreign counterparts who are not fully committed to implementing and enforcing the proposed technical solutions and who nullify training by inappropriately reassigning specifically trained personnel.

Questions and Discussion. Task Force Members raised questions regarding the absence of a national AML/CFT strategy – similar to the national drug control strategy - and whether more Treasury personnel should be attached to embassies abroad. Questions were also raised concerning how exactly FinCEN plans on adapting to new technologies, what role the National Security Council plays in prioritizing and directing interagency efforts, the limits of GTOs, and what could be done to increase the effectiveness of these instruments. Finally, the repercussions of "de-risking" were also discussed. "De-risking" occurs when financial institutions terminate or restrict business relationships with categories of customers. For example, many financial institutions have made a business decision to terminate correspondent banking relationships in Somalia. While mitigating the financial institution's financial exposure, some Members said such actions can be devastating to an underserved community and suggested that issues related to de-risking merited further examination.

April 19, 2016: "Preventing Cultural Genocide: Countering the Plunder and Sale of Priceless Cultural Antiquities by ISIS"

Overview. The Task Force reviewed the current state and emerging challenges of the exploitation of art and antiquities from Syria and Iraq for terrorism financing. The Task Force heard from five witnesses: (1) Robert M. Edsel, Chairman of the Board of the Monument Men Foundation; (2) Yaya J. Fanusie, Director of Analysis at the Center on Sanctions and Illicit Finance of the Foundation for Defense of Democracies; (3) Patty Gerstenblith, Professor at the DePaul University College of Law; (4) Amr Al-Azm, Associate Professor at Shawnee State University; and (5) Lawrence Shindell, Chairman of ARIS Title Insurance Corporation.

Witness Testimony. Edsel stressed that the lack of regulation and transparency in the art industry, compared to other sectors, offers an opportunity to both terrorists and criminals. Fanusie advocated four measures to be implemented: (1) establishing a targeted sanction regime for artifact smugglers and dealers; (2) making antiquities looting an intelligence and law enforcement priority; (3) providing specific training on these issues to the intelligence community and Special Operation Forces; and (4) expanding registries of art and antiquities. Gerstenblith suggested four measures as well: (1) imposing import restrictions on cultural materials illegally removed from countries at risk; (2) strengthening customs enforcement of existing laws; (3) shifting away from forfeiture and repatriation and toward criminal prosecutions; and (4) fostering greater transparency and accountability in the market by requiring documentation of arts and antiquities ownership. Finally, Gerstenblith pointed out that measures should not only be reactive, but also proactive – specifically mentioning Libya as the probable next target of illicit trafficking of cultural materials. Al-Azm pointed out that while ISIS was not the first to loot, smuggle and destroy arts and antiquities, it has institutionalized and intensified the practice. He stated that ISIS sells what it can and destroys what it can't or is too difficult to move, and that official regime forces have also looted cultural artifacts – even though 70 percent of the Syrian territory now lies outside their control.

Shindell underlined the need of improved AML compliance provisions for art and cultural objects and reported that the adoption of emerging information-based technology solutions - such as the one offered by the Global Center of Innovation for i2M Standards - might increase transparency in global art and antiquities transactions. Additionally, Shindell pointed out that FinCEN and Treasury have a role to play in detecting and sharing anomalies in the flow of transactions originating within the art industry financial sector. To that end, Shindell proposed that FinCEN extend to art title insurance companies the provisions of the Bank Secrecy Act (BSA). Finally, Shindell noted that the main obstacles to overcome are the unregulated nature of the industry, the lack of record-keeping in the source and market nations (which obscures the origin, legal status and beneficial ownership of items sold), and the presence of free ports and tax free zones, that are used to store items for extended periods of time to mask their origin.

Questions and Discussion. Task Force Members questioned how looted material can appear to be legitimate because of the lack of mechanisms to prevent and detect forged documentation. The absence of a sanction regime targeting Syrian antiquities and criminal provisions for the smuggling of cultural material were also raised. Finally, some Task Force members discussed the necessity of improved information sharing and coordination between government agencies, with foreign partners, and with the private sector. Specifically, Members examined the idea of prescribing export declarations for art worth more than $10,000, as well as an import tariff.

March 1, 2016: "Helping the Developing World Fight Terror Finance"

Overview. On March 1, 2016, the Task Force reviewed the effectiveness of U.S. technical assistance in developing countries to counter terrorism financing with the aim of determining what works, what doesn't, and what Congress can do to improve the situation. The Task Force heard from four witnesses: (1) Robert M. Kimmitt, Senior International Counsel at WilmerHale; (2) Clay Lowery, Vice President of Rock Creek Global Investors and Visiting Fellow at the Center for Global Development; (3) James W. Adams, former Vice President for East Asia and the Pacific Region at the World Bank; and (4) William F. Wechsler, Senior Fellow at the Center for American Progress.

Witness Testimony. Kimmitt pointed out that facing the threat posed by terrorism financing requires smart, creative and adaptable solutions, as well as a "whole-of-governments" approach involving the international community (including competitors like China and Russia) and the private sector. Effective responses, Kimmitt pointed out, must not be "one size fits all," but should instead be country-specific. He pointed out that United Nations Security Council resolutions should be the preferred framework for joint action and coordination, and that, when such a framework is not possible, the United States should resort to bilateral agreements with individual partners, which would make U.S. assistance dependent on effective policing of their financial system.

Kimmitt stressed the importance of effective interagency processes involving the U.S. Departments of State, Treasury, Defense, Justice, and Homeland Security, under the supervision of the National Security Council, and with the support of the intelligence community. He advocated for a wider use of Treasury liaison officers in embassies and military commands abroad, as well as Defense liaison officers within the Treasury. Finally, Kimmitt stressed the importance of avoiding regulatory action that produces unintended "de-risking" in post-conflict and developing countries.

Lowery elaborated on Kimmitt's argument about the necessity of preventing "de-risking" in poor countries as it undermines the very objectives of AML/CFT policies. Lowery also pointed out that "de-risking" negatively affects remittance flows and correspondent banking relationships. Lowery suggested clarifying the intent and scope of the existing AML/CFT regulations and enforcement procedures and a concerted effort to lower the costs of compliance.

Adams conveyed his skepticism about the performance of technical assistance programs in developing countries. He pointed to both their limited scope (15 percent of total donor commitments) and unsatisfying track record. Adams stressed the unwillingness and incapability of some beneficiary countries to fully avail of the assistance received, as well as the lack of coordination and unrealistic expectations among international donors. To offset the above issues, Adams advocated three solutions: (1) a rigorous process of verification of the beneficiary country's commitment to achieve self-sustainable, long-term capacity improvements; (2) the establishment of a priority framework of action among all participating donors and the clear definition of a country lead; and (3) the donor's longer-term commitment to ensure obtaining that capacity (beyond the standard five-year period).

Wechsler offered four lessons: (1) in the absence of the host nation's full and unconditional support and commitment, technical assistance is doomed to be ineffective; (2) a good technical assistance program is one that also tackles associated capabilities such as the judiciary and law enforcement; (3) a good program "targets narrowly and is executed broadly," meaning that it should be focused on a small corps of professionals who can receive the proper training and assistance; and (4) the most successful assistance programs are those run by capable ambassadors assisted by committed country teams. In conclusion, Wechsler offered two recommendations: (1) to increase budget allocations and personnel assigned to technical assistance missions at the Departments of State and Treasury; and (2) to export abroad the U.S. format of a dedicated intelligence component within the financial ministry such is Treasury's Office of Intelligence and Analysis.

Questions and Discussion. Questions were raised on the decision-making process that determines which embassy will have a Department of the Treasury attaché and why Treasury is not represented in each embassy. Questions were also raised about the reasons why the main interagency coordination body in the U.S. to fight the financing of terrorism, the Terrorist Financing Working Group, has not convened since July 2015. Task Force Members asked what incentives would compel host countries to commit to long term AML/CFT reforms and if enough priority is assigned to monitor and assist countries of origin of ISIS foreign fighters. Finally, questions were raised about the degree of cooperation in AML/CFT between the Departments of State and Treasury and the coordination provided by the National Security Council.

February 3, 2016: "Trading with the Enemy: Trade-Based Money Laundering is the Growth Industry in Terror Finance"

Overview. At this hearing, the Task Force reviewed trade-based financial crimes as a source of funding for terrorist organizations in order to pinpoint effective measures to counter them. The Task Force heard from four witnesses: (1) John Cassara, former intelligence officer and Treasury Special Agent; (2) Louis Bock, former Agent with the former United States Customs Service; (3) Farley Mesko, Co-Founder and Chief Executive Officer of Sayari Analytics; and (4) Nikos Passas, Professor of Criminology and Criminal Justice at Northeastern University.

Witness Testimony. Cassara reported that trade-based money laundering (TBML) is the least understood, largest, and most pervasive system used by criminals and terrorists to fund their operations, and estimated that between six and nine percent of U.S. trade annually might be affected by it. He stressed that the phenomenon affects every country but is especially acute in countries with weak economies, high corruption and limited rule of law. Cassara stated that the current countermeasures to chart and regulate unofficial, informal, and alternative remittance systems – such as Hawala and fei-chien – are ineffective, and stressed the need of increased international trade transparency. Cassara added that improvements in advanced data analytics provide the capability to increase transparency in the sector and could result in additional government revenues. Finally, Cassara recommended four measures: (1) conduct a systematic and thorough study of the phenomenon; (2) expand the funding, manpower and scope of the Department of Homeland Security's Trade Transparency Unit (TTU); (3) anchor any trade agreement binding the U.S. to the partner's specific commitment to set up a TTU; and (4) provide specific TBML-training to federal, state and local law enforcement agencies throughout the nation.

Bock reported that, under DHS, the TTU lost its initial customs and financial focus, that it has been focused more on immigration from South America than on trade-based money laundering, and that it has been understaffed and undermanned. He therefore advocated that the TTU be given increased resources and placed under the authority of Treasury's FinCEN.

Mesko underscored that in providing a seemingly legitimate cover for their activities, criminal and terrorist enterprises leave a paper trail that could and should be followed. He also suggested an overhaul of Office of Foreign Assets Control (OFAC) rules that presently only apply to entities on the Treasury's Specially Designated National (SDN) list if their ownership share is above 50 percent. Passas advised that all facets of financial and trade monitoring functions be consolidated under FinCEN, and encouraged the use of academia and advanced analytics to drive intelligence and investigative efforts.

Questions and Discussion. Questions were raised by Task Force Members about the feasibility and desirability of provisions mandating the disclosure of beneficial ownership information prior to company formation and whether the issue of effective monitoring and enforcement would be better addressed with additional funding or changes in the institutional architecture and ultimate authority within the government. Additional questions were raised concerning harmonization of the format in which U.S. and foreign trade data is collected, why this is not being done systematically, and what it would cost to fund the centralizing of all U.S. trade data into a single stream useful to and readable by several departments. Finally, questions were raised about how to counter cross-border money laundering without damaging legitimate commercial activities.

September 9, 2015: "Could America Do More? An examination of U.S. Efforts to Stop the Financing of Terror"

Overview. This hearing reviewed U.S. efforts to degrade and inhibit terrorism financing and money laundering, with the aim of ensuring that the government-wide effort is accomplishing its intended purposes and identifying areas in need of improvement. Additionally, the Task Force sought to evaluate the degree of cooperation between the various federal agencies involved in AML/CFT efforts as well as coordination with private sector entities.

The Task Force heard from four witnesses: (1) Scott Modell, Managing Director of The Rapidan Group; (2) Louise Shelley, Director of the Terrorism, Transnational Crime and Corruption Center at the George Mason University; (3) Daniel Larkin, Former FBI Unit Chief and Founder of the National Cyber Forensics & Training Alliance; and (4) Elizabeth Rosenberg, Director of the Energy, Economics and Security Program at the Center for a New American Security.

Witness Testimony. Modell advanced a series of recommendations: (1) a greater degree of international cooperation and a methodical campaign based on shared financial intelligence and law enforcement; (2) the need to overcome parochial bureaucratic cultures and obtain a greater interagency collaboration as a prerequisite for truly effective transnational operations; (3) more proactive efforts against key financial safe havens exploited by terrorism networks such as Qatar, Kuwait and Lebanon, possibly including unilateral covert action; (4) increased investigative focus by Treasury's OFAC, including its own operational element; (5) widespread Information Operations (IOs) to target the public and the private sector and expose violations by governments, corporations and individuals; and (5) systematic and creative pay-outs from the Department of Justice to incentivize confidential sources, facilitators, and those who would testify in court. Modell suggested providing domestic law enforcement with the financial resources they need to mount a sustained and strategic campaign of criminal investigations against terrorist financing facilitators; making better use of the intelligence provided by FIUs, and decisively targeting Iran for its failure to comply with international AML/CFT best practices.

Shelley advised moving past the concept of terrorism financing, which she described as reactive and take a more proactive stance by focusing on terrorist marketing, business strategies and targets of opportunity. She stressed the need to deal with terrorists like business competitors, and to make broader use of public-private partnership to do that. Additionally, Shelley advocated the necessity of a holistic view of crime and terrorism responses, and of focusing specifically on drug trafficking, small-scale illicit trade, and corruption – which continue to provide the bulk of terrorism financing. Finally, she prescribed establishing advisory and working groups with private entities that are more likely to be targeted by terrorist organizations, such as manufacturers of consumer goods, pharmaceuticals and cigarettes, and devoting additional resources to monitoring cryptocurrencies such as Bitcoin. Larkin underlined the need to establish public-private task forces to protect privacy, promote transparency, and to offer the private sector a neutral space to share their intelligence with law enforcement. He described a public-private partnership of government, business and academia that allows a real-time exchange of information to stop cyber attacks, and said he believed a similar model would be effective in stopping terror finance and related illicit finance.

Rosenberg echoed the testimonies by the previous witnesses and said that the current statutory treatment of information concerning shell companies and beneficial ownership presents an untenable risk for the U.S. financial system. She also stressed the need for more incisive Know Your Customer (KYC) and CDD provisions – which she advocates be extended to corporate formation agents, investment advisors, real estate agents, and the new digital currencies. Rosenberg advocated the allocation of additional resources to the U.S. Departments of State, Defense, and Treasury and to law enforcement to expand counterterrorism and CFT activities (with a specific focus on the threats emanating from Iran), and to coordinate with foreign counterparts to share information and intelligence.

Questions and Discussion. Task Force Members raised questions regarding how best to counter the largely domestic stream of revenue that the Islamic State generates within the territory it controls. The possibility of extending Section 314 of the USA PATRIOT Act and provisions of the Bank Secrecy Act beyond the financial services realm – to the real estate sector, for example – was also discussed. Other questions were raised about the repercussions of sanctions relief that would be made available to Iran under the provisions of the Joint Comprehensive Plan of Action (JCPOA) and on extending to other national police forces the integrated crime/terrorism model of both the New York and Los Angeles Police Departments.

Methods to reduce the permeability of the financial system due to nested foreign correspondent banking relationships were also debated. Finally, questions were raised about the level of regulatory responsiveness toward alternative financing methods such as virtual currencies, mobile payments, and prepaid rechargeable credit cards, and new areas of concern such as cyberspace and the dark web.

July 22, 2015: "The Iran Nuclear Deal and its Impact on Terrorism Financing"

Overview. The Task Force reviewed the negotiation of the Joint Comprehensive Plan of Action (JCPOA) with Iran and the impact of the relief of sanctions to Iran on terrorism financing. The Task Force heard from five witnesses: (1) Ilan Berman, Vice President of the American Foreign Policy Council; (2) Mark Dubowitz, Executive Director of the Foundation for Defense of Democracies and Director of the Center on Sanctions and Illicit Finance; (3) Steven Perles, Attorney at Perles Law Firm; (4) Olli Heinonen, Senior Fellow at the Belfer Center for Science and International Affairs, Harvard University; and (5) Richard Nephew, Director of the Economic Statecraft, Sanctions and Energy Markets Program at Columbia University.

Witness Testimony. Berman stressed that the provisions of the deal signed in Vienna on July 14, 2015, will slow down for about a decade but not completely stall Iran's ambition to develop and field a full-fledged nuclear program. At the same time, Berman contended the monitoring and verification requirements of the deal do not provide adequate guarantees against the resumption of clandestine activities or procurement from foreign suppliers. He also stressed the significant economic relief that Iran stands to benefit from if it complies with requirements to divulge the details of its military-related nuclear program. While Berman conceded that it is possible that Iran will use the funds made available to improve its economy and pay down its national debt, he stressed that the funds could as well be used to finance terrorist activities abroad via proxies such as Hezbollah, Hamas, and the Palestinian Islamic Jihad. Finally, Berman continued that Iran has been funding and arming regime forces in Syria, Houthi rebels in Yemen, and Shi'ite militias in Iraq.

Dubowitz echoed the criticism of the JCPOA voiced by Berman and stressed the need for Congress to correct the current deal's shortcomings to more effectively block Iran's path to the nuclear bomb and maintain effective non-military tools of pressure and enforcement against illicit behavior. Dubowitz stressed that the Iran sanctions regime had also held as a goal protecting the integrity of the U.S. and international financial systems and said the JCPOA weakens the U.S.'s ability to continue doing so. Dubowitz also warned that under the provisions of the JCPOA, Iran will regain access to the Society for Worldwide Interbank Financial Telecommunication (SWIFT) system, which services the vast majority of transactions in the global financial system, and Iran's Islamic Revolutionary Guard Corps (IRGC) will receive significant additional resources. He produced data pointing to the fact that Iran will be spending the additional resources on its military, intelligence and domestic repressive security apparatus.

Perles applauded Congress for enacting measures such as the Flatow Amendment of 1996, which entitles U.S. citizens to seek monetary compensation from state sponsors of terrorism, and the Terrorism Risk Insurance Act (TRIA) of 2002, which included a provision to provide them with tools for enforcing judgments. Perles stressed that Iran is certain to allocate a portion of the funds that could be made available by the JCPOA to continue to train, finance, and supply proxies to conduct illicit foreign ventures. Additionally, Perles disagreed with the legal argument advanced by the Luxemburg-based and German-owned company Clearstream S.A. that, as long as the financial records of an entity with substantial presence in the U.S. are maintained exclusively outside the U.S., such entities are not subject to OFAC's AML/CFT regulations. In conclusion, Perles affirmed his belief that private litigation is a very effective way of identifying assets that sanctioned entities have hidden in the U.S., thus raising the cost of financing terrorism.

Heinonen stressed that under the JCPOA Iran is likely to maintain a sizeable nuclear program and is not bound by effective oversight. Further, the JCPOA does not fully address the possibility of Iran continuing its nuclear program with material in undeclared facilities, he said.

Nephew testified that the JCPOA provides a credible guarantee that Iran's declared nuclear program will not produce weapons-grade nuclear material for use in a bomb for at least ten years, and that the breakout period will be at least one year. Concerning sanctions and CFT measures, he said that the U.S. maintains pressure on Iran via: (1) the secondary sanctions provisions (that is – by virtue of U.S. and dollar centrality in global finance – penalties that are directed against third-party, foreign companies doing business with sanctioned entities) contained in the Comprehensive Iran Sanctions, Accountability and Divestment Act (CISADA); and (2) against individuals and entities trading conventional arms and ballistic missiles.

Questions and Discussion. Task Force Members raised questions concerning how to ensure that the funds made available to Iran under the JCPOA do not fund terrorism, debated a rehabilitation program establishing a set of benchmarks for the reintegration of sanctioned Iranian institutions and individuals into the SWIFT system, and concluded by discussing the possibility of interagency and private sector cooperation.

June 24, 2015: "Evaluating the Security of the U.S. Financial Sector"

Overview. The Task Force reviewed how the growth and complexity of the international financial system makes the system susceptible to cyber-attacks and has enabled illicit actors to move money and hide assets. The Task Force received testimony from three witnesses: (1) the Honorable Cyrus Vance, Jr., District Attorney, New York City; (2) Mr. Chip Poncy, Founding Partner, Financial Integrity Network, Senior Counsel, Center on Sanctions and Illicit Finance at the Foundation for Defense of Democracies; and (3) Mr. John W. Carlson, Chief of Staff, Financial Services Information Sharing and Analysis Center.

Witness Testimony. Vance testified concerning the perspective of state and local law enforcement on non-transparent beneficial ownership of corporate entities. He used examples of cases from New York to explain how companies often incorporate in the United States because the U.S. does not collect beneficial ownership information and that this can often make it difficult to identify and prosecute terrorist financers. Vance stressed the importance of verification on incorporation documents and the importance of safeguarding the privacy of beneficial ownership information. Poncy explained the importance of working with international regional bodies like the G7, the G20, and the Financial Action Task Force (FATF) to improve financial integrity and transparency around the world. He described systemic challenges to financial transparency based on his work at Treasury for 11 years following the terrorist attacks of 9/11. He reiterated common forms of terrorist financing— kidnapping for ransom, collaboration with criminal organizations, fundraising and recruitment— as well as the necessity of adequate "Customer Due Diligence" rules and beneficial ownership requirements for legal entities. Poncy also reiterated the importance of intermediation and strengthening the information-sharing of Section 314 of the USA PATRIOT Act, as well as the importance of FinCEN's work to issue and enforce AML/CFT preventative measures in accordance with the BSA. Carlson described the role of the Financial Services – Information Sharing and Analysis Center (FS-ISAC) working with individual financial institutions to disseminate and foster the sharing of relevant and actionable information to protect the financial services sector against cyber and physical threats. He explained how the current cyber threat environment continues to evolve and intensify and reiterated the importance of compliance with federal cybersecurity requirements and guidance as well as the National Institute of Standards and Technology (NIST) Cybersecurity Framework.

Questions and Discussion. Task Force Members raised questions about Treasury's beneficial ownership rulemaking, and provided suggestions on information sharing, including amendments to Section 314 of the USA PATRIOT Act. Additional questions were raised regarding compliance with FATF standards – specifically with Customer Due Diligence standards and beneficial ownership, as well as relating to reforms of the company formation process. Members asked about improving implementation of effective AML/CFT programs among financial institutions with correspondent banking relationships. There was discussion of improving cyber-crime prevention, including harmonizing requirements at the policy and examination levels across different U.S. based financial regulatory agencies, and the possible passage of cyber-threat information-sharing legislation. Some discussion was also given to sanctions relief under the JCPOA and whether Iranian banks would have access to SWFIT.

May 21, 2015: "A Dangerous Nexus: Terrorism: Crime, and Corruption"

Overview. The Task Force reviewed the current techniques employed by terrorist organizations and transnational crime syndicates, the effectiveness of current U.S. policies and whether or not there is room for improvement moving forward. The Task Force heard from four witnesses: (1) Celina Realuyo, Professor at the William J. Perry Center for Hemispheric Defense Studies of the National Defense University; (2) David Asher, Board of Advisors at the Center on Sanctions and Illicit Finance of the Foundation for Defense of Democracies and Fellow at the Center for a New American Security; (3) Douglas Farah, President of IBI Consultants LLC, Associate at the Center for Strategic and International Studies, and Fellow at the International Assessment and Strategy Center; and (4) Richard Barrett, Vice President at the Soufan Group.

Witness Testimony. Realuyo stressed that illicit actors need critical enablers to obtain their political and economic objectives and that some of today's global terrorist and criminal networks are better armed and funded than the governments responsible for countering them. She proposed five measures: (1) increasing funding for the agencies involved in investigating and prosecuting criminals, terrorists and corrupted officials; (2) maintaining the Iraq-Afghan Threat Finance Cell and using the format to counter emerging crime-terrorism hybrid threats such as ISIL; (3) revitalizing the interagency Terrorist Financing Working Group to coordinate all activities of the above-mentioned agencies; (4) using a portion of the fines from sanctions evasion and money laundering to finance counter-threat programs; and (5) designing public-private partnerships to make the private sector the primary early warning source for financial crimes detection.

Asher briefly stated that despite successes such as those against the Lebanese Canadian Bank, U.S. interagency and international cooperation efforts have not been successful. He stressed that banks today still accept payments from Lebanese sources to buy used cars going to West Africa and pointed to the necessity of stricter enforcement and more generalized prosecution for the trend to be corrected. Asher proposed extending the provisions of the Racketeering Influences and Corrupt Organizations Act (RICO) to terrorist groups.

Barrett stressed that, given its asymmetric nature, terrorism does not require big funds to be effective and that those funds can be procured via legal, quasi-legal and illegal means, depending on what is easiest and most effective. He noted that terrorists tend to flock to less-governed areas of the globe where they can establish bases and control territory. In Barrett's opinion, even though terrorists and criminals might be co-located in the same area, the former tend more to take a cut from the latter rather than joining ranks or competing with them. Barrett said that, in his opinion, criminals tend to see terrorists as bad for business because they are dangerous and bring too much attention to illicit activity. Similarly, he continued, terrorists are not ideologically aligned with criminals and their economic goals, and see them as not sufficiently committed to their ideological cause. In conclusion, Barrett testified that the hybridization of crime and terrorism might actually be more nuanced than what is generally described by others.

Farah described the convergence of transnational crime, terrorism and corruption in Latin America as a phenomenon possibly leading to the advent of "criminalized states" – that is, states actively utilizing transnational organized crime as an instrument of tradecraft, relying on oil revenues and illicit activities to fund themselves and often overlapping with terrorist organizations. Farah contended that Venezuela was a good example of such convergence because, rather than operating on the margins of the state or seeking to co-opt small pieces of state machinery, criminal networks concentrate their efforts directly at the core of the state.

Farrah added that Venezuela is not alone in this trend, and that Ecuador, Bolivia, Nicaragua, El Salvador and the former government of Argentina have engaged in illicit activities. Farah contended that this so-called Bolivian alliance resulted in massive corruption, rising violence, and a weakening of the rule of law and institutions. The alliance proceeded to establish strategic partnerships based on the cocaine trade, with both state and non-state actors participating including Hezbollah, Iran, Russia, China, and the Revolutionary Armed Forces of Colombia, or FARC. In particular, Farah testified that Iran benefitted from unsanctioned Venezuelan, Ecuadoran and Bolivian financial institutions that laundered money into the global financial system.

Questions and Discussion. Task Force Members raised questions about the feasibility and efficacy of replicating the system of the Iraq-Afghanistan Threat Finance Cell in Latin America, the viability of extending USA PATRIOT Act Section 311 to nations complicit in illicit finance activities, and the extent of the effectiveness of U.S. interagency AML/CFT efforts. Additional questions were raised related to how to more strictly control the smuggling of oil from ISIL-controlled areas via Turkey, the possible repercussions in AML/CFT terms of lifting the current sanctions regime to Iran, the ease with which anonymous foreign individuals can buy luxury real estate in the U.S., and ensuring the inclusion of informal value transfer systems (IVTS), such as hawala, in a manner that precludes possible AML/CFT abuses, but guarantees the flow of remittances to developing countries such as Somalia. Finally, Task Force members raised questions about reforming the 1971 Bank Secrecy Act as well as whether regulations inhibited banks from exchanging and acting upon potential AML/CFT violations.

April 22, 2015: "A Survey of Global Terrorism and Terrorist Financing"

Overview. The Task Force reviewed the policies, rules, and regulations implemented to date by the federal government in AML/CFT to determine if their effectiveness as well as potential areas of improvement. The Task Force heard from three witnesses: (1) Juan Zarate, Advisor at the Center for Strategic and International Studies and chairman at the Center on Sanctions and Illicit Finance of the Foundation for Defense of Democracies; (2) Jonathan Schanzer, Vice President of the Foundation for Defense of Democracies; and (3) Seth G. Jones, Director of International Security and Defense Policy Center, RAND Corporation.

Witness Testimony. Zarate suggested that the successes of the past decade notwithstanding, the effort to thwart the financing of terrorism must continue to evolve according to the changing landscape of the financial system. Schanzer focused on two areas of concern: Iran and Turkey. He opined that if Iran sanctions relief is fully implemented, resources newly available to Iran would go to terrorist groups such as Hezbollah, the Palestinian Islamic Jihad, the Houthis, and Shi'ite militias in Iraq. He urged Congress to closely oversee the process to make sure that the eventual implementation of such relief does not result in increased financial support for terrorism worldwide. Schanzer also testified that the eastern border of Turkey with Syria is a major area of concern and described it as the primary gateway for jihadists of ISIL and the al-Nusra Front. He quoted unspecified reports describing Turkish authorities as turning a blind eye or even abetting terrorism-related trafficking across its borders. Schanzer added that, according to his sources, terror financiers from Persian Gulf countries have been camping in hotels along the Turkish southeast frontier; Turkey has been assisting Jihadists in Libya since 2013 in violation of the U.N. arms embargo; Hamas has established a foothold in the country; and Turkey violated Iran sanctions in 2012-2013. In conclusion, Schanzer advocated exerting increased pressure on Turkish authorities to curb their widespread support for illicit actors.

Jones described the new, complex financing trends of groups such as al Qaeda, ISIL, and Hezbollah as potentially very dangerous. He highlighted that the United States continues to have proven capabilities to curb the strategic reach of the core of terrorist networks actively planning to strike the U.S. mainland and its assets worldwide, and to use AML/CFT tools targeting individuals and charitable organizations; however, he testified, the United States is not yet able to efficiently target local sources of revenue abroad. For instance, he argues that the United States cannot adequately target revenue that ISIL has marshalled from the territory it controls.

Questions and Discussion. Task Force Members raised questions about how exactly terrorism financing has changed in the past decade; best practices to monitor cross-border resource transfers; and how FinCEN can be better equipped to deal with these evolving issues. Other questions addressed regulations affecting hawalas and financial inclusion, and if such regulations need reforming; the likely consequences of the sanctions relief measures to Iran; the state of information sharing among agencies of the federal government with the private sector and what can be done to improve public-private coordination; the lack of transparency regarding beneficial ownership of real estate and corporations; the connection of Hezbollah to drug syndicates in Latin America and its overall impact on terrorism financing; and, finally, whether the United States could use the United Nations to efficiently target terrorism financing.

Appendix C: "A Survey of Global Terrorism and Terrorist Financing" (Apr. 22, 2015)

Appendix D: "A Dangerous Nexus: Terrorism, Crime, and Corruption" (May 21, 2015)

Appendix E: "Evaluating the Security of the U.S. Financial Sector" (Jun. 24, 2015)

Appendix F: "The Iran Nuclear Deal and Its Impact on Terrorism Financing" (July 22, 2015)

Appendix G: "Could America Do More? An Examination of U.S. Efforts to Stop the Financing of Terror" (Sept. 9, 2015)

Appendix H: "Trading with the Enemy: Trade-Based Money Laundering is the Growth Industry in Terror Finance" (Feb. 3, 2016) [Appendix H is on file with the Committee. A link will be added when available].

Appendix I: "Helping the Developing World Fight Terror Finance" (Mar. 1, 2016) [Appendix I is on file with the Committee. A link will be added when available].

Appendix J: "Preventing Cultural Genocide: Countering the Plunder and Sale of Priceless Cultural Antiquities by ISIS" (Apr. 19, 2016) [Appendix J is on file with the Committee. A link will be added when available].

Appendix K: "Stopping Terror Finance: A Coordinated Effort" (May 24, 2016) [Appendix K is on file with the Committee. A link will be added when available].

Appendix L: "The Enemy in Our Backyard: Examining Terror Funding Streams from South America" (June 8, 2016) [Appendix L is on file with the Committee. A link will be added when available].

Appendix M: "The Next Terrorist Financiers: Stopping Them Before They Start" (June 23, 2016) [Appendix M is on file with the Committee. A link will be added when available].